1982

# *Epistolarity*

JANET GURKIN ALTMAN

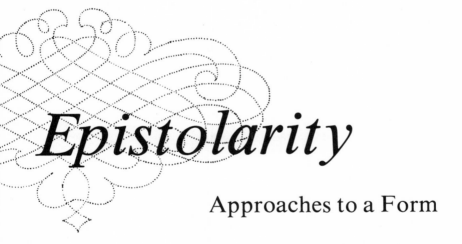

# *Epistolarity*

## Approaches to a Form

OHIO STATE UNIVERSITY PRESS : COLUMBUS

*Library of Congress Cataloging in Publication Data*

Altman, Janet Gurkin, 1945–
    Epistolarity: approaches to a form.

    Bibliography: p.
    Includes index.
    1. Epistolary fiction—History and criticism.
I.   Title.
PN3448.E6A4            809.3              81-16866
ISBN 0-8142-0313-2                       AACR2

# Contents

# ACKNOWLEDGMENTS

The most traceable inspiration for this book on epistolary literature is Jean Rousset's article "Le Roman par lettres,"
which drew me toward both a corpus of literature and an initial
strategy for reading. My own subsequent readings of epistolary
fiction have particularly benefited from stimulating discussion
with Georges May (with whom I originated this work at Yale),
Ronald Rosbottom (similarly drawn to write about this curious
form), and the students of my comparative literature seminar on
letter narrative at the University of Iowa in 1977.

Special thanks also go to Félix Martínez-Bonati, Rick Altman,
Paul de Man, Charles Porter, Jean Boorsch, and Philip Lewis for
their astute criticism and helpful suggestions at various stages of
my writing. Carol Sykes at Ohio State University Press has been a
model editor for lucidity and care in manuscript preparation, and
Kim Smith's talent and wit assisted me immeasurably during the
proofing and indexing processes. To all of these colleagues I am
extremely grateful.

The following pages constitute an attempt to push a certain
kind of formalist reading to its limits on a particularly intriguing
"form." I have tried to sketch out the gains of this kind of reading
while remaining aware of its problematics and limitations. Although my methodology is very much one of my own creation, I
owe a clear debt to Jean Rousset, François Jost, the Russian formalists, and the German and French narratologists who have

practiced and theorized about formalist reading. I also owe a more hidden debt to Jacques Derrida and others who have critiqued this type of reading. I wish to acknowledge here, therefore, all of the writers and readers, past and future, who are drawn to wrestle with the problematic relationship between "form" and "meaning," those slippery and unstable terms that we seem forever condemned to reify in order to talk about them.

I dedicate this book to my remarkable mother and to the memory of my father—to Sylvia and Roy Gurkin.

*Epistolarity*

Die leichte Möglichkeit des Briefschreibens muss—bloss theoretisch angesehn—eine schreckliche Zerrüttung der Seelen in die Welt gebracht haben. Es ist ja ein Verkehr mit Gespenstern und zwar nicht nur mit dem Gespenst des Adressaten, sondern auch mit dem eigenen Gespenst, das sich einem unter der Hand in dem Brief, den man schreibt, entwickelt oder gar in einer Folge von Briefen, wo ein Brief den andern erhärtet und sich auf ihn als Zeugen berufen kann.

The great feasibility of letter writing must have produced—from a purely theoretical point of view—a terrible dislocation of souls in the world. It is truly a communication with spectres, not only with the spectre of the addressee but also with one's own phantom, which evolves underneath one's own hand in the very letter one is writing or even in a series of letters, where one letter reinforces the other and can refer to it as a witness.

Franz Kafka, *Briefe an Milena*

# INTRODUCTION

When I first began reading epistolary novels, there was little visible critical or artistic interest in the letter form. It was commonly assumed that the form was a historically limited, archaic one, describable in terms of its "rise and fall." The last decade, however, has seen the development of a new critical interest in letter fiction and a clear revival of the form by creative writers. Demonstrably, the epistolary novel is a hardy species that continues to produce lively strains in various parts of the world. Recently, writers of as diverse sensibilities as Michel Butor in the "half-dead letters" ("missives mi-vives") of *Illustrations III* (1973), the three Marias in Portugal who coauthored the feminist *New Portuguese Letters* (1972), and Bob Randall in his popular American suspense novel *The Fan* (1977) have reinvented the letter form for equally diverse readerships.[1] Although historically speaking the epistolary genre peaked in eighteenth-century Europe, producing such classics as Montesquieu's *Lettres persanes*, Richardson's *Pamela* and *Clarissa*, Rousseau's *La Nouvelle Héloïse*, Smollett's *Humphry Clinker*, Goethe's *Werther*, and Laclos's *Les Liaisons dangereuses*, the letter's potential as artistic form and narrative vehicle has been explored by writers of many nationalities and periods—from Ovid in the *Epistulae Heroidum* to Saul Bellow in *Herzog*.

Such well-known works present obvious diversity in style and content; yet they reveal a surprising number of similar literary

structures and intriguingly persistent patterns when read together
with other examples of the epistolary genre. These structures—
recurring thematic relations, character types, narrative events,
and organization—can in turn be related to properties inherent to
the letter itself. In numerous instances the basic formal and
functional characteristics of the letter, far from being merely
ornamental, significantly influence the way meaning is consciously and unconsciously constructed by writers and readers of
epistolary works.

In the following chapters I use the concept of a work's "epistolarity" (working definition: the use of the letter's formal properties to create meaning) as a parameter for reading epistolary
literature. At this point the notions of "epistolarity" and "meaning" must remain partially vacant terms, since the framework in
which they acquire cumulative value is constituted by the analyses
that follow. It should be clear, however, that the concept of
epistolarity is primarily a frame for reading. A work's epistolarity
cannot be scientifically measured. It can only be argued by an
interpretative act, which involves the critic's description of a letter
novel's epistolarity as much as the novelist's or novel's actualiza-
tion of the letter's potential to create narrative, figurative, and
other types of meaning.

Epistolary novels make meaning in a variety of ways. The
production of meaning may be directly dependent on the epistolary form of the novel or it may depend on the multitude of other
factors that make novels such complex artifacts. Conversely,
novels that at first appear not to be epistolary may in fact create
meaning through the literary structures particular to the letter or
the letter form. By concentrating on epistolarity I am focusing on
those occasions, wherever they may be found, when the creation
of meaning derives from the structures and potential specific to
the letter form. In following this strategy I am seeking to offer
interpretative approaches to individual works (including many
not traditionally called "epistolary novels" and excluding many
that traditionally have been), as well as a reading of a genre as a
whole. Within the field of phenomena susceptible to "interpretation" I include not only the more covert, "obscure," and problematic aspects of complex epistolary works but also the overtly

exploited conventions that structure letter fiction as narrative and make it possible to specify the epistolary novel as a genre.

Epistolary literature has only recently become the object of close critical scrutiny, but it has already proven a fertile field for a variety of approaches different from mine. Literary historians who investigate the origins and fortunes of the letter genre necessarily contribute to our general understanding of the rise of the novel itself, since epistolary narrative is primarily a product of that formative era in which the novel staked out its claim to status as a major genre. Moreover, the unusual phenomenon of story-telling through letters has been in itself sufficiently intriguing to attract attention from those followers of Henry James, Percy Lubbock, and Wayne Booth who are interested in narrative technique.[2] More generally, the letter's multivalency—as a linguistic phenomenon, as a real-life form, as an instrument of amorous or philosophical communication—has appealed to critics with other interests and approaches.[3]

Prior to the last decade, the very few studies of the epistolary genre were primarily historical in nature. As early as 1933 Godfrey Singer attempted to trace the history of the genre from its origins to the twentieth century in his thesis *The Epistolary Novel*. Although Singer's book contains a potentially interesting chapter on early American novels, his work on the whole remains a superficial and unfortunately unreliable enumeration of items. Much more thorough research with a serious historical perspective is available in Charles E. Kany's *The Beginnings of the Epistolary Novel in France, Italy, and Spain* (1937), which Kany wrote to rectify the notion that the epistolary form was a late-seventeenth- and early-eighteenth-century English creation. Kany traces the origins of the genre back to classical times, follows its progress through the Middle Ages, and terminates with Boursault's works in the mid seventeenth century, after establishing the previously unrecognized importance of Spanish contributions to the genre. F. G. Black's study *The Epistolary Novel in the Late Eighteenth Century* (1940) and R. A. Day's subtle account of the pre-Richardsonian period *Told in Letters: Epistolary Fiction before Richardson* (1966) continue Kany's historical work for England. Most recently, Laurent Versini, in *Le Roman épistolaire* (1979), has embraced the genre's chronology from ancient Greece to the present in a relatively short but highly informed and informative survey, which concentrates on France.

Such studies, though useful in providing perspective and bibliography, are essentially unifunctional. They inform us of the existence of certain works, but they do not suggest models for reading them. Far more interpretative, though also historical in approach, are the chapters that Vivienne Mylne devotes to epistolary works in her study *The Eighteenth-Century French Novel: Techniques of Illusion* (1965). Mylne's point of departure is Georges May's theory that the development of the eighteenth-century novel was significantly influenced by hostile contemporary criticism.[4] Building upon this theory, Mylne examines the narrative techniques that novelists developed in order to create an illusion of reality and authenticity, in response to criticism's accusations of unrealism and the public's distrust of fiction. Consequently, in her chapters on letter novels—a form in which fiction conventionally masquerades as a real-life product—she examines the advantages and pitfalls of the letter as an instrument for creating the illusion of reality. When analyzing individual works, Mylne often deals with problems and techniques arising from the letter form itself, pointing out inconsistencies and implausibilities that violate the code of verisimilitude as well as identifying some effective uses of the form.

Mylne's interest in the epistolary genre is of course secondary to her larger thesis concerning the representation of reality in the eighteenth-century French novel, just as Tzvetan Todorov's discussion of the letter in the first chapter of his study of *Les Liaisons dangereuses* is subordinate to his interest in building a poetics of literary discourse in general.[5] Nevertheless, the brief chapters of readers such as these are often more attentive to the particular properties of the letter form and more suggestive of interpretative models than the major studies of literary historians like Kany, Day, and Black. It is precisely the subordination of individual analyses to a larger goal that transforms Mylne's and Todorov's books into useful instruments for further research. Mylne not only tells us what a handful of eighteenth-century novelists have done with the epistolary form but suggests how to deal with the problem of verisimilitude in any letter narrative. In the same way Todorov, by attempting to fit *Les Liaisons dangereuses* into the larger perspective of literature as a system of communication, is able to identify much of what is particular to the letter in Laclos's novel as a specific instance of communication.

Laclos's monumental example of the epistolary genre has in fact been instrumental in attracting critical interest to the form itself. No one interested in interpreting *Les Liaisons dangereuses* can fail to examine the central role of the letter in creating meaning. Jean-Luc Seylaz devotes part of his excellent study *"Les Liaisons dangereuses" et la création romanesque chez Laclos* (1958) to Laclos's exploitation of the form's resources, as does Dorothy Thelander to a lesser extent in *Laclos and the Epistolary Novel* (1963).[6] It remained for Laurent Versini to examine the relationship of Laclos to his generic predecessors, as he does with admirable thoroughness in *Laclos et la tradition* (1968).[7] Since Versini's approach is largely historical, his premise being that *Les Liaisons* constitutes "à la fois le sommet et la liquidation de la littérature épistolaire" (p. 251), in discussing Laclos's numerous predecessors he makes many illuminating comments on the evolution of epistolary techniques.[8]

Several recent studies of works other than *Les Liaisons* have emphasized their epistolary aspects. Such exemplary analyses as those of Testud, Kearney, and Duchêne confirm the importance of approaching meaning as a function of form in interpreting the letter work.[9] Although studies of other individual letter novels occasionally appear, few critics have addressed themselves exclusively and explicitly to the ways in which letters create meaning from a general or generic perspective. In 1962 Jean Rousset broke the ground for synchronic generic studies of this type with his seminal chapter on the letter novel in *Forme et signification*, in which he briefly explores the potential of the epistolary instrument, sketches a simple typology, and presents illustrative interpretations of three works.[10] François Jost likewise has made a significant contribution in his article "Le Roman épistolaire et la technique narrative au XVIIIe siècle" (1966).[11] Distinguishing between two fundamental uses of the letter, Jost outlines a

typology of epistolary narrative. On the one hand, he identifies
the "static" or "passive method," characterized by the "lettre-
confidence," in which the letter merely reports events and the
writer and receiver play a passive role. This method is contrasted
with the "active" or "kinetic method," characterized by the
"lettre-drame," in which the action progresses through the letters
themselves, which provoke reactions or function as agents in the
plot.[12] Each of the two major types has three subsets, based on the
number of correspondents; Jost's description of the six fundamental epistolary types suggests several properties of the letter
and the ways they have been exploited. Today, over a decade
later, Rousset's and Jost's articles, preliminary and brief though
they may be, remain unique in their formalist approach to the
epistolary genre as a whole.[13]

> *A concept of form in a new meaning had now come into
> play—not just the outer covering but the whole entity,
> something concrete and dynamic, substantive in
> itself.—Boris M. Eichenbaum*[14]

Whether under the tutelage of the New Critics, the recently
rediscovered Russian formalists, or the popular Marshall
McLuhan, we have come increasingly to appreciate that form can
be more than the outer shell of content, that the medium chosen
by an artist may in fact dictate, rather than be dictated by, his
message. The enterprise that Jean Rousset undertook in *Forme et
signification*—"saisir des significations à travers des formes"—
can describe the activity of the writer as well as the reader of
literature. The writer who chooses to construct a novel in letters
may find his material growing out of his chosen form and not vice
versa. If the exploration of a form's potential can generate a work
of art, it can also contribute to our understanding of that work.

Such has not, however, always been the assumption of critics of
the epistolary novel. Frank G. Black's observation is a case in
point:

> The reader of fiction does not wish to be reminded over frequently of
> a device which exists for the sole purpose of conveying the story. . . .
> [An] inappropriateness is felt in this novel [Gunning, *Memoirs of
> Mary*] and in others where the letters—their loss, concealment,
> forgery, and so on—become motives in the plot. One dislikes the

apparent confusion of method and matter. . . . Though skill in
particular cases qualifies the statement, it would seem that in letter
fiction the epistle should be kept as a means of presenting the story
and not be unduly obtruded as an agent in the narrative.[15]

Such restrictive tastes could lead us to dismiss the work of Joyce,
Proust, Pirandello, and Brecht, as well as Richardson and
Laclos.[16]

Black assumes that the epistle is chosen "as a means of
presenting the story." His statement gives primacy to plot, which
the letter should merely function to relate. Yet as any reader of
letter narrative should know—particularly those familiar with the
French tradition (Crébillon, Rousseau, Laclos)—often relatively
little "happens" independently of the letters. Although Clarissa's
and Pamela's "story" might well have been told (albeit in a
different way) without letters, Laclos's method *is* his matter; not
only are the physical letters primary agents in the plot, but the
entire psychological action in the novel advances through the
letter writing itself.

Black did not, of course, set out to define "epistolarity" in his
work on the late-eighteenth-century letter novel. Yet his assumptions about the form subordinate it to an esthetic value—
suppression of the acts that produce the narrative—which reflects
a taste more heavily influenced by the nineteenth-century novel's
mimetic esthetic than the eighteenth century's novelistic values. If
we are to understand epistolary literature more fully and appreciate its art, some inquiry into its particular modes of communication is in order.

The chapters that follow represent an effort to approach
epistolary literature on its own terms. Underlying this method are
two assumptions related to the observations at the beginning of
this section: (1) that for the letter novelist the choice of the epistle
as narrative instrument can foster certain patterns of thematic
emphasis, narrative action, character types, and narrative self-
consciousness;[17] and (2) that for the reader of epistolary
literature, the identification of structures common to letter novels
can provide (and expose) important models and perspectives for
interpretation of individual works.

An inductive survey of a wide range of letter narrative has led
me to focus on six key aspects of the epistolary genre because of

their power to subsume or emblemize a number of the letter's
properties and to ground readings of a variety of works. Each of
the chapters of this study explores one of these six aspects as an
independent approach to the entire genre; many of the same
works are therefore treated in several chapters. In choosing these
six I have not restricted myself to purely technical or formal
aspects, as do Jost and Rousset. I have been at least as concerned
with thematic constants, recurring character types, and patterns
of narrative organization in epistolary literature as with the
narrative techniques particular to it. In so doing I hope to be
laying the ground for a more serious consideration of the
epistolary form as a genre rather than merely as one type of
narrative technique.

In each chapter generalizations grow out of concrete analyses
of texts; the dual objective of defining "epistolarity" and interpreting literature is maintained by deriving each parameter of
epistolarity from a variety of examples and validating its
usefulness as an interpretative tool by more extended consideration of individual works.

My choice of texts has necessarily been eclectic, based on
neither historical, national, nor esthetic considerations but rather
on a work's instructive manifestation of epistolarity. Both my
own field of expertise and French predominance in the genre (see
Jost's bibliography) have led me to concentrate somewhat more
on the French corpus.[18] I hope that whatever disproportion has
thereby resulted will be balanced by the fact that the French
territory is less charted than its British counterpart and yields (for
reasons that should become apparent) more insights into
epistolarity as I have defined it.

1. The authors known as the three Marias (Maria-Isabel Barreno, Maria-
Teresa Horta, and Maria-Fátima Velho da Costa) were inspired by both the
form and content of Guilleragues's influential *Lettres portugaises* (1669) to write
their *Novas Cartas portuguesas* in order to demonstrate how little the isolation
and alienation of women in Portugal had changed over three centuries. Bob
Randall, who uses nothing but letters to create suspense quite cleverly in *The
Fan*, declared in a television interview that he thought he had invented the
epistolary novel. Indeed, the writers who have recently taken up the letter form
have done so with the enthusiasm of a new discovery. Jacques Derrida is the
latest to renew ties energetically with this ancient genre; the epistolary section

*Envois* (pp. 5–273 of *La Carte postale*, which appeared in 1980) participates fully in the conventions of letter fiction. *Envois* offers, moreover, a richly provocative meditation on telecommunication, on the experience of "en-voyage" (sending messages—*envois*—while traveling), in which the post card and the "postal effect" become dynamic metaphors for Derrida's complex concepts of writing, dissemination, and *différance*.

2. See, for instance, Bertil Romberg's chapters on the letter form in her *Studies in the Narrative Technique of the First-Person Novel*, or E. Th. Voss, *Erzählprobleme des Briefromans*. (For complete publication information on these and other pertinent works that I cite, please refer to my Selected Bibliography.) Although James experimented with the epistolary form as author, leaving us the two short stories "The Point of View" and "The Bundle of Letters," he never addressed himself to the genre as critic. Neither Lubbock in *The Craft of Fiction* (London: J. Cape, 1921) nor Booth in *The Rhetoric of Fiction* (Chicago: University of Chicago Press, 1961) deals specifically with the genre, although their approach is evident in Romberg's chapters.

A number of German dissertations on the letter novel appeared in the 1960s: N. Würzbach, "Die Struktur des Briefromans und seine Entstehung in England" (1961); D. Kimpel, "Entstehung und Formen des Briefromans in Deutschland" (1961); W. Gauglhofer, "Geschichte und Strukturprobleme des europäischen Briefromans" (1968), and H. Picard, "Die Illusion der Wirklichkeit im Briefroman des 18. Jahrhunderts" (1971). In spite of the titles, these dissertations typically analyze a limited number of works, but they do deal with more general questions of narrative technique, largely within the tradition of analysis of "Erzähldistanz" (narrator's relationship to story) defined by Käte Friedemann (*Die Rolle des Erzählers in der Epik* [1910]), Käte Hamburger (*Die Logik der Dichtung* [1957]), and Franz Stanzel (*Die typischen Erzählsituationen im Roman* [1955]).

3. In addition to numerous isolated studies of the letter (as distinct from letter narrative), there has been a regular seminar on "The Familiar Letter in the Seventeenth Century in England" at Modern Language Association meetings in recent years. In France the Société d'Histoire Littéraire de la France organized a colloquium on "La Lettre au XVIIe siècle" in 1977 (papers published in the *Revue d'histoire littéraire de la France*, Nov.–Dec. 1978), and critics like Duchêne, Beugnot, and Bray have regularly dialogued with each other on the problematic relationship of reality and art in real and literary correspondences.

4. In *Le Dilemme du roman au XVIIIe siècle* (1963), Georges May identifies and examines the effects of the dilemma that criticism created for the French novelist: the impossibility of avoiding simultaneously criticism's accusations of *invraisemblance* and its attacks on immoralism.

5. Tzvetan Todorov, *Littérature et signification* (1967), pp. 13–49.

6. Thelander's title is somewhat misleading. Her short study serves more as an introduction to Laclos than to the epistolary novel.

7. Versini actually examines Laclos's relationship to a variety of preceding traditions: dramatic and thematic as well as epistolary.

8. Versini's more recent study, *Le Roman épistolaire* (1979), provides clearer historical perspectives than the more diffuse thesis of *Laclos et la tradition*. It is, moreover, a highly readable book, the best place to begin for a sense of the epistolary novel's history.

9. Pierre Testud, "Les *Lettres persanes*, roman épistolaire" (1966); Anthony Kearney, "*Clarissa* and the Epistolary Form" (1966); and Roger Duchêne, *Réalité vécue et art épistolaire: Madame de Sévigné et la lettre d'amour* (1970).

10. Jean Rousset, "Une Forme littéraire: le roman par lettres," chapter four of his *Forme et signification*. A considerably shorter version of the chapter (without the individual analyses and bibliography) was serialized under the same title that year in the *Nouvelle Revue Française* 10 (May–June 1962): 830–41, 1010–22.

11. The same article, revised, appeared in Jost's collection *Essais de littérature comparée* (1968), 2:89–179, with a bibliographical appendix (pp. 380–402). This appendix contains 520 entries and includes almost all of the major (as well as most of the minor) epistolary works of world literature from classical times to the mid twentieth century; it has been my single most useful bibliographical tool. Other helpful listings are: for France, Yves Giraud's *Bibliographie du roman épistolaire en France des origines à 1842*, Martin, Mylne, and Frautschi's *Bibliographie du genre romanesque français, 1751–1800*, and Versini's bibliography in *Laclos et la tradition*; for England, the lists in Black's *The Epistolary Novel in the Late Eighteenth Century* and Day's *Told in Letters*; and for Germany, the bibliographies in Voss's and Kimpel's dissertations.

12. Vivienne Mylne makes a similar distinction between "memoir-letters" and "event-letters" (p. 151) and points out the analogy between these and two types of scenes in plays.

13. In 1976 the Association Internationale des Etudes Françaises devoted a full day of its annual meeting to a colloquium on "Le Roman par lettres." All seven of the communications dealt with one or two individual works, with *an* rather than with *the* epistolary novel. The papers and discussion are published in the association's *Cahiers*, no. 29 (1977), pp. 131–241 and 348–59.

14. Boris M. Eichenbaum, "The Theory of the Formal Method," in *Readings in Russian Poetics*, ed. L. Matejka and K. Pomorska (Cambridge: MIT Press, 1971), p. 12.

15. Black, p. 58.

16. Other readers, schooled by Shklovsky or the modernists, would of course attribute esthetic value precisely to that "laying bare of the device" (Shklovsky's term) which Black deplores and which Shklovsky illustrates in his own epistolary novel, *Zoo, or Letters Not about Love*, which has recently been widely translated (1923; English translation, 1971).

17. I would not argue, however, as M. Roelens has in "Le Texte et ses conditions d'existence," that the letter is a "forme nécessitante" whose adoption is a servitude determining all aspects of a work. Roelens reads *Les Liaisons* in terms of a rigid logic whereby conformity to the esthetic of verisimilitude leads to the choice of the letter, which subordinates all aspects of the novel (psychology, ideology, and so forth) to the necessity of bringing the novel into existence. Although this reading is seductive, it is nonetheless reductive as an absolute claim for Laclos's novel and is less applicable to other epistolary works.

18. I have accordingly assumed that anyone led to read this book will have sufficiently comparatist interests to read French. French texts are quoted only in the original; for other languages translations are given. The spelling in all quotations from eighteenth-century and earlier editions has been standardized and modernized; punctuation, however, has not been altered.

# CHAPTER ONE

# EPISTOLARY MEDIATION

Given the letter's function as a connector between two distant points, as a bridge between sender and receiver, the epistolary author can choose to emphasize either the distance or the bridge. When Ovid began to explore the letter's narrative potential in the *Epistulae Heroidum,* he was already aware of both aspects of the letter's intermediary nature. Many of the *Heroides* are fictional letters from abandoned heroines, who repeatedly bemoan the distance separating them from their lovers. Even lovers on good terms, when they are obliged to communicate by letter, lament the instrument's inadequacy. "Mittit Abydenus, quam mallet ferre, salutem, / si cadat unda maris, Sesta puella, tibi" ("he of Abydos sends to you, Maid of Sestos, the greetings he would rather bring, if the waves of the sea should fall"), writes Leander to Hero, when a storm prevents him from crossing the Hellespont.[1] The very hand that usually bears him across these waves is now reduced to constructing an inferior bridge: "at quanto mallem, quam scriberet, illa [dextra] nataret" ("but ah! how much rather would I have it swim than write" [v. 21]).

Other Ovidian letter writers choose to deemphasize the gulf in favor of the letter's power to span it. Phaedra, who cannot communicate with Hippolytus by speech because of both her own modesty and his hardheartedness, places all her hopes in the epistle:

> inspicit acceptas hostis ab hoste notas.
> Ter tecum conata loqui ter inutilis haesit
>    lingua, ter in primo destitit ore sonus.
> qua licet et sequitur, pudor est miscendus amori;
>    dicere quae puduit, scribere iussit amor.

Even foe looks into missive written by foe. Thrice making trial of speech with you, thrice hath my tongue vainly stopped, thrice the sound failed at first threshold of my lips. Wherever modesty may attend on love, love should not lack in it; with me, what modesty forbade to say, love has commanded me to write. [Phaedra Hippolyto, vv. 6–10]

Paris in his letter to Helen, like Phaedra, confesses his love and tries to persuade the object of his passion to reciprocate. The letter in both cases is seen as facilitating a union: "Iamdudum gratum est, quod epistula nostra recepta / spem facit, hoc recipi me quoque posse modo" ("Long now have I had cheer, for your welcoming my letter begets the hope that I also may be likewise welcomed" [L. 16, Paris Helenae, vv. 13–14]). Helen's response, which begins with a protest but ends with a suggestion of capitulation, demonstrates the letter's usefulness as a tool for seduction.

Ovid claimed that the *Heroides* constituted a new literary genre;[2] whether he was in a strict sense right or not, these *Epistulae* were to have a long line of descendants. From the *Lettres portugaises* in the seventeenth century to Montherlant's *Les Jeunes Filles,* epistolary heroines and heroes have embroidered with frequency on themes already present in Ovid.

In fact, the letter form seems tailored for the love plot, with its emphasis on separation and reunion. The lover who takes up his pen to write his loved one is conscious of the interrelation of presence and absence and the way in which his very medium of communication reflects both the absence and presence of his addressee. At one moment he may proclaim the power of the letter to make the distant addressee present (the "je crois te parler" of so much French fiction) and at the next lament the absence of the loved one and the letter's powerlessness to replace the spoken word or physical presence (the theme throughout Leander's letter to Hero). A scriptomaniac like Andrée Hacquebaut, in Montherlant's quartet of novels *Les Jeunes Filles*, writes paradoxically to Pierre Costals that separation draws people closer ("l'éloignement rapproche" [vol. 1, p. 115])[3] because letters permit an intimate, interiorized communion ("dans votre silence je vous recrée et vous retrouve, tel que je vous ai aimé" [vol. 2, p. 26]), and yet Andrée laments at another date that letters serve only to increase the distance between two people (vol. 2, p. 50). The metaphor of the letter as a chain connecting two lovers is concretized in an unusual image in the *Lettres d'une Péruvienne* of Mme de Graffigny. Zilia, captured by the Spanish, communicates with her fiancé Aza through Peruvian letters— *quipos*—which are none other than knotted ropes that can be passed back and forth between the two: "les mêmes noeuds qui t'apprendront mon existence, en changeant de forme entre tes mains, m'instruiront de ton sort" (L. 1), "ces noeuds, qui me semblaient être une chaîne de communication de mon coeur au tien" (L. 17). The letter is here literally a chain of communication, one whose physical shape metamorphoses according to the sentimental forces acting upon it.

THE SEDUCTION NOVEL

An entire plot tradition, the novel of seduction through letters, is built around the letter's power to suggest both presence and absence, to decrease and increase distance. Typically, in such works as Crébillon's *Lettres de la marquise*, Mme Riccoboni's *Fanni Butlerd*, Dorat's *Les Malheurs de l'inconstance*, or in the présidente-Valmont plot of *Les Liaisons dangereuses*, the letter is an insidious device used by the seducer to break down his victim's resistance. The seduction (Paris-Helen type in the *Heroides*), with its emphasis on the letter as bridge, is followed by abandonment (Dido-Aeneas type in Ovid), with its appropriate stress on the letter as emblem of separation.[4]

These thematic emphases (rapprochement-separation) and the letter's relationship to them (bridge, emblem of distance) are not quite so neat, however, as our bipartite division of the seduction novel may imply. Even a work given over entirely to the abandonment part of the usual seduction-abandonment plot, such as the *Lettres portugaises*, will not emphasize the theme of separation exclusively. The Portuguese nun, who usually feels so cut off from her lover that she resents even the letter's good fortune of "falling into his hands" (L. 1) when she herself cannot, can at one point look upon the letter as making her feel her lover's presence rather than his absence: "il me semble que je vous parle, quand je vous écris, et que vous m'êtes un peu plus présent" (L. 4). Similarly, in novels that develop the seduction plot, whereas the seducer regards the letter as his arm for overcoming the barrier between him and his lady, the lady paradoxically regards the letter as an extension of this barrier, as her weapon of protection. Each time the présidente de Tourvel breaks her vow of silence to respond to Valmont, it is by way of self-defense. The letter affords her a greater distance and perspective from which to justify herself. A correspondence is less dangerous than private conversations, "ces entretiens particuliers . . . où, par une inconcevable puissance, sans jamais parvenir à vous dire ce que je veux, je passe mon temps à écouter ce que je ne devrais pas entendre" (L. 90). The présidente's letters, moreover, are always requests for further separation, asking Valmont to assume a more distant position, and consequently in her eyes function doubly as bulwarks.

Claude-Joseph Dorat's *Les Malheurs de l'inconstance* should serve as an exemplum of the subtle ways in which the letter mediates seduction. Dorat's novel represents a particularly complex confluence of seduction motifs present in other epistolary novels; moreover, in its title, characters, and plot it strongly prefigures *Les Liaisons dangereuses*, presenting a présidente-like figure, the marquise de Syrcé, who succumbs to the comte de Mirbelle only after a long and valiant epistolary resistance. A brief summary of this lesser-known eighteenth-century work, published in 1772, ten years before *Les Liaisons*, will make the parallels with Laclos's novel clearer.

The duc de***, so far unsuccessful in his attempt to seduce the marquise de Syrcé, decides to seduce her "par procuration" (L. 6). He chooses as his proxy the comte de Mirbelle, a promising but as yet unformed libertine, whose current affair with Lady Sidley is beginning to bore him. Most of the novel is devoted to Mirbelle's long but ultimately successful epistolary seduction of Syrcé, who attracts him at first only by the strength of her resistance, but with whom he winds up falling in love. The duke meanwhile tries (unsuccessfully) to seduce Lady Sidley through letters sent behind

Mirbelle's back. When Sidley discovers Mirbelle's infidelity, she retires to a convent. Syrcé confesses her sins to her mother and dies in childbirth. Recognizing the duke as "le bourreau de Madame de Syrcé, de Sidley, le mien" (pt. 2, L. 48), Mirbelle kills him in a duel and goes off to expiate his sins in solitude.[5]

The scene of the marquise de Syrcé's defeat and the circumstances surrounding it, like the parallel episode in *Les Liaisons*, are based on the letter's dual mediatory aspect. Mme de Syrcé, like the présidente de Tourvel, has just fled from the dangerous presence of her pursuer. She continues to receive his letters, however, and, unlike the présidente, reads them and responds. In a curious letter to Mirbelle, she describes in pastoral terms the labyrinth that is her customary afternoon retreat:

> J'oubliais un labyrinthe presque magique: il faut ma prudence pour ne pas m'y égarer. [. . .] Les routes en sont bordées d'un double rang de rocailles, où serpente une eau vive sur un sable colore. Les statues n'y représentent que des fictions, car ce sont des femmes qui cèdent, et je n'aime point cela.  On consacre nos faiblesses, où sont les monuments érigés à nos vertus? c'est le tort des hommes non le nôtre. Où en étais-je? je n'en sais rien . . . Dieu me préserve de mettre de l'ordre dans ce que j'écris! Je me depêche d'arriver à la grotte charmante qui termine le labyrinthe. Quand on y est, il semble qu'on soit séparé de l'univers; on y marche sur les roses, et on en est couronné. J'y vais souvent, surtout quand le soleil se couche. L'attrait y mène, l'enchantement y retient, on y rêve . . . à ce qu'on veut.
> 
> A propos de rêves, il faut que je vous raconte celui que j'ai fait. [She continues with a description of her dream of loving a sylph.] [Pt. 1, L. 41][6]

In a candid style quite different from the controlled, ordered, formal style of the présidente (who nonetheless discloses her underlying emotions to Valmont in her letters), the marquise de Syrcé gives herself totally away to Mirbelle (who, being more emotional and less intelligent than Valmont, would never be able to perceive the real sentiments of a less frank mistress than Syrcé). The marquise naively divulges everything—from her emotional state to the time and place she can be located—while consciously believing (as she writes to her confidante Mme de Lacé) that her flight and her letters will keep Mirbelle at a safe distance. The "égarement" of her writing reflects her erotic state, and the labyrinth is a convenient emblem for both. The "où en étais-je?" of the letter will be echoed in the "où suis-je?" of the seduction scene, as Mirbelle records it:

> ce voluptueux dédale . . . Quel objet! quel moment! à travers une charmille, je l'aperçois lisant une Lettre, et cette Lettre était une des miennes! [. . .] son sein n'avait d'autre voile qu'une gaze légère que le zéphyr dérangeait. [. . .] Je m'enhardis, la porte du sanctuaire s'ouvre, je parais aux regards de la déesse: elle jette un cri, sa main tremblante abandonne la Lettre qu'elle tenait. [. . . Elle ne songe pas] à réparer le désordre de sa parure. [. . .] "Je suis l'amant que vous avez rêvé . . . Oui, oui, reconnaissez un Sylphe à mon respect." [. . .] "malheureuse!" dit-elle, "où suis-je" . . . Elle retombe sans force et sans couleur sur le lit du gazon. [. . .] un voile de verdure enveloppa la pudeur; le Sylphe devint homme, et l'homme devint un Dieu. . . .[7]

The letter from Mirbelle that the marquise is holding is an ambivalent intermediary between the two lovers. It is almost simultaneously the breach in the bulwark that facilitates the conquest, having predisposed the marquise to amorous reverie, and the bulwark itself, insofar as it is one of the last protective coverings to fall; not coincidentally, the wind brushes aside the veil covering her breast at almost the same moment that she drops the letter.

The présidente de Tourvel succumbs to her much more aggressive and calculating seducer in circumstances governed by a strikingly similar epistolary mediation. Although Valmont invades her retreat with her permission, he enters Tourvel's house only on the pretense of returning her letters to her. In Dorat's novel Mirbelle's letter (and the preceding revelatory letter from Syrcé about the labyrinth) is instrumental in facilitating his victory; in the *Liaisons* scene, however, it is less the content of the letter than its physical aspect (the letter as object rather than the letter as message) that serves as catalyst. The turning point of the scene occurs when Valmont offers his collection of letters to the présidente, attributing to the package itself an ultimate signifying power that the individual letters never had: "Et tirant de ma poche le précieux recueil: 'Le voilà, dis-je, ce dépôt trompeur des assurances de votre amitié. Il m'attachait à la vie, reprenez-le. Donnez ainsi vous-même le signal qui doit me séparer de vous pour jamais' " (L. 125). The concerned présidente of course refuses to transform the letters, which she has nevertheless always naively regarded as instruments of "éloignement," into the "signal" for final separation; they remain instead what Valmont has always intended them to be: distance breakers instead of distance makers.

As a mediator of desire in the communication process, the letter functions on two figurative levels. On the one hand, as we saw in Dorat, the epistolary situation in which one writes to an absent lover fosters the generation of substitute images of the lover (e.g., the sylph that Syrcé dreams of and that Mirbelle decides to incarnate). On the other hand, as we saw in Laclos, the letter as a physical entity emanating from, passing between, and touching each of the lovers may function itself as a figure for the lover (rejection of the letters is the "signal" for rejection of the lover). Applying Jakobson's terminology somewhat loosely, we might distinguish these two types of figures so frequently fostered by letter writing as *metaphoric* (a metaphor of the lover is generated by the epistolary situation, which conjures up interiorized images and comparisons) and *metonymic* (the letter itself, by virtue of physical contact, stands for the lover).[8] Both types of figures have a long history in epistolary literature. The letter as lover (metonymy of the self) appears any time the letter is perceived as having the virtue of "falling into his hands when I cannot" (*Lettres portugaises*); in the hands of some lovers, what Saint-Preux designates as "un vain papier [qui] me tenait lieu de toi" may even become a fetish in sexual fantasies. Mr. B's, Lovelace's, and Valmont's rape of their women's private correspondence prefigures their attempted violations of their persons. The letter's figurative function as generator of metaphors, on the other hand, assumes importance in epistolary literature any time the substitute image or illusion of a lover created during absence is confronted with his presence; epistolary romantics frequently try to become each other's illusions or lament the difference between the image created by letters and the real lover. In both cases the fundamental parameters of the epistolary situation act in specific catalytic and inhibiting ways upon the seduction process.

The seduction novel provides a privileged situation for emphasizing the letter's ambivalence as intermediary. The marquise de Merteuil devotes an entire letter (L. 33) to an argument against the epistolary approach to seduction, citing the slowness of letters, the time for reflection and refusal that they allow the victim, the difficulty of writing what one does not feel, and the general inferiority of long-distance love to actual presence. In a rebuttal letter (L. 34) Valmont justifies his approach with the argument of necessity (since the présidente refuses to talk to him he has no choice), but in an earlier letter he has suggested a more interesting reason: "J'ai beau me rappeler mes heureuses témérités, je ne puis me résoudre à les mettre en usage. Pour que je sois vraiment heureux, il faut qu'elle se donne; et ce n'est pas une petite affaire" (L. 6). If Valmont chooses to write rather than act, it is partly for the same reasons that Pierre Costals, Montherlant's latter-day Valmont, chooses to write Solange when she has reacted totally passively to him: "En fait je vais lui écrire. . . . Par cette lettre, je retourne la situation, la mets au pied du mur. J'ai abattu ma carte, à elle d'abattre la sienne" (*Les Jeunes Filles*, vol. 1, p. 184). Both seducers use the letter to force their women into a more active posture, to elicit a response in both the epistolary and the sexual sense, in which she must reveal and give of herself.

The epistolary romance thus differs significantly from the libertine affair, in that it takes more time and forces the seduced as well as the seducer to play a more aggressive role. It would be difficult to imagine a long sequence of "lettres galantes" exchanged by the same two lovers; the novel that Fontenelle entitles *Lettres galantes de monsieur le chevalier d'Her\*\*\**, in fact, is a collection of letters addressed by the chevalier to numerous women, not one of whom receives more than four or five letters in sequence. An instructive contrast to Valmont's affair with the présidente is provided by the marquise de Merteuil's escapades with Prévan and the chevalier de Belleroche, or even by the vicomte's own libertine exploits with Emilie, Cécile, and the vicomtesse de M\*\*\*: each of these is the affair of one or two evenings and can be told only in "bulletin" form by the aggressor. Valmont's affair with the présidente, on the other hand, is conducted by means of a real exchange of letters and takes four months. Merteuil constantly rebukes Valmont for taking so much time, in repartees that contrast her own approach with Valmont's divergence from libertine etiquette and accuse him of having fallen in love. Whether Valmont is actually "in love" with the présidente or not is an open question; that he has invested significantly more emotion in this affair than in his usual ones is not. Moreover, the fact that Valmont conducts this particular romance through letters, whether by choice or necessity, is bound up with his emotional involvement.

The pure epistolary romance would be exactly the opposite of the libertine affair; by definition, it would be platonic. Crébillon's *Lettres de la duchesse de \*\*\* au duc de \*\*\** provides an unusual example of a uniquely epistolary romance (the duke and duchess glimpse each other only once during the entire exchange), but the typical romantic correspondence serves rather to punctuate and further an affair that is going on between the letters. If the letter in Crébillon's *Lettres de la duchesse* becomes an emblem of the physical and psychological distance between the duke and duchess, in *Lettres de la marquise de M\*\*\* au comte de R\*\*\**, by the same author, the letter is an instrument of rapprochement, at least in the first half of the novel. What is common to both novels, however, is that the use of the letter to mediate the romance entails an increased emphasis on psychological nuance and the details of everyday life.

The epistolary romance is a slow-motion affair, in the same way that an exchange of letters is a dialogue *ritardando*. It follows that stress will be thrown off events and onto psychology. What we observe in the letters of the marquise de M\*\*\* or in the Tourvel-Valmont exchange are the vicissitudes of a heart or the subtle interplay of conflicting personalities. In each case the use of the letter as the vehicle of seduction produces erotic and psychological effects that may surprise the seducer as much as his victim. The libertine Valmont begins to savor slowness, becoming "moins pressé de jouir" (L. 57); Dorat's rake Mirbelle winds up falling in love with a woman he had intended merely to conquer. In a not dissimilar fashion, Crébillon's marquise, Dorat's Syrcé, and Laclos's Tourvel are surprised to find that correspondence has served less to preserve than to erode emotional indifference. For both the calculating seducer and his virtuous victim the vehicle for detachment can operate insidiously to produce attachment, which perhaps unconsciously motivated the continuation of the correspondence all along. The letter is an ambivalent instrument and as such lends itself to a correspondent's self-deception.

The seduction novel is not the only type concerned with the effects of epistolary mediation. Of the four novels that we shall now examine, not one portrays a seduction via letters, and only one presents an epistolary romance. All, however, are built around the letter's power to connect or to interfere.

CLARISSA

*Clarissa* is certainly one of the most distinguished examples of the seduction novel.[9] Yet the conquest of Clarissa by Lovelace does not take place via correspondence; only 6 of the 537 letters composing Richardson's novel are exchanged between the heroine and her tormentor. It is true that Clarissa, in traditional epistolary fashion, does begin her relationship with Lovelace through letters, in which she tries to reconcile him with her family, but the reader sees these only occasionally and indirectly, when Clarissa inserts or quotes from them in her letters to Anna Howe. The novel, as François Jost has pointed out, differs from *Les Liaisons* in being composed primarily of "lettres-confidence," letters written to confidants, rather than "lettres-drame" written to the adversary.[10] The letter in *Clarissa* is thus neither a primary instrument of seduction nor a means for holding the seducer at a distance. Once Clarissa has fled her father's house with Lovelace, she is his prisoner, and the seduction scenes leading up to the rape take place in closed rooms. Yet this novel, more perhaps than any other, emphasizes epistolary mediation.

Let us examine Clarissa's reasons for writing Lovelace those first letters that we rarely glimpse. She writes originally at her relatives' request, to ask Lovelace questions regarding his European travels. After the duel between her brother and Lovelace, her parents forbid her to continue the correspondence, but she writes secretly, having determined that serious violence might occur if she did not try to placate Lovelace. Clarissa's letter writing from the very beginning serves a mediatory function; she writes to reconcile Lovelace to her family, just as she will later hope to be reconciled herself to her family through Lovelace: "If the circumstances of things are such that I can have no way for reconciliation with those who would have been my natural protectors from such outrages, but through *you* (the only inducement I can have to stay a moment longer in your knowledge), pen and ink must be at present, the only means of communication between us" (8 June, to Lovelace).

Clarissa's pen and ink will more than once be her only means of communication. While still in her parents' house, she is reduced to communicating with her relatives and her suitor Solmes through letters, having been locked up in her room and forbidden "to come into their presence" (6 March). When she exchanges her parents' prison for Lovelace's, and even after her escape, she is afraid to intrude into her relatives' presence bodily but sends instead an epistolary way-paver (29 July). It is only in the letter to be sent posthumously that Clarissa can write her father: "With exulting confidence now does your emboldened daughter come unto your awful presence by these lines, who dared not but upon this occasion to look up to you with hopes of favour and forgiveness" (9 September). Similarly Lovelace, when told after the rape that it would be "death immediate" for Clarissa to see him, writes her a penitent letter, calling it "a more pardonable intrusion, perhaps, than a visit would be" (7 August). The suppliant letter in *Clarissa* thus typically mediates and mitigates a forbidden contact.

Frequently, particularly at the end of Richardson's novel, one character "comes into the presence" of another by letter only, and not necessarily through a letter addressed to that person. Thus a kind of double mediation occurs when Mrs. Norton shows to Clarissa's family the letter Clarissa sent Mrs. Norton. Only then does the family begin to believe that Clarissa is really ill. They are not sufficiently convinced to repeal their curse, however, viciously blaming their own emotional reaction to the letter on Clarissa's talent for writing and moving the passions (31 August). If Clarissa dies in solitude, it is because only those who actually see her (Belford and Morden) are convinced of her illness. Even Anna Howe, who never makes it to Clarissa's bedside, cannot believe Clarissa's dire condition on the basis of letters alone: "But methinks your style and sentiments are too well connected, too full of life and vigour, to give cause for so much despair as the staggering pen seems to forbode" (5 September). The rhetorical thrust of such moments is clear: the letter is a poor substitute for direct contact. By mediating reality, it screens the *im*mediacy of Clarissa's plight.

The letter already constitutes a mediation between sender and receiver, but Richardson complicates this kind of interference with additional mediatory devices. Clarissa's correspondence with Anna Howe is frequently intercepted and even forged by Lovelace. After her escape from him, few of her letters to her family are answered directly. When she writes her mother, her Uncle John responds for the mother; Clarissa then writes her Uncle John, but her Uncle Antony replies for him; when Clarissa writes her Uncle Antony, her sister answers brutally.

In this novel where so little direct communication takes place, the letter writer himself assumes an important mediatory role. Clarissa requests Anna Howe's "epistolary mediation" (term actually used by Clarissa) on many occasions: between Clarissa and Lovelace's aunts (27 July), between Clarissa and her family. Even Belford abandons his role of simple confidant toward the end of the novel to assume a much more active mediatory one. When circumstances bring him into direct contact with the dying Clarissa, he experiences what is essentially a doubting Thomas's conversion; subsequently he will serve in multiple fashions as mediator between sinner and saint. From 16 July on, Belford remains close to Clarissa, serving as Lovelace's only means of communication with her. Lovelace, frequently dissatisfied with such indirect means, demands "pardon from her *lips*, which she has not denied me by pen and ink" (31 August) but is foiled in his efforts to storm Clarissa's retreat. Belford actually serves Clarissa as intermediary better than he serves Lovelace. As Clarissa's first disciple he ultimately transmits both the information for her story (handing over Lovelace's letters to her) and the story itself (when he becomes executor of her estate and protector of her memory). Belford will perform one final mediatory act, when he attempts to keep distance between Lovelace and Clarissa's avenging angel, Colonel Morden, in order to reconcile them (3 October).

Clarissa also tries to intervene between Lovelace and her cousin Morden. In posthumously delivered letters to Lovelace (24 August) and to her cousin (included in Belford's of 21 September) she begs the former to repent and the latter not to take vengeance.

These letters actually fulfill Lovelace's earlier dream of Clarissa's "sweet mediation," as Lovelace had transcribed it:

> At that moment her cousin Morden, I thought, all of a sudden, flashed in through a window with his drawn sword. Die Lovelace! said he. . . .
>
> I was rising to resent this insult, I thought, when . . . instantly my charmer, with that sweet voice which has so often played upon my ravished ears, wrapped her arms round me. . . . O spare, spare my Lovelace! and spare, O Lovelace, my beloved Cousin Morden! Let me not have my distresses augmented by the fall of either or both of those who are so dear to me!
>
> At this, charmed with her sweet mediation, I thought I would have clasped her in my arms: when immediately the most angelic form I had ever beheld, all clad in transparent white, descended in a cloud, which, opening, discovered a firmament above it, crowded with golden cherubs and glittering seraphs, all addressing her with: Welcome, welcome, welcome! and, encircling my charmer, ascended with her. . . . I lost sight of *her*, and of the *bright form* together. . . . And then . . . the floor sinking under *me* . . . I dropped. . . . [22 August]

Lovelace in his dream mistakes the mediating Beatrician Clarissa for a human figure, just as he later interprets literally Clarissa's promise to write him "from her father's house." Clarissa's "letter from her father's house" is precisely the Beatrician plea for repentance that is sent to Lovelace posthumously, inviting him "to follow me, as soon as you can be *prepared* for so great a journey" (24 August). If the dream sequence typifies the thematic emphasis on mediation and intercession in this novel, the post-humous letter foreshadowed by the angelic dream figure exemplifies the extent to which Richardson uses the letter's mediating property to reinforce his thematic emphasis.

*Clarissa* is constructed as a tragedy of indirect communication. Anna Howe's anguished letter to Charlotte Montague articulates the powerlessness of the letter writer: "I wrote to her [Clarissa] the very moment you and your sister left me. . . . Having no answer I wrote again. . . . But judge my astonishment, my distraction, when last night the messenger, returning posthaste, brought me word that she had not been heard of since Friday morning! And that a letter lay for her at her lodgings which came by the post; and must be mine! . . . Lord, have mercy upon me! What shall I do! I was a distracted creature all last night!" (18 July). The unopened letter, the intercepted letter, the forged letter, the deceitful letter, letters that arrive too late (relatives' messages of forgiveness posted the day of Clarissa's death), letters to parents written while still in their house: all of these compose the novel of a heroine who, if she writes at all, is using the only form of communication left open to her. The use of letters in *Clarissa* serves to emphasize the estrangement and isolation of the title character, such an indirect device being emblematic of the psychological and physical barriers separating her from her family, Lovelace, and friends.[11] From the beginning of the novel to the end, Clarissa writes from a situation of solitary confinement and avails herself of the prison letter as the only instrument that could, and yet fails to, free her.

In Richardson's puritan novel the moral landscape is clearly divided into three domains: heaven, the world, and hell. Clarissa's banishment from Harlowe Place, her descent into Mrs. Sinclair's infamous house, and her ultimate return to her "father's house" retrace, albeit ambiguously, the biblical myth of man's pilgrimage from Eden to paradise.[12] Direct communication between these three worlds is emphatically forbidden; the landscape that emerges is one of zones of sacred space from which "sinners" are excluded. Clarissa's invisible father sits within an inner room, a holy of holies from which he sends out directives of banishment via the son and the mother. Throughout the novel Clarissa abortively seeks communication with the father. As the sacred space is displaced from Harlowe Place to Clarissa's body and she is increasingly isolated within inner rooms, mediatory efforts diversify and multiply. Communication between Clarissa and the world, between Clarissa and Lovelace, must be effected via an elaborate system of transmission and intercession, of which the letters are emblematic. Richardson increasingly uses letters to emphasize the moral distance between sender and receiver and to underline the difficulties of communication between the sacred and the profane. Alternately viewed as sinner and saint, Clarissa is prevented from bridging the gap between herself and the world. Interceding letters trace the history of that gap but are powerless to span it. They can record, but not affect, *The History of Clarissa Harlowe.*

MITSOU

If *Clarissa* dramatizes in many ways the abortiveness of indirect communication, *Mitsou, ou comment l'esprit vient aux filles* portrays the failure of direct contact. Only twenty-four of the ninety pages of Colette's novel are in epistolary form; the rest is composed of narrative, description, and primarily dramatic dialogue. Yet the epistolary passages inform the entire work, since *Mitsou* depicts an epistolary romance that breaks down when it is no longer mediated by letters, as we can see by reviewing Colette's organization of her narrative.

Sections 1–3 (three "scenes" in dramatic style) present Mitsou, a melancholy, simple showgirl, who is briefly introduced to a Blue Lieutenant in her dressing room and begins to correspond with him. Little by little in section 4 (epistolary), Mitsou and the soldier grow to love each other through letters. The Blue Lieutenant admires Mitsou's simple, frank style and replies in the same fashion. When he returns home on leave, however, in sections 5–8 (dramatic), their first meeting is awkward. The more sophisticated Robert is repelled by Mitsou's apartment; in the restaurant Mitsou makes social blunders and they discover their tastes are different. Mitsou is shy and Robert becomes her lover reluctantly. The following day (section 9, dramatic and epistolary), expecting Robert, Mitsou receives instead a long letter from him informing her that he had to leave suddenly. In an equally long reply (section 10, epistolary) she analyzes the real reason for his leaving.

The above analysis of this simple story, told by Colette in a whimsical, almost Giralducian style, should suffice as a background for analyzing the role of the letter in the novel and the images that Colette creates to describe that role. In letters Mitsou and Robert must remain at the "vous" level, for "Le premier *tu* est un cri irrépressible, et on ne crie pas dans une lettre" (p. 96). The letter both maintains and bridges a physical gap across which the two can gradually reveal to each other their inner selves and their daily existences before the shock of physical contact would render such spiritual communication impossible. "Ah! chère, chère Mitsou," writes Robert as he is getting to know Mitsou through her letters, "que tout me plaît en vous, et surtout ce souci qu'ont vos lettres de me peindre votre existence morose et claire, et vide comme une mansarde neuve!" (p. 105).

When they meet in the flesh after their correspondence, "pas encore habitués aux nuances de leurs voix" (p. 118), they can only experience a malaise. To understand Mitsou, Robert must actually translate her spoken words into epistolary form: "la phrase que vient de prononcer Mitsou, il lui semble qu'il la lit et la relit, là-bas, dans un lieu dépouillé. . . . 'Je n'ai jamais été amoureuse, à présent je la [sic] suis. . . .' 'Elle aurait sans doute mis un z à été. . . . Que j'aime ce z' " (p. 137). Robert relies even more heavily than Mitsou on the letter as a mediator, however. Just as he needs the covetous glances of others in the restaurant to move him toward her, he goes through the motions of sexual love to accomplish an image of masculinity rather than out of personal desire.[13] Analyzing his situation when he awakens just before dawn, Robert recognizes that "c'est que j'ai cessé, en la voyant, d'être amoureux de Mitsou" (p. 167). Still troubled by the strength of his feelings for her, however, he realizes that "trop tôt, le hasard a fouillé un sillon où dormait vivante, mais non complète et frappée d'impuissance, la larve onduleuse de mon amour futur" (p. 170).

In his farewell letter to Mitsou, Robert returns to the "vous" form, after having used the familiar "tu" throughout their evening together. The Blue Lieutenant confesses in this figuratively rich letter that, erotically speaking, he prefers the slow rhythm of a correspondence to the accelerated one of the love affair: "Je n'ai pas encore . . . quitté cette habitude chère et énervante d'attendre longtemps—quatre jours chaque fois—la chute d'un de vos voiles et l'écho d'une de vos paroles. Ce dialogue, attardé aux obstacles de la route, m'avait donné de vous une idée de langueur et de nonchalance; je l'ai perdue cette nuit, entre des bras dont l'étreinte explicite et rythmée—plus vite, encore plus vite— éperonnait ma hâte" (pp. 177–78). Robert continues to find epistolary metaphors for his erotic state, as he expresses the desire to reflect upon the discrepancy between images of Mitsou on two different "sheets": "Je ne sais pas quand je reviendrai. Je ne sais pas si je reviendrai. . . . Il faut seulement m'écrire, Mitsou. Cynique à mes heures, je vous avoue que je meurs de la curiosité de confronter, maintenant que je les ai l'une et l'autre froissées contre mon coeur, Mitsou sur batiste et Mitsou sur papier. . . . Je ne baise que vos mains, ma chérie, et j'éloigne sagement, amèrement de moi, pour un temps, le souvenir de tout votre corps sensible" (pp. 178–79).

Mitsou responds in an equally colorful letter that she too felt that she had developed a great deal through their correspondence, but that the actual sight of him made all her "petals curl up"; she still loves Robert enough to try to "become his illusion" (p. 187). Less platonic than he, however, she reproaches him for trying to jump "à piéjoints [sic] par-dessus notre rencontre d'hier" (p. 184), suggesting that if he will grant her "la confiance et la bonne amitié de votre corps, peut-être qu'une nuit, à tâtons, tout doucement, elles m'amèneront enfin jusqu'à vous" (p. 187). Mitsou feels the same need for slowness ("tout doucement") that the epistolary romance offers, but for her the slow rhythm must now take place in a physical context ("à tâtons").

The mediatory property of the letter makes Colette's novel more than a simple variation on the old myth that "wit" comes to girls through love or sexual initiation. To be sure, Colette probably borrowed her subtitle from La Fontaine's verse tale "Comment l'esprit vient aux filles," in which the village simpleton is sent to a lascivious monk to get some "sense" and quickly learns the art of ruse. Mitsou, like the Agnès of Molière's *Ecole des femmes* or Arlequin of Marivaux's *Arlequin poli par l'amour*, starts out as the empty mind ("empty as a new attic" is Colette's image) to be schooled by love, and like them learns to lie to hide her affairs. The key experience in Mitsou's development, however, is not simply the birth of desire but the experience of writing about that desire. Not only love, but letters and writing are an "event" in Mitsou's life; she has never experienced either before. Mitsou begins her exchange with Robert naively; ironically he initially interprets her candid remarks as sarcasm and responds in kind, whereas she initially prefers not to try to decipher his ironies but to "look at his lovely handwriting" instead (p. 84). Only gradually do they become skilled readers of each other's letters, and Mitsou makes the most dramatic progress.

Throughout the novel Colette uses natural imagery of growth (seeds, buds, larvae) to emphasize that Mitsou is in early stages of development. Perhaps the key image, although a less obvious one, is the mirror. When Robert and Mitsou first meet, their images appear fleetingly in Mitsou's music hall mirror together: they look like twins. Later, when Mitsou is speaking to her middle-aged lover, l'Homme Bien, she realizes that while she has just spoken the truth about Robert, it sounds like a falsehood; she makes this discovery while glancing at her image in the mirror. In the course of her exchange with Robert, Mitsou begins not only to write letters but to see how she is being read: letters become the mirrors in which she develops awareness of how her self and her language appear to others. In short, the experience with Robert marks not only the birth of desire but a developmental phase for the childlike Mitsou, in which she first confronts a variety of mirror images and develops a sense of her self concurrently with a sense of language.[14] Mitsou also discovers the disparity between the self as seen from the outside (in the physical mirror) and the self as seen from the inside (in the letter as mirror). This discovery is not fully brought home to her until the physical encounter with Robert, during which Robert does not recognize the Mitsou of the letter in the Mitsou he sees. Only at that point does it become clear that epistolary mediation has functioned differently for the two letter writers and has produced unforeseen effects. Mitsou, who has physically desired Robert since the first brief meeting, suggests that the correspondence, by mediating the expression and deferring the realization of her desire, has deepened it into "love" (p. 108). Whereas epistolary mediation reinforces and develops Mitsou's desire, for Robert it appears the sole creator and sustainer of desire.

Concurrent and strikingly parallel to Mitsou's development is an evolution in authorial voice. This voice, present in all of the nonepistolary sections, shifts point of view radically during the course of the novel. The author who speaks directly to the reader in the first three sections prior to Mitsou and Robert's letter experience views Mitsou ironically and disdainfully, from the outside, with the same snobbism that Robert will later express. After the long epistolary section, this authorial voice will be submerged. The narrator who tells of Mitsou and Robert's night together will alternate between Mitsou's and Robert's perceptions of each other. In other words, the vision is no longer that of the ironic exterior observer but continues the essential technique of the epistolary section. The experience of composing the epistolary section has seemingly mediated and interiorized the author's vision.[15] Letter writing is a consequential event in this novel, and not only for Mitsou, who acknowledges it as such. The letter's mediation acts subtly, not only in the ambivalent ways it bridges the distance between lovers, but also in the gradual and cumulative way it operates upon the narrator's *Erzähldistanz*.

The idea of making love through letters is subject to many colorations, some contradictory, in the hands of various epistolary novelists. If the parents of Restif de la Bretonne's latter-day Abelard (*Le Nouvel Abélard*, 1778) decide to have their son court his Heloise through letters only, without ever seeing her, it is because they share the Blue Lieutenant's belief that relationships can best be developed slowly and at a distance. Abelard, however, does not recognize Heloise when he meets her for the first time, although—unlike Robert—he loves the girl he sees, and fears he is in love with two different women. Andrée Hacquebaut, Montherlant's most persistent writer of unanswered fan mail to Pierre Costals, justifies her monologue in illusionistic terms reminiscent of *Mitsou*: "dans votre silence, je vous recrée et vous retrouve, tel que je vous ai aimé" (*Les Jeunes Filles*, vol. 2, p. 26). Correspondence for young girls, Montherlant points out very early in the first volume of the same quartet, can be "un ersatz d'homme" (vol. 1, p. 62). The same Andrée who praises epistolary re-creation complains to Costals that perhaps if she had not given so much of herself to him in her letters he would have loved her, and she would not feel like an "empty envelope" (vol. 2, p. 50). The advantages and pitfalls of *l'amor de lonh*, which Denis de Rougemont sees as the essence of romantic love,[16] are nowhere better analyzed than in the epistolary mode, as *Mitsou* illustrates.

## MADEMOISELLE LA QUINTINIE

Just as *Mitsou* maintains the ambiguity of epistolary mediation while tending to stress the power of absence (rather than presence) to draw humans closer, *Mademoiselle La Quintinie* maintains that ambiguity with the opposite emphasis on the letter as an obstacle between people. If *Mitsou* presents mediation in a favorable light, George Sand's work is emphatically the novel of antimediation.

Almost half of *Mademoiselle La Quintinie* (publ. 1863) is composed of letters written by Emile Lemontier to his father, M. Honoré Lemontier, confiding in him his nascent love for Lucie La Quintinie and the vicissitudes of their courtship. Since Emile has been raised by his father in the best of the Enlightenment tradition, his idealistic vision of marriage as a total union of ideals and beliefs encounters a significant stumbling block in Lucie's religious mysticism. When the priest Moréali makes several mysterious appearances at Lucie's estate, Emile begins to be jealous of "l'image du prêtre entre Lucie et moi" (L. 2, p. 42) and suspicious of "le rôle du prêtre entre les époux" (L. 2, p. 43). Emile's father presents his argument against priestly mediation in terms more consonant with his Enlightenment ideal: "jamais plus d'ombres, toujours plus de lumière entre Dieu et l'homme" (L. 3).

Meanwhile we begin to see letters to Lucie from Moréali, complaining that she has written him too rarely, arguing that her possible marriage with Emile may endanger her salvation, and asking her to receive him in disguise. Lucie opposes such dissimulation and points out furthermore that "entre Dieu et moi je n'ai jamais pu apercevoir le diable" (L. 10, p. 106).

As Lucie and Emile make slow, subtle, but definite progress toward reconciling their differences, the obstacles to their marriage become more and more external. Moréali begins a series of machinations to prevent the marriage of the girl who (it is now revealed) had been the most promising student in the convent school he directed; considering Lucie his "spiritual" daughter, Moréali has destined her to head the nuns' convent of a new austere order founded by Father Onorio. Moréali sends for Father Onorio and the two prevail upon Lucie's father, General La Quintinie, to intervene. The plot now briefly resembles that of *Tartuffe*, with the general playing the role of Orgon.

Although this novel is not as epistolary as some (the last tenth of the novel is in the third person, and many of the letters themselves are given over to straight narration), the use of letters is consonant with the chosen theme. If we consider this theme to be essentially a debate between the forces of priestly mediation

(Onorio, Moréali, General La Quintinie) and the antimediatory Enlightenment forces (Emile, his friend Henri, Lemontier), we note that the letter in the hands of the former is an instrument of dissimulation, of mystification and concealment, often used to avoid direct confrontation between two people living close together, whereas the letters written by the group opposing priestly mediation are candid reports exchanged between persons separated by physical distance only. Emile learns through one of Lucie's convent friends halfway through the novel that when Moréali was director of the convent, "si quelqu'une avait un petit secret à lui confier, elle lui écrivait, et il répondait d'assez longues lettres, fort belles" (L. 24, p. 189). Moréali maintains his relationship with Lucie through letters, complaining that she does not write often enough; these letters moreover are full of mysterious affectations and suggestions of deceit. Emile and Lucie, significantly enough, never write each other, but explore each other's ideas in lengthy conversations, recognizing that "pour que nos idées arrivent à se fondre, il ne faut pas qu'on nous sépare" (L. 14, pp. 144–45).

Moréali, on the other hand, continues to use letters as barricades. He tries to prevent Emile from pleading his case to the general in person by insisting on carrying instead a message from Emile to Lucie's father and bringing Emile a letter in response. Emile refuses, demanding direct confrontation: "le fils de mon père ne sera jamais éconduit par une lettre" (L. 25, p. 211). At the end of the novel, when the priest insists on reading a letter addressed by Lucie's dying mother to her husband, invoking his role as the mother's confessor, Lemontier is horrified: "le prêtre . . . reparaissait toujours debout et omnipotent entre la femme et le mari, même au delà de la mort" (p. 330).

Father figures in this novel, like letters, constitute either an arbitrarily imposed obstacle to direct contact or a freely chosen, occasional resource to facilitate communication. Although Henri's father, in his capacity as counselor and friend, is called a "père spirituel" (L. 19, p. 152), he differs radically from Père Onorio or Moréali. His mediation is conducted directly in a triangle with "deux époux attirés vers lui d'un commun accord par une égale confiance" (L. 17, p. 153) and with the ultimate goal of self-effacement: "lorsqu'il ne les verrait pas venir à lui, il remercierait Dieu de ce qu'ils n'ont pas besoin de lui" (p. 153). The priests, on the other hand, insist on maintaining a triangle of indirect communication, in which one participant is always kept in the dark, just as Lucie's father (another of the many father figures vying for authority in this paternity case) refuses to understand that anyone could love his daughter and "s'adresser à elle-même au lieu d'aller demander aux autorités civiles ou militaires l'autorisation préalable" (L. 18, p. 166).

From beginning to end *Mademoiselle La Quintinie* sheds an unfavorable light on all institutionalized forms of mediated communication but principally on priestly intercession. This novel, in contrast to *Mitsou*, does not present a single letter that serves to draw the correspondents closer (even Emile and his father do not improve upon their previously established close relationship through letters). On the other hand, letters do often serve to separate people, to stave off direct confrontation, to cloud issues. Epistolary mediation in George Sand's novel tends to share, and reinforce, the same unflattering coloration that characterizes all imposed intervention—paternal or ecclesiastical—in this work. *Mademoiselle La Quintinie* is thus in many respects an intriguingly atavistic nineteenth-century novel, adopting a favored eighteenth-century form—the letter—in order to develop Enlightenment themes.

### HERZOG

When we turn to a more recent fictional occurrence of epistolary mediation, in Saul Bellow's *Herzog*, we must speak of mediation in new terms.[17] Whereas until now we have spoken of the letter as connecting two persons, in Bellow's novel the addressees never even receive Herzog's letters. Whether written on paper or merely mental, all but three of these letters are never mailed.[18] We can hardly speak in our accustomed fashion of mediation between Herzog and the dead or shadow figures to whom he writes.

From the beginning of *Herzog* it is evident that the past is to play an important role in the novel. In the first few pages terms like "formerly" appear frequently: "his friend, his former friend, Valentine" (p. 8); "his ex-wife Madeleine" (p. 8); "he was a formerly handsome man" (p. 10). The novel has hardly announced its time and setting as summer in the Berkshires when we are immediately plunged into a flashback—the preceding spring in New York. Formal flashbacks, which establish a new novelistic time, and frequent use of the past anterior tense to transport us briefly into an earlier past, set the tone of a novel whose time pattern will not come full circle to the summer in the Berkshires until just before its conclusion.

Moses Herzog's preoccupation with the dead is an important aspect of his concern with the past. He views himself as a "survivor" and seeks the meaning of his survival among the dead: "To realize that you are a survivor is a shock. At the realization of such an election, you feel like bursting into tears. As the dead go their way, you want to call to them, but they depart in a black cloud of faces, souls" (p. 96). On his trip to Europe he saw "everybody but the dead. Whom perhaps I was looking for" (p. 87). In order to capture the dead, to justify himself to the dead, to discover himself through the dead, Herzog writes letters. From the first paragraph of the novel we understand the role the epistolary form is to play:

> If I am out of my mind, it's all right with me, thought Moses Herzog.
> Some people thought he was cracked and for a time he himself had doubted that he was all there. But now, though he still behaved oddly, he felt confident, cheerful, clairvoyant, and strong. He had fallen under a spell and was writing letters to everyone under the sun. He was so stirred by these letters that from the end of June he moved from place to place with a valise full of papers. He had carried this valise from New York to Martha's Vineyard, but returned from the Vineyard immediately; two days later he flew to Chicago, and from Chicago he went to a village in western Massachusetts. Hidden in the country, he wrote endlessly, frantically, to the newspapers, to people in public life, to friends and relatives and at last to the dead, his own obscure dead, and finally the famous dead. [P. 7]

These introductory paragraphs summarize the episodes that will form the temporal base of all but the last chapter of *Herzog*. The first eight chapters deal with four days in the life of Moses Herzog, from the day in June when, after a checkup with Dr. Emmerich, Herzog decides to get away from his problems to Martha's Vineyard until the day of his return from Chicago to his house in the Berkshires. Although these four days constitute the

only continuous time in the novel, they account for only part of
the total narrative time. More than half the novel is given over to
random flashbacks, as they occur in Herzog's head, inspired by
various incidents during the four days.

Almost all of these flashbacks are preceded by what we might
call "epistolary seizures" on the part of Herzog. Typically, Herzog
picks up the pen to begin a letter ("Dear Zelda," for example);
after a few sentences or paragraphs we travel back with him to the
time that person suggests (in this case to March in Chicago, when
he conversed with Aunt Zelda in her suburban kitchen).
Fragments of the letter being written may alternate with
memories for several pages. A complete list of all the occurrences
of the pattern "letter/flashback" would account for half of the
narrative:

| | |
|---|---|
| p. 40: | "Dear Tennie, I went to see Simkin . . . " Flashback to visit to Simkin, who tells him ex-wife Mady's mother Tennie is hurt. Visit to Tennie. Flashback to Moses' boyhood. (Pp. 40–46) |
| p. 47: | "Dear Zelda, Of course . . . " Flashback to conversation with Mady's Aunt Zelda. (Pp. 47–56) |
| p. 56: | Letter to friend Asphalter. Flashback to March visit to Asphalter, who gives him letter from girl who babysits for Mady. (Pp. 56–61) |
| pp. 61–68: | Series of philosophical letters and flashbacks. |
| p. 69: | "So, Edvig . . . " Flashback to visits to Dr. Edvig, psychiatrist, where they discuss Mady's religion. Flashback to marriage with Mady. Flashback to incident when Mady insisted Herzog go to church with her. Letter to Edvig questioning Mady's "religion." (Pp. 69–84) |
| p. 88: | "Shapiro, I should have written sooner . . . " Flashback to Shapiro's visit to Moses and Mady's place in Ludeyville. (Pp. 88–99) |
| p. 100: | "Sandor! Last time we were in touch . . . " Flashback to autumn when Sandor and Bea looked after him after Mady threw him out. (Pp. 100–16) |

p. 128: Letter to Monsignor who converted Mady. Flashback to beginning of marriage with Mady, who quickly abandoned religion. Flashback to earlier marriage with Daisy. (Pp. 128–60)

p. 161: "Dear Nachman . . ." Flashback to his boyhood friendship with Nachman. Flashback to Herzog family life when Moses was a boy. (Pp. 161–85)

p. 207: "Dear Sono . . ." Flashback to life with his Japanese mistress who had warned him against Mady. (Pp. 207–16)

The next one hundred fifty pages are concerned more with the events of the third and fourth days of the primary time level: Herzog's night with his current mistress Ramona, his visit to a courtroom, and, primarily, his trip to Chicago to see his daughter Junie in the hope of gaining her custody. During these pages we see very few letters and even fewer flashbacks (the principal incursions of the past being Herzog's memories of his mother's death and his father's remarriage).

The pairing of epistolary seizures with flashbacks alerts us to the function of the letter in Bellow's novel. The epistolary medium here is a "medium" in the spiritualistic sense; it is the intermediary through which Herzog reestablishes contact with the shades of his past: "I've been writing letters helter-skelter in all directions. More words. I go after reality with language. Perhaps I'd like to change it all into language, to force Madeleine and Gersbach to have a Conscience. . . . and I've filled the world with letters to prevent their escape. I want them in human form, and so I conjure up a whole environment to catch them in the middle" (pp. 332–33). In every case the writing of a letter is the means through which Herzog "haunts the past" (p. 177). Herzog's letters serve as a bridge to the past even when he writes to the living. In the letter to Spinoza Herzog himself becomes conscious of the lack of difference between his dead and living addressees: "*It may interest you to know that in the twentieth century random association is believed to yield up the deepest secrets of the psyche.* He realized he was writing to the dead. To bring the shades of great philosophers up to date. But then why shouldn't he write the dead? He lived with them as much as with the living—perhaps more; and besides, his letters to the living were increasingly mental, and anyway, to the Unconscious, what was death?" (p. 225).[19] In Herzog's incoherent, unfinished, unmailed letters, it makes little difference whether the addressee is a real shade or merely a shadow figure.

The passage just quoted points to a second function of Herzog's letter scribbling. Not only does the letter serve as an approach to Herzog's past, but it also has a quasi-psychoanalytic function. The very "random association" about which Herzog wishes to inform Spinoza is an accurate description of Herzog's incoherent epistolary style. Herzog's scrawling resembles automatic writing. He himself speaks in the above-quoted passage of the role of the "Unconscious" in his writing as he does elsewhere:

> He had letters to write. He was busy, busy, in pursuit of objects he was only now, and dimly, beginning to understand. His first message today, begun half-consciously as he was waking up . . . [P. 128]
>
> He knew his scribbling, his letter-writing, was ridiculous. It was involuntary. His eccentricities had him in their power. [P. 19]

If Herzog writes in the first place, it is less out of a desire to communicate with his past than out of a need to justify himself. His flashbacks are full of allusions to the things he never said: "His mother had instructed him. 'You must never say' " (p. 33). His letters and reminiscences are an outpouring of repressed feelings, confession, and self-apology, "putting into words what he had often thought but, for the sake of form, or something of the sort, had always suppressed" (p. 398). In Bellow's novel, letters serve the same function for a post-Freudian hero that the epistle served for Ovid's Phaedra: what modesty has forbidden one to speak, passion impels one to write.

Letters serve a cathartic function for Herzog that often verges upon the role of opiate or crutch: "He dreaded the depths of feeling he would eventually have to face, when he could no longer call upon his eccentricities for relief" (p. 19). But the letter, as Geraldine Portnoy writes to Herzog, can also "give one a chance to consider—think matters over, and reach a more balanced view" (p. 127). In fact, by the end of the novel it becomes clear that Herzog's scriptomania is a temporary insanity and has actually been a tool for recovery of greater stability. Through his letters Moses pieces together his past and vents his pent-up emotions. It becomes clear that almost all of them are addressed, indirectly, to the one character to whom Moses Herzog never actually writes a single letter: his ex-wife Madeleine. Only after he has physically confronted Mady in Chicago can he return to himself, find peace, and begin life anew.

The "unfinished business" motif runs throughout Bellow's novel. Herzog leaves his friends at Martha's Vineyard a few hours after he has arrived, explaining "Have to go back. . . . Unfinished business" (p. 124). When he thinks of marrying Ramona, he remembers that "he was not through with love and hate elsewhere. Herzog had unfinished business" (p. 86). His letters and writing are emblematic of that unfinished business; Herzog somehow cannot seem to turn his current research into books, for lack of a "focus" (p. 11) and his discontinuous, incoherent, unfinished, unmailed letters are part of the same syndrome. So much have the letters become identified with "unfinished business" that when Ramona responds to Herzog's excuse not to go out, we appreciate the pun:

> "I shouldn't go out—I have a lot to do—letters to write."
> "What letters! . . . Business?" [P. 190]

Herzog's "business letters," though not of the type Ramona imagines, are only one aspect of the uncompleted "assignment" (p. 283) that Moses feels responsible for but cannot seem to define. Only in Chicago can he finally exorcise the "love and hate" that have kept him from functioning so far. In Chicago Herzog performs two significant acts that are the logical conclusion of the letters he has been writing all along. If Herzog's letters have revealed his obsession with Madeleine, his confrontation with his ex-wife in Chicago ends in a feeling of relief, and Moses finally wills his own separation from her.

A second logical conclusion to Herzog's letter writing is his conversation in Chicago with his old friend Luke Asphalter. Early in the novel (pp. 56–61) Herzog had taken up the pen to write Asphalter out of concern that Luke had become too close to his monkey Rocco. When he stays with Luke in Chicago, Moses discovers that Luke is obsessed by some of the same problems as he: love and hate, repressed feelings, death; in an attempt to cure his depression, Luke is doing an exercise prescribed by Tina Zokóly in which he pretends he has already died. Moses sympathizes with Luke but gently upbraids him for self-ridicule and self-punishment to the point of anguish and bitterness. His long speech to Luke terminates with the following self-discovery:

> When the preachers of dread tell you that others only distract you from metaphysical freedom then you must turn away from them. The real and essential question is one of our employment by other human beings and their employment by us. Without this true employment you never dread death, you cultivate it. And consciousness when it doesn't clearly understand what to live for, what to die for, can only abuse and ridicule itself. As you do with the help of Rocco and Tina Zokóly, as I do by writing impertinent letters. . . . I feel dizzy. Where's that bottle of Cutty Sark? I need a shot. [P. 333]

For once Herzog exhibits strength; instead of asking advice, he gives it. This is the first long speech of Herzog's that is coherent, that makes sense. Whereas he had not been able to finish the earlier letter to Luke (let alone mail it), Moses now is able to carry his thought through to recognition of the illusory role letter writing is playing in his own life. He realizes this only out of his concern for another person, however; in the midst of his first instance of other-directedness, he makes the most important discovery about himself. We might say that the earlier letter to Luke, which tapered off into soliloquy, has become a real communication, completed and delivered in a context of dialogue. Herzog reacts out of genuine solicitude for Luke, and in helping Luke confront problems he begins to pull out of his own mire.

After these recognition scenes in Chicago, Moses returns to Ludeyville. The time of the novel comes full circle as we follow Herzog through the last chapter. In Ludeyville he writes three letters (to Luke, Ramona, and his son Marco), which he posts and which we read. We are also given excerpts from a rash of unmailed letters. "Thus began his final week of letters. He wandered over his twenty acres of hillside and woodlot, composing his messages, none of which he mailed" (p. 387). These are Herzog's final exorcisms. Significantly enough, he can now briefly address Madeleine and her lover Gersbach: "*Dear*

*Madeleine—You are a terrific one, you are! Bless you!* What a creature! To put on lipstick, after dinner in a restaurant, she would look at her reflection in a knife blade. He recalled this with delight. *And you, Gersbach, you're welcome to Madeleine. Enjoy her—rejoice in her. You will not reach me through her, however. I know you sought me in her flesh. But I am no longer there*" (pp. 387–88). Herzog feels "a deep dizzy eagerness to begin" (p. 392). Death, even his own, no longer troubles him; as he looks at the middle-aged body in which he has heretofore felt uncomfortable, he acknowledges that it will die but also that he is "pretty well satisfied to be, to be just as it is willed, and for as long as I may remain in occupancy" (p. 414). As he putters about, tidying up the summer house that Mady had left in a mess, he wonders

> what further evidence of his sanity, besides refusing to go to the hospital, he could show. Perhaps he'd stop writing letters. Yes, that was what was coming, in fact. The knowledge that he was done with these letters. Whatever had come over him during these last months, the spell, really seemed to be passing, really going. . . . As he stretched out, he took a long breath, and then he lay, looking at the mesh of the screen, pulled loose by vines, and listening to the steady scratching of Mrs. Tuttle's broom. He wanted to tell her to sprinkle the floor. She was raising too much dust. In a few minutes, he would call down to her, "Damp it down, Mrs. Tuttle. There's water in the sink." But not just yet. At this time he had no messages for anyone. Nothing. Not a single word. [Pp. 415–16]

On this note Bellow's novel terminates.

Herzog's "dizziness" (pp. 333, 392) is that of the scales reestablishing their equilibrium. The letter writing of the first half of the novel is emblematic both of what has thrown Moses "off-balance" and of the introversion necessary to maintain one's sense of balance. Counterweighing the letter writing is the half of the book in which Herzog confronts the outside world and people directly.

Letters in Bellow's novel, metaphorically speaking, serve a psychotherapeutic function. Herzog's epistolary style of free association enables him to recall his past, to bring to the conscious level repressed emotions. In many cases we could speak analogically of a transference taking place within the letters, the shadow figures addressed in them being substitutes for the real objects of the repressed feelings. But just as the visits to the psychiatrist's office have achieved maximum usefulness when the patient can give them up, so Herzog's abandonment of his scribbling at the end of his novel constitutes a declaration of mental stability. Letters in *Herzog* are both symptoms of the neurosis and the means for the cure.

Epistolary mediation in *Herzog* is a mediation with the subconscious and with the past. As we have noticed, letters frequently serve as transitions to flashbacks. They are Herzog's "madeleines," his "instants privilégiés," the medium through which he resurrects and reconstructs his past—a past that extends through his marriages back to his boyhood and even back to the Jewish extermination of World War II: "These personal histories, old tales from old times that may not be worth remembering. I remember. I must. But who else—to whom can this matter?" (p. 184). Herzog's preoccupation with memory is Proustian in nature but actually shares more with that of Resnais's characters in *Hiroshima, mon amour*. Wolfgang Luchting's comments on Resnais's film are equally applicable to Bellow's novel:

> *Proust's* two main themes are, first, the time that destroys; second, the memory that conserves. *Resnais* treats these themes, too, but the other way round: first, for his protagonists, memory destroys; second, time restores. *Proust* is interested in memory. *Resnais* studies forgetting. . . .
> Resnais does not wish the past to reside in the present, he pushes it back into its own realm. Proust celebrates the past, searches it, makes it into the present, and lives in it. . . .
> Proust, although he knew of course as well as Resnais that the past cannot be revived except in memories, prefers the memories and finds his redemption in them. Resnais believes one can keep on living only by forgetting.[20]

Whereas Proust celebrates the past, Bellow and Resnais resurrect the emotions of the past to exorcise them. Only after the past has been conquered and classified as past can Herzog begin anew. The epistolary medium through which Moses conjures up the shades and shadows of his past is more than a "psychic" medium; it is the instrument through which he arrives at self-knowledge and regains sanity. Epistolary mediation in *Herzog* is both psychic and psychotherapeutic.

The letter's mediatory role in epistolary narrative derives precisely from its position as a halfway point, as an "either-or," "neither-nor" phenomenon. As an instrument of communication between sender and receiver, the letter straddles the gulf between presence and absence; the two persons who "meet" through the letter are neither totally separated nor totally united. The letter lies halfway between the possibility of total communication and the risk of no communication at all. In seduction correspondence is an intermediate step between indifference and intimacy; on the other side of seduction it is an intermediate step between conquest and abandonment. The same seducer who uses the letter to engage his victim at the beginning of a relationship may substitute the letter for his actual presence when he wishes to disentangle himself.

Even in *Herzog* the letter derives its mediatory function from its "halfway" nature. The letter writer writes in the present to a person whom he remembers from the past; as a transition to flashbacks in *Herzog*, the letter is intermediate between present and past. As a psychotherapeutic device the letter is both the symptom of the neurosis and the instrument for its cure, but it lies halfway between neurosis and cure; to regain total sanity Herzog must give up message writing.

Because of its "both-and," "either-or" nature, the letter is an extremely flexible tool in the hands of the epistolary author. Since the letter contains within itself its own negation, epistolary narrators regularly make it emphasize alternately, or even simultaneously, presence and absence, candor and dissimulation, mania and cure, bridge and barrier.

1. Letter 18, Leander Heroni, vv. 1–2, of the *Heroides*. Both the original and the translations from Ovid are taken from the Loeb Classical Library edition of *Heroides and Amores*.

2. See Howard Jacobson's recent study *Ovid's "Heroides"* for a detailed, insightful discussion of Ovid's originality.

3. All paginations refer to the edition listed in the Selected Bibliography. Wherever the author or editor has numbered or dated the letters, I use the letter number (e.g., L. 1) or date to identify material quoted.

4. The units of seduction-abandonment may be repeated, as in Crébillon's *Lettres de la marquise*, where the count reseduces the marquise after a period of neglect.

5. Those familiar with *Les Liaisons dangereuses* will immediately notice the similarities between the two seduction novels. The number of correspondents in each novel is limited (seven principal correspondents and five secondary in *Les*

*Liaisons*, six main and four minor correspondents in *Malheurs*). Although there is hardly a one-to-one analogy between the characters of *Les Liaisons* and those of *Les Malheurs*, many of the functions and relationships of Laclos's characters are present already in Dorat's work. When Merteuil at the beginning of *Les Liaisons* seeks revenge on Gercourt through either Valmont's or Danceny's corruption of Gercourt's fiancée, she is proposing the same kind of "seduction by proxy" that the duke plots at the beginning of *Les Malheurs*: to strike at the marquise de Syrcé through Mirbelle. Mirbelle's tutorial relationship to the duke anticipates Danceny's relationship to Valmont, but his affair with Syrcé is more comparable to Valmont's with the présidente, particularly since Syrcé follows a passion curve so similar to that of Mme de Tourvel. The marquise de Syrcé, like the présidente, has two confidantes—Mme de Lacé and her mother; the mother, like Mme de Rosemonde (whom the présidente moreover regards as a "mère"), makes her entrance close to Syrcé's defeat and sends a letter praising her daughter's virtue (pt. 2, L. 13—parallel to Rosemonde's L. 126), which arrives ironically just after her daughter's fall. In both novels we find a *chassé-croisé* of romances: Merteuil and Valmont switch partners with Cécile-Danceny, just as Syrcé and the duke switch with Lady Sidley–Mirbelle. It is surprising that Laurent Versini, who has explored in such detail Laclos's debt to his predecessors (*Laclos et la tradition*), should mention *Les Malheurs de l'inconstance* only in passing allusions without noting the high instance of parallel structures in the two novels.

6. In passages that already contain auctorial ellipses, my own ellipses are indicated by brackets.

7. Pt. 1, L. 43. It would be hard to overlook the erotic overtones of the sylph image as used by both lovers. In Syrcé's letter every detail describing the labyrinth that leads to the grotto-paradise evokes forbidden sexual pleasures, and the dream of loving a sylph that she naively recounts is a thinly veiled expression of subliminal desire. Mirbelle of course quickly perceives this. His reuse of the image in his letter is more openly suggestive of the male stages in the sexual encounter: "Je m'enhardis, la porte du sanctuaire s'ouvre. . . . le Sylphe devint homme, et l'homme devint un Dieu."

8. Roman Jakobson, "Two Aspects of Language and Two Types of Aphasic Disturbances," in R. Jakobson and Morris Halle, *Fundamentals of Language* (The Hague: Mouton, 1956), pp. 53–82.

9. Within the large corpus of criticism devoted to Richardson, relatively little discussion has focused on the novelist's use of the epistolary form. In 1951 the distinguished Richardsonian A. D. McKillop devoted a short article to analysis of "Epistolary Technique in Richardson's Novels." More recently Anthony Kearney related technique to subject in an impressive article that goes a long way toward establishing the thematic significance of Richardson's formal choice— "*Clarissa* and the Epistolary Form." The general consensus, however, continues to be that Richardson is less an "epistolary" than a "dramatic" novelist; cf. Ira Konigsberg, *Samuel Richardson and the Dramatic Novel* (Lexington, Ky.: University of Kentucky Press, 1968) and Mark Kinkead-Weekes, *Samuel Richardson, Dramatic Novelist* (Ithaca: Cornell University Press, 1973). It is not my intention to enter into a debate over taxonomy, since these descriptions of the novelist's technique are hardly mutually exclusive, each accounting for different sets of characteristics. I merely wish to illuminate further some epistolary aspects of Richardson's novel that have not been brought out in

previous studies, stressing as my argument in this chapter the extent to which thematic emphases in *Clarissa*, as well as in a variety of other novels, grow out of the mediatory property of the letter. To do so I shall build upon, rather than challenge, previous interpretations.

10. Jost, "Le Roman épistolaire," pp. 407–8.

11. Clarissa's letters are thus much more motivated than those of Pamela, who far too often "scribbles" out of habit only and continues writing even after she has rejoined society.

12. One must emphasize the extent to which Richardson displaces the biblical myth. Clarissa's banishment from her father's house carries all the marks of Adam's banishment from Eden, but only from Clarissa's point of view. Harlowe Place—where daughters and marriages are handled in mercantile fashion—is clearly as much a "Harlot Place" as Mrs. Sinclair's hellish world.

13. Those familiar with René Girard's work *Mensonge romantique et vérité romanesque* will note that in Colette's novel the theme of mediation as Girard has identified it (mediated desire) coincides with the particularly epistolary phenomenon that we have been analyzing in this chapter (mediated communication). That is, the letter here is accomplishing the same function as a mediating figure in the triangle of desire that Girard studies. Robert can desire Mitsou only indirectly, through the intermediary of the letter.

14. The mirror image appears frequently in Colette's work, but it is usually linked with narcissism. See, for instance, Joan Hinde Stewart's article "Colette: The Mirror Image," which deals chiefly with the relation between solipsistic writing and female identity in Colette's partially epistolary novel *La Vagabonde* (1911). In the same article Stewart deals relatively briefly with *Mitsou*, arguing that *La Vagabonde* better illustrates the epistolary "form's suitability for the development of questions of self image" (p. 199). I would argue, on the contrary, that the solipsistic, specular use of the letter in *La Vagabonde* is fundamentally nonepistolary and dramatizes in its very nonepistolarity the heroine's refusal to address the other and move beyond diaristic, narcissistic writing. What is striking in *Mitsou*'s use of the mirror image, on the other hand, and more closely related to the choice of the letter form, is its nonnarcissism. Mitsou's and Robert's letters, desire, and even their specular glances are addressed to the other, not turned uniquely back upon the self; the self is progressively discovered and developed through the other, in an exchange that is more arguably and profoundly epistolary.

15. Neither I nor the students with whom I have read *Mitsou* would agree with Elaine Marks, who finds the subjective, epistolary sections much less successful than the objective presentation of the narrative in this novel (*Colette*, p. 102). I contend that the exchange between Robert and Mitsou involves much of the subtle interplay between perception of self and other that characterizes the most interesting epistolary writing. These letters are perhaps less easily readable than the third-person sections (and an inquiry into the readability of letters at various historical moments would be in itself an interesting topic), but they repay close analysis in terms of the epistolary tradition and effectively modify even the "objective" presentation during the course of the novel.

16. In *L'Amour et l'occident* (Paris: Plon, 1939).

17. Bellow's novel is not, of course, an epistolary novel in the traditional, strictly formal sense. As in *Mitsou* the epistolary sequence alternates with other

narrative forms, yet the use of the letter is so inseparable from the thematic emphases of these works and is so based on the mediatory property particular to the letter that both novels merit treatment in this chapter, all the more so since criticism of these works has disregarded their epistolary aspects. In fact, I hope that my discussion will ultimately show that, though novels like *Mitsou* and *Herzog* would have to be classified as "mixed forms" in terms of narrative technique, they arguably are *epistolary* novels in a more specifically generic sense (see my Conclusion).

18. Yet Herzog's letters are not to be confused with diary entries or even stream-of-consciousness narration. The existence of a real addressee, whom Herzog perceives as "other" than himself, is a distinction that is crucial to interpretation of the novel, as we shall see in chapter 2.

19. In Bellow's text, all epistolary material is italicized.

20. W. Luchting, "*Hiroshima, mon amour*, Time, and Proust," *Journal of Aesthetics and Art Criticism* 21 (Spring 1963): 312–13.

# CHAPTER TWO

# OF CONFIDENCE AND CONFIDANTS

In chapter 1 we examined one set of thematic emphases and character types in epistolary literature that derive from a property inherent to the letter. We shall now turn to an even more visible characteristic of the letters that typically compose epistolary narratives—their confidentiality—which structures the thematics, character relations, and narrative action of letter novels to a remarkable degree. The confidant that the letter novel appropriated from classical theater is exploited in particular ways in narrative. In specifying the confidant's functions, this chapter will bring out a number of the conventions that give epistolary literature its generic coherence. Moreover, after detailing the conventional ways in which these functions organize letter narrative, we should be in a better position to analyze the more subtle ways in which a writer like Laclos works with or against them.

With or without the aid of a computer, we cannot fail to notice the frequent conjunction in French epistolary fiction of the themes of "confiance" and "confidence."[1] Clifton Cherpack was the first to yoke the two terms as a critical construct; in his review of J.-L. Seylaz's analysis *"Les Liaisons dangereuses" et la création romanesque chez Laclos*, Cherpack faults Seylaz for neglecting the *confiance-confidence* theme in *Les Liaisons*, asserting that only the marquise de Merteuil's hunger for the *confiance* and *confidences* of her cohort can account for the fact that this archproscriber of compromising messages should confide in anyone at all.[2] Far from being limited to Laclos alone, the theme that Cherpack finds in *Les Liaisons* is present to a greater or lesser degree in countless letter novels and seems to derive from their epistolary nature itself, from the very fact that correspondence is essentially a private affair. Expressions such as *(se) confier, (se) fier, confidence,* and *confiance* form a family from which French letter writers borrow constantly, just as the confidant(e) is a stock role in this type of narrative.

THE CENTRALITY OF CONFIDENCE

In order to make a *confidence*, as epistolary characters so often do, one must have *confiance* in the *confident.* If *confidences* constitute part of the epistolary medium (letters written to confidants being one of the fundamental vehicles of epistolary narrative), the loss and winning of *confiance* are part of the epistolary subject. A necessary first step in seduction, countless protagonists tell us, is gaining the confidence or becoming the confidant of the person to be seduced. "Je ne suis encore que sa confidente; mais sous ce voile de l'amitié, je crois lui voir un goût très vif pour moi," writes Merteuil of Danceny (L. 113). Lovelace calculatedly inspires Clarissa's trust with his famous "Rosebud" letter.

Often the seducer wins, loses, and regains the *confiance* of his victim during the course of the plot; the présidente de Tourvel, Mme Riccoboni's Fanni Butlerd, and Crébillon's marquise de M*** all realize at one point that their lovers have betrayed their trust, withdraw their *confiance*, but are reseduced. In *La Nouvelle Héloïse* there are likewise two important stages of *confiance*, but here the second is radically different from the first. The first stage is characterized by many of the *confiance* themes of the seduction novel; Saint-Preux pleads with Julie, "prends confiance en un ami fidèle . . . daigne te confier aux feux que tu m'inspires" (pt. 1, L. 5). In reciprocally confiding in each other at the very beginning, each asks the other to strengthen him, to help him resist in parallel letters (1:1, 4). *Confiance* is assumed to be a source of strength, yet it has the same result as in the seduction novel: leaning upon each other, the lovers fall into the very abyss that they fear, and they will blame their fall on the same "aveugle confiance" (1:7) cited by

Fanni Butlerd, Crébillon's marquise, or the présidente de Tourvel.

The second stage of the novel presents us with a new vision of *confiance*, in keeping with Julie's status as a "new" Heloise. If too much *confiance* is seen as the source of the lovers' fall in the first half of the novel, too little is viewed as an impediment to their redemption in the second half. The same Claire who called Julie d'Etange's misfortune "l'effet d'une téméraire confiance" (1:30) criticizes Julie de Wolmar's lack of faith in herself when Wolmar wants to leave his wife alone with Saint-Preux: "Je te reprochais alors ta confiance comme je te reproche aujourd'hui ta frayeur" (4:13). Wolmar's strategy consists precisely in overwhelming Julie and Saint-Preux with his trust in order to prove to them that they are worthy of it. The Saint-Preux who had abused "la confiance d'une mère" (3:7) is given a second chance by the fatherly Wolmar; *confiance* is a test for Saint-Preux and Julie that they had earlier failed but now pass. As Saint-Preux proves his trustworthiness, he is initiated into the salon d'Apollon—"l'asile inviolable de la confiance . . . une sorte d'initiation à l'intimité" (5:2)—and becomes worthy of the "confiance" (5:1) that Edouard wants to accord him concerning the conduct of Edouard's personal affairs. The untenable lovers' intimacy of the first half of the novel gives way to communal intimacy; private confession becomes semipublic and communal with the omnipresent Wolmar presiding, just as the intimate correspondence between Saint-Preux and Julie has vanished in favor of letters that could be read by other members of "la petite communauté."

Too much or too little *confiance*, extremes to be avoided in *La Nouvelle Héloïse*, are perceived as the source of ills in numerous other epistolary works. The incestuous marriage at the end of Restif de la Bretonne's *Le Paysan perverti* results from Zéphire's and Mme Parangon's having failed on several occasions to confide in each other the name of their children's father. On the other hand, the key element in Ursule's corruption in Restif's *La Paysanne pervertie* is her initiation into Mme Parangon's confidence and her reading of confessional letters from Mme Parangon to Edmond. Likewise, the *défaut de confiance* theme generates much of the plot of Mme Riccoboni's *Lettres de Sophie*

*de Vallière,*[3] whereas the misfortunes of Mme Riccoboni's Fanni
Butlerd and Richardson's Clarissa derive from their having
trusted their lovers or themselves too much. Any of the latter
heroines might lament with Aphra Behn's Sylvia, after she loses
her virginity: "Where got I so much Confidence?"[4]

### THE EPISTOLARY CONFIDANT

The confidant who inspires, wins, or loses trust is an essential
figure in epistolary literature, called into existence by the need of
every letter writer to have a "friendly bosom" into which he can
"disburthen his cares," as Smollett's Lydia Melford so often
expresses it to her friend Laetitia Willis in *Humphry Clinker*. So
important is the confidant that François Jost has based his cogent
typology of epistolary narrative on the criterion of two possible
types of addressees, confidant or antagonist, distinguishing
thereby between the narrative technique of *La Vie de Marianne*,
*Clarissa*, and *Lettres persanes* as opposed to, respectively, *Lettres
portugaises*, Abelard and Heloise's correspondence, and *Les
Liaisons dangereuses.*[5]

Confidants also play an important role in the theater, however,
a role so similar to that of their epistolary counterparts that it is
tempting to assume that there is nothing uniquely epistolary
about the figure. Indeed, Merteuil's and Valmont's frequent
recourse to theatrical imagery in *Les Liaisons*, their tendency to
see themselves as confidants in a play, encourage us in this
assumption. A schematic analysis of the function of the confidant
in general should help us to understand better the role of the
epistolary confidant and in what ways he might differ from his
dramatic counterpart.[6]

### *The Passive Confidant: Information Receiver*

At what we might call the "degré zéro de la confidence," the
confidant fulfills his minimal, passive, twofold function: he listens
to confessions, he listens to stories. Often at the beginning of both
play and letter narrative he has the vital function of triggering the
exposition. What he hears is an account of past events; this
narrative-connected role, obviously unsustainable in the dramatic medium, continues throughout the text to be part of the
epistolary confidant's raison d'être. Absent by definition, he

cannot witness the events to which the dramatic confidant is most often third party; they must be told to him. The only sustained role shared by epistolary and theatrical confidants at this minimal passive level, therefore, is that of sounding board to the hero's sentiments. Even here, however, we must make a distinction: the theater can do without the confidant, in monologue, whereas the letter cannot;[7] furthermore, as a tangible document the confidential letter is subject to being "overheard" by anyone at any time, with all of the resulting consequences.

## The Active Confidant

The confidant is rarely a purely passive listener. Even in letter narrative that includes no letters from the confidant, his voice is heard within the hero's letters through quotation or paraphrase. There are varying degrees to his activity, according to whether he merely contributes information relevant to the hero's story or actually influences it.

### Information Contributor

In both epistolary narrative and the theater, the confidant's voice constantly relieves that of the hero; he asks questions, fills in parts of the exposition, gives advice. The confidant may also be a source of new information unknown to the hero. On the stage as well as in the letter novel he may report events that he, but not the hero, has witnessed. Thus Julie in Corneille's *Horace* tells her mistresses the outcome of the battles, and Anna Howe gives Clarissa an account of a visit Lovelace made to her. Whereas this new information in an epistolary work usually takes an extended narrative form, in the theater it consists more often of brief announcements of marriages, deaths, arrivals. Such announcements, moreover, can produce a peripeteia in the plot, which the epistolary confidant's messages do less frequently, because of his usual absence from the center of the action.

### Independent Agent

An even more active role is played by the second category of confidants, who not only listen to, comment upon, and relate part of the hero's story, but actually influence it. The counselor whose advice is taken, particularly the evil counselor, would figure in this category (Oenone of *Phèdre*, Narcisse of *Britannicus*). This more enterprising type of confidant usually has a well-delineated personality, independent from the hero's; after listening to the hero's plight, he decides either to help him attain his goal or to hinder him. The confidant who betrays the hero's confidences (Narcisse in *Britannicus,* Euphorbe in *Cinna*) and the servants of comedy who both run and steal the show are the logical extension of this role.

When the confidant becomes such an important agent in the plot as to be a protagonist or antagonist in his own right (from Corneille's "Suivante" to Beaumarchais's Figaro), we begin to question whether he is actually still functioning as a confidant. If our examples in the preceding paragraph have been drawn from the theater, it is because at this level it becomes increasingly difficult to speak of epistolary and dramatic confidants in parallel terms. When the confidant takes over as *meneur du jeu* in the theater, his role becomes increasingly independent of the *confiance-confidence* relationship, whereas the epistolary confidant's continuing importance, even in his most active moments, derives precisely from this relationship. Even in Marivaux's *Les Fausses Confidences*, for example, we never see Dorante actually confide in the much more active valet Dubois (unless, significantly enough, it is in Dorante's *letter,* which Dubois arranges to have stolen and read in public at the end of the play). It is from the trumped-up *confidences* made by Dubois himself, rather than from those he receives, that Dubois, like Scapin, derives his importance.[8] Similarly, Narcisse in *Britannicus*, double agent though he may be, tells Néron secrets about Britannicus that are more of his own creation than his master's. Furthermore, if he can betray Britannicus's love for Junie to Néron, or the fact that the two young lovers are meeting secretly (act 3, scene 6), it is because of what he has *seen*, not heard.[9] The physical presence of the theatrical confidant determines his role as strongly as physical absence does for his epistolary counterpart. The dramatic confidant, originating in the "suite" of the hero, derives his power from following the hero around.

The epistolary confidant, on the other hand, derives his importance from the friendship of the hero, a friendship that is emphasized throughout and whose formation may even be portrayed.[10] If the action-oriented theater has little time after the exposition for the confidant to listen to the sentimental effusions of his friend (he tends rather to witness them as they take place between protagonists), the epistolary confidant will spend much of his time doing just that. Moreover, whereas the primary source of the dramatic confidant's power is his advisory capacity, the epistolary confidant derives additional power and perhaps his most essential role from the mere fact of receiving letters—as those most epistolary of all confidants, the marquise de Merteuil and the vicomte de Valmont, demonstrate all too well. The duke who is the corruptor-friend of Dorat's comte de Mirbelle (in *Les Malheurs de l'inconstance*) insists that as soon as Mirbelle seduces the marquise de Syrcé, "il est essentiel que je sois instruit" (pt. 1, L. 37), just as Merteuil wants the présidente's first letter after her fall. The epistolary confidant is most fundamentally an archivist.

It is therefore the passive rather than the active aspect of the confidant that is the more epistolary quality; indeed, the very activity that the epistolary confidant engages in depends on his having received *confidences* or on his effort to obtain them. In the theater the confidant, as he develops, tends to abandon his confidential role to become another protagonist or antagonist. Cliton, for example, Dorante's valet in Corneille's *Le Menteur*, talks too much himself, and particularly at ill-advised moments, to remain a mere confidant, and Dorante lies to him as well as to others. Dorante promises twice to make Cliton the unique "secrétaire" of his heart and "dépositaire" of his secrets, but when Cliton uses Dorante's refrain for the third time in the play, "A moi, de votre coeur l'unique secrétaire, / A moi, de vos secrets le grand dépositaire!" (act 4, scene 3), he is only acknowledging his loss of this role.

If the theater, more frequently than the letter novel, tends to develop the confidant into an antagonist, the letter form tends to develop the antagonist into a confidant. The exchange between lovers can rarely be prolonged without their beginning to make confessions to each other and to tell each other anecdotes about their daily existence. Thus Crébillon's marquise de M*** keeps the count apprised of the developments in her husband's love affair and her own reactions to it, and Saint-Preux writes Julie of his experiences in Paris.

The epistolary confidant shares much more with his classical theater counterpart than he differs from him. What differences there are arise from three obvious differences between the two media:

1.  The information that the confidant receives, as well as that which he supplies, is more likely to take a long narrative form in the narrative medium.

2.  Historically, conventions and *bienséances* work *for* the presence of the confidant as a third party to meetings between protagonists (lovers) in the classical theater, *against* it in the epistolary novel; and communication with an absent confidant of course differs immensely from communication with a present one. Even in meetings between lovers, the *bienséances* work against their making confidences or confessions to each other on stage, whereas the letter between lovers originates precisely in order to circumvent that *bienséance* for purposes of intimate, private communication.

3.  The tangible, documentary nature of the letter is the most fundamental source of difference and makes the epistolary confidant more important as information receiver than as information supplier (the source of the theatrical confidant's influence). Because the letter writer hesitates to make a *confidence* that can at any time through interception or misuse become an arm against him, and because the confidant wishes to overcome this hesitation, the theme of *confiance* will be emphasized more frequently in letter narrative than in the theater.

A CHANGE IN CONFIDANT

The epistolary medium, more than the theater, continues throughout to use the confidant in his most characteristic capacity—as receiver (rather than transmitter) of *confidences*. Perhaps for this reason, a change in confidants can often signal an important moment in the epistolary hero's development. As many readers of Laclos have already noticed, both Cécile and the présidente drop one confidante (Sophie, Mme de Volanges) in favor of another (Merteuil, Mme de Rosemonde) at crucial and parallel points;[11] both women switch to more indulgent confidantes at the moment that they perceive themselves as having lost innocence.

The inverse of this change occurs in *Les Malheurs de l'inconstance*. At the beginning of Dorat's novel, the marquis de Mirbelle confides to the duke the background of his secret affair with Lady Sidley. Mirbelle's honest friend Gérac enters shortly afterward as a rival confidant to the libertine duke. As long as Mirbelle's sentiments toward his new love interest, the marquise de Syrcé, are of a libertine nature, he continues to confide more in the duke than in Gérac. When he recognizes that his sentiments are those of love, however, he abandons the duke and confides in Gérac exclusively: "je ne me confierai qu'à vous, à vous seul dans l'univers" (pt. 1, L. 43). The account of his garden seduction of Syrcé is thus addressed to Gérac rather than to the duke, who had requested the first news. By refusing to confide in the duke and choosing only a trustworthy friend, Mirbelle—unlike Danceny and Cécile—keeps his affair within the private domain.

Mme Elie de Beaumont's marquis de Roselle rejects his sister as a confidante at the beginning of *Lettres du marquis de Roselle* because his sister has censured him. Soon afterward he declares Valville (in a letter to same) to be his unique confidant, this libertine being the only one to whom Roselle can speak of his love for the opera dancer Léonore. Throughout the novel Roselle's proper but well-meaning sister tries to win back his confidence; she finally succeeds in the second half by confiding her brother to a surrogate confidante, Mme de Narton, who gains Roselle's *confiance* and provides him with a well-brought-up girl to replace Léonore. The movement from sister to Valville and back to sister (through Narton) traces the stages of Roselle's development.

The conflict between relatives and libertines for the trust of a young man likewise organizes the first half of Restif's *La Malédiction paternelle*. N***'s libertine associations and marriage merit him a break with his family and a curse from his father; subsequently, N*** can confide only in his libertine friends, whom he transforms into surrogate "frères" and "soeurs." If N*** changes confidants so frequently (from his sister to his successive libertine

friends Loiseau, Zoé, Regnault, and "l'Américain") it is because
all of them seem touched by the father's curse—most die almost as
soon as they become his confidants. His first confidante, his
sister, outlasts the others but dies, as if by contamination, reading
a letter from N***. Libertine *confiance*, Restif's novel seems to
suggest, is tenuous and can never replace that of the unified
family.

In each of the above examples, the choice or change of
confidant is an integral part of the novel's signifying system. In
classical theater, protagonists tend to keep the same confidants,
who function to witness and intervene in the ongoing action. In
the letter novel, however, where the confidant is not already part
of the protagonist's entourage, and where confidential communication is more difficult and dangerous, the very formation and
dissolution of confidential ties become part of the action and acts
of communication become moral choices.

These choices are not without moral ambiguity. As Tourvel
turns from Volanges to Rosemonde, she annexes both an indulgent listener and a superego: "ainsi engagée à vous dire tout, je
m'accoutumerai à me croire toujours en votre présence. Votre
vertu remplacera la mienne. Jamais, sans doute, je ne consentirai
à rougir à vos yeux, et retenue par ce frein puissant, tandis que je
chérirai en vous l'indulgente amie confidente de ma faiblesse, j'y
honorerai encore l'ange tutélaire qui me sauvera de la honte" (L.
102). Valmont's need for his confidante Merteuil is surprisingly
similar to Tourvel's bond with Rosemonde. Valmont often writes
to Merteuil to distract himself from Tourvel, to regain his
libertine control. By returning to Merteuil as monitor of his
actions, by thinking himself "in her presence," he strives to
maintain the libertine identity that he associates with her, just as
Tourvel sees in Rosemonde an indulgent "guardian angel" of her
virtue. The confidant in both of these cases is perceived by the
writer as an alter ego who will help prevent alteration of his own
ego; yet this confidant who ostensibly is chosen to inhibit
forbidden desires actually allows the writer the pleasure of
speaking of them. Merteuil's wry description of the motivation
behind Cécile's confessions to God is readily applicable to
Valmont's confidential relationship with the marquise or the
présidente's with Rosemonde: "Tourmentée par le désir de
s'occuper de son amant, et par la crainte de se damner en s'en

occupant, elle a imaginé de prier Dieu de le lui faire oublier, et comme elle renouvelle cette prière à chaque instant du jour, elle trouve le moyen d'y penser sans cesse" (L. 51). In epistolary narrative more regularly than in the theater, confidants are chosen, not given. The choices as well as changes of confidant reflect the letter writer's own shifting values, selves, and self-perceptions.

## ECLIPSE OF THE CONFIDANT

If the turn toward a particular confidant can be an important articulation in the narrative structure, those moments when there is no confidant at all, rare though they may be, are likewise privileged. In narrative composed exclusively of letters, occasionally there may appear "fragments" written by one character to no particular official addressee (although they usually find their way into someone's hand). These are those points of high tension, of tragic isolation, in *Clarissa, Les Liaisons, La Nouvelle Héloïse,* or *Delphine,* when Clarissa (immediately following her rape), the présidente (after Valmont's desertion), Saint-Preux (forcefully separated from Julie by Edouard), and Delphine (after her sacrifice of Léonce) enter a state of shock. Traumatized, these writers close in upon themselves and let their inner turmoil pour out incoherently onto the paper. Delphine's comment in her first fragment could apply to all of the above characters' situations: "Je suis seule, sans appui, sans consolateur . . . c'est à moi seule que je parle de ma douleur . . . quel triste confident que la réflexion solitaire!" (pt. 5, frag. 1). Let us now focus briefly on each of these moments.

The only letter in *Les Liaisons* that does not have a specific addressee, letter 161 ("La Présidente de Tourvel à . . . "), is addressed alternately to everyone. The présidente's "tu" changes both tones and identities—from husband, to Valmont as deceiver, to Valmont as lover. Her "vous" is alternately Mme de Rosemonde and Mme de Volanges. In her desperation, the présidente fears a Valmont who is "il," throws herself into the arms of a Valmont who is "tu," and bids adieu to a Valmont (now "vous") who is tormenting her. The présidente's pronouns are as protean and confusing as the images that Valmont has alternately presented to her.

In *Clarissa* the scraps of paper that the heroine writes upon, tears up, and throws away are incomplete efforts to confess her fallen state, to articulate her feelings of guilt, betrayal, and anguish—to Anna Howe, her father, her sister, and Lovelace. The rambling incoherent nature of these messages, the eclipse of Clarissa's real confidante in favor of a series of shadow confidants to whom she can neither complete nor mail her thoughts, all translate the depths of mental isolation into which Lovelace's crime has plunged the heroine.

As Saint-Preux is being sped away from Julie in Edouard's stagecoach (pt. 2), his distracted state is similarly revealed by the short, elliptical sentences he jots down, addressed alternately to friends who are "vous" or to a "tu" who is Julie—internalized rather than real addressees. In Delphine's fragments (written, like those of Saint-Preux, in the stagecoach that is speeding her away from the one she loves), the heroine likewise responds in her imagination to people to whom she could not actually write what she is thinking: "Thérèse, que m'écrivez-vous? . . . Je voudrais lui répondre; mais non, je ne pourrais lui dire ce que je pense, ce serait la troubler" (*Delphine*, pt. 5, frag. 7). Alternating between "vous" and "elle" for Thérèse, between "tu" and "il" for Léonce, Delphine reflects in her fragments the same frustrated desire to communicate that Saint-Preux expresses when he moves from "tu" to "elle": "Tu m'as chassé avec barbarie, je fuis plus vite que le vent. . . . Ah! l'air emporte mes plaintes! . . . et cependant je fuis! Je vais vivre et mourir loin d'elle . . . vivre loin d'elle!" (*La Nouvelle Héloïse*, pt. 2, frag. 3).

In each of these four instances the impulse to communicate with the accustomed confidant persists, but is constantly frustrated by the eclipse of the addressee or by the proliferation of fragmented images of addressees. A hallmark of the resulting interior monologue is pronoun ambiguity (the présidente's use of the same pronoun for different unidentified persons) or alternation ("vous"-"elle," "tu"-"il" for the same person), which translates the writer's inner confusion. At such points in letter narrative, the sudden disappearance of a real confidant emphasizes the mental isolation of a traumatized epistolary hero who continues, even in his imagination, to address an unseizable and unreachable addressee.

What is merely a brief interlude in *Les Liaisons, Clarissa, La*

*Nouvelle Héloïse*, or *Delphine* becomes the basis for all of the hero's epistolary efforts in Bellow's *Herzog*. Herzog's trauma, unlike that of the others, constitutes a lengthy mental crisis, reflected in his case not by the temporary eclipse of a confidant but by a long anguished search for one. Like Clarissa and the others, he turns to a series of shadow confidants, scribbling fragmentary, unmailed letters that reach out toward an "other" not yet real. This shadow confidant, in spite of being addressed as "Dear Luke" or "Dear Zelda," is a part of Herzog's *traum*, yet is different from Herzog's own "self." Herzog's epistolary stream-of-consciousness is so "other"-directed as to have its logical culmination in the three real, mailed letters at the end of the novel, posted to Ramona, Luke, and Marco, whom Herzog can now confront directly. Moses' earlier unmailed letter to Luke expressing concern for Luke's health, for instance, has its parallel in Clarissa's unposted fragment to Anna, "But say are you really ill?" (*Clarissa,* 16 June). Moses Herzog is entirely in the tradition of earlier traumatized epistolary heroes and heroines insofar as his scribblings reflect a state of shock (caused in this case by his divorce), mental isolation, and a frustrated desire to pour out confused deep feelings of guilt, betrayal, and even concern for the person addressed, to an addressee who remains "other," however internalized a confidant he may be.

EPISTOLARY CONFESSION: The Fatality of Confidentiality

If the point signaled by a switch in confidants or the sudden disappearance of this figure constitutes an important articulation of letter narrative, no less marked a moment is that of confession.[12] Correspondence, whether between friends or lovers, is often carried on secretly, thus making any letter a potential disclosure if it falls into the wrong hands, even when its subject matter does not constitute a particularly secret revelation to the intended recipient. Conspiratorial letters, for instance, are the basis of Thornton Wilder's *Ides of March* (1948), a historical novel composed of chain letters supposedly circulated among the group that plotted the assassination of Julius Caesar. The truly confessional letter, containing a disclosure to the addressee, is thus shrouded in double secrecy. Secrets are a frequent source of suspense in letter fiction, their imminent revelation often being announced long before actual disclosure. In Mme Riccoboni's *Lettres d'Adélaïde de Dammartin, comtesse de Sancerre,* Adélaïde refuses three times to satisfy a friend's curiosity about her past before finally ceding. Mme Riccoboni delights in this fairly mechanical suspense technique, postponing until the end of *Lettres de Juliette Catesby* Milord d'Ossery's confessional letter explaining the mysterious actions described at the beginning, while Juliette reproaches him throughout for his lack of *confiance* in her. The end of a novel is an obvious locus for confessional letters; *La Nouvelle Héloïse, Mademoiselle La Quintinie,* Mme Elie de Beaumont's *Lettres du marquis de Roselle,* and Nodier's *Adèle* all close with confessions that have been duly anticipated. In countless letter novels suspense is thus transferred from the level of *action* (the adventure novel's mode of suspense) to the epistolary mode's essential level of *communication.*

Rousseau is no less fond of this suspense technique than Mme Riccoboni, although more inventive in multiplying both the secrets and the excuses for postponing their revelation. When Julie forbids her lover to ask about her secret activities to unite them (pt. 1, Ll. 33, 46), lest he cause them to fail, Saint-Preux agrees to respect "un si doux mystère . . . l'aimable secret" (1:34). Although the reader may guess that these plans have to do with Julie's pregnancy, he does not have his suspicions confirmed and learn the details until her confessional letter (3:18). Much is made of the "fatal secret" that prevents Julie from being totally happy in marriage; Saint-Preux is forced to interrupt his letter to Edouard just before revealing it, yet the next letter that Edouard receives does not mention it. Only later do the two determine that the letter in which Saint-Preux had actually revealed the secret has gone astray, and Saint-Preux writes anew. Meanwhile, the disclosure has been postponed for some eighty pages of the novel.

Even confessions that are not delayed for such long intervals are usually heralded by the letters that precede them. Thus Julie's admission of love at the very beginning of the novel ("Il faut donc l'avouer enfin, ce fatal secret trop mal déguisé!" [1:4]) is preceded by stalling messages and a final note: "Je suis obsédée, et ne puis ni vous parler ni vous écrire jusqu'à demain. Attendez" (pt. 1, billet 3). Such announcements, like the pointing finger of John the Baptist, emphasize the importance of the revelation that follows (cf. the pairs pt. 3, Ll. 17 and 18; pt. 5, Ll. 9 and 10; pt. 6, Ll. 11 and 12). In the case of these letter pairs, the epistolary form's potential to delay communication—even for brief intervals—promotes a thematics of secrecy.

Secrets, particularly in *La Nouvelle Héloïse*, are often fatal. "Ce fatal secret" is Julie's term for her love for Saint-Preux as well as Saint-Preux's expression for Julie's disclosure of Wolmar's atheism. Confessional letters and indeed all secret correspondence are likewise tinged with fatality. Julie and Saint-Preux realize from the very beginning that having once written each other of their love, they cannot stop writing. Saint-Preux refers to his first letter as "cette fatale lettre" and observes in his second letter, "Je n'écrirais point celle-ci, si je n'eusse écrit la première." When Julie takes up the pen for the first time she remarks, "de ce premier pas je me sens entraînée dans l'abîme." The very continuation of their correspondence reflects the fatality of their passion.

In many an epistolary seduction novel, letters are the instrument of destiny. The woman who receives a letter and responds, be she Crébillon's marquise, Mme Riccoboni's Fanni Butlerd, Dorat's Syrcé, or countless others, is taking a first step along a fatal path. Typically, she protests constantly that she should not write, and threatens repeatedly to cease the correspondence. But to the reader who turns the page and finds another letter, each letter appears a link in a fatal chain, at the end of which the writer must recognize, as does Crébillon's marquise, that, "A force de vous écrire que je ne vous aimais pas, je vins enfin à vous écrire que je vous aimais" (L. 40). Confessions of love, whether the result of a long epistolary exchange or the beginning of it, reveal the energy that forges the links together.

If we move from the seduction plot to other types of confessional or confidential exchange in letter narrative, we find the same apparent determinism operating. Any confidential exchange is motivated by psychological need, and the letter writer's own emphasis on that need (from Lydia's reiterated desire to "disburthen her cares" to Merteuil's and Valmont's impulse to provoke each other's admiration) often makes the confidential bond appear a bondage. To be sure, the continuation of correspondence constitutes a practical narrative necessity for the epistolary novelist, but his characters also charge the chain of communication with psychological necessity whenever the desire for self-expression, self-justification, revelation, or admiration becomes a major propelling force behind the narrative. The more confidential and secret the relationship between writers, the more dangerous and necessary the maintenance of their tie becomes; the confidential relationships in *Les Liaisons dangereuses* prove to be the most fatal liaisons of all, when the most confessional of the letters are exposed at the end.

CONFESSOR VERSUS CONFIDANT

In works where the theme of confession is important, it is not surprising to find the priestly confessor figure. What is more interesting to observe in epistolary fiction is the way in which the confessorial role is metaphorically combined with or played off against the confidential role. Restif's "paysan perverti," Edmond, is corrupted by two libertine friends, Gaudet and le Père d'Arras. The latter, with his built-in confessorial role, is easily able to win also the confidence of the naive Laure and her mother as their *directeur de conscience*. Edmond borrows from religious vocabulary to describe even his letters to his friend Gaudet: "c'est une confession que je te fais, comme je la ferais au Père d'Arras, entends-tu bien?" (L. 40). Interestingly enough, in Restif's synthesis of the *Paysan* and the *Paysanne—Le Paysan et la paysanne pervertis*—he combines also the roles of Gaudet and d'Arras into a single priest-confidant, le Père Gaudet d'Arras.

The ecclesiastical confessor and the secular confidant are emphatically opposed in George Sand's *Mademoiselle La Quintinie*. This novel, which was analyzed in chapter 1, is a serious treatment of an old fabliau theme: "le mari confesseur de sa femme." Here, however, the fiancé Emile, rather than donning an ecclesiastical frock to learn Lucie's secrets, wins her *confiance* on purely secular grounds and even divests the priest in her life of his confessorial role. Within his own secular domain, Emile is not averse to borrowing from religious vocabulary to describe the relationship of *confiance-confidence* that can be established between two people. He and Lucie use the expression "nous confesser l'un l'autre jusqu'au fond de l'âme" (L. 14); after

Moréali's first "confession" to Emile, Emile "absolves" the priest (L. 25).

Although ecclesiastical and secular confession are not distinguished on the metaphorical level in the novel, their difference is maintained on the ideological plane. In letter 17 Emile differentiates clearly between institutionalized, forced confession and the free confession made to a friend who has legitimately gained one's confidence. If Lucie is easily converted to Emile's way of thinking about confession, it is because she already has a notion of the value of the secular *confidence*. Early in the novel she points out that she is making a "confidence" rather than a "confession" to Moréali (L. 10). By letter 17 she is asking Moréali to gain Emile's "confiance" as a friend rather than as a priest. When Moréali tells Emile in letter 20, "je ne prétends à votre confiance qu'autant qu'il vous plaira de me l'accorder," he finally seems willing to abandon the role of priest-confessor in favor of the status of friend-confidant. Much of the action of *Mademoiselle La Quintinie* can be expressed in terms of the secularization of the confessor, in keeping with George Sand's philosophical polemic against the church's claim to a monopoly on morality and salvation. The replacement of the priest-confessor by the friend-confidant, or the transformation of the former into the latter, is part of this polemic, and it is fitting that the letters discovered at the end of the novel (the deathbed confession of Lucie's mother), which Moréali assumed were addressed to him, should be addressed instead "au véritable confesseur" (p. 287)—her husband.

DELPHINE: The Tragedy of Confidence

Mme de Staël builds a drama of *confiance* of a different nature around the heroine of *Delphine* (1802). *Delphine*, a model of post-Rousseauist epistolary composition, has unfortunately been overshadowed by Mme de Staël's third-person autobiographical novel *Corinne* (1807). *Confiance*—understood in all three senses of self-confidence, faith in others, willingness to confide—is one of Delphine's primary characteristics; much of her story concerns the betrayal of that confidence by her successively chosen confidants. Indeed, an analysis of this work should reveal the extent to which the narrative structure of the epistolary *Delphine*—unlike that of the autobiographically similar *Corinne*—is informed by the thematics of *confiance*.

A brief summary of the factors generating the plot of *Delphine* may help those unfamiliar with the novel to follow my analysis. At the center of *Delphine* are two star-crossed lovers—Delphine d'Albémar and Léonce de Mondoville—who, even before they meet, are described by their respective confidants as being destined for each other. Unfortunately, from the very beginning a primary obstacle to their union presents itself: the first letter of the novel announces that Delphine, by donating a dowry to Mathilde de Vernon, has just facilitated Mathilde's betrothal to Léonce, a Spanish nobleman whom neither Mathilde nor Delphine has yet met. Throughout the novel dramatic interest is generated by the sudden appearance or disappearance of obstacles to the Delphine-Léonce union: (1) a calculating, dissimulating mother (Mme de Vernon), who uses her friendship with Delphine to ensure her own daughter Mathilde's happiness and to destroy Delphine's; (2) Léonce's marriage; (3) the legalization of divorce by the Revolution; (4) Mathilde's pregnancy; (5) a Gothic-novel rival for Delphine's love, M. de Valorbe, who imprisons Delphine when she refuses to marry him, thereby ruining her reputation; (6) Delphine's convent vows; (7) Mathilde's death; and (8) the Revolution's legalization of the breaking of religious vows. Even when the last external obstacle is removed, however, the two lovers fail to get together, for, as at previous crucial points in the novel when their union seemed possible, the internal obstacles take over. By a quirk of fate these two lovers are not so well matched as all else would imply: Delphine's political liberalism and disregard of public approval in favor of personal integrity repeatedly clash with Léonce's conservative sense of honor and his sensitivity to public opinion.

Parts 1 and 2 emphatically establish Delphine as a kind of "héroïne de la confiance" and present as Delphine's foil the first character who takes advantage of this trait, her friend and aunt Sophie de Vernon. Orphaned at an early age and educated by her much older, fatherly husband, Delphine d'Albémar has been brought up in an atmosphere of trust and openness (of "confiance"), as she explains in a letter to Mme de Vernon's daughter, Mathilde, early in the novel (pt. 1, L. 3). This letter, concerning

Delphine's rather unconventional education, has its counterpart in Mme de Vernon's deathbed letter to Delphine, where Sophie de Vernon, likewise orphaned as a baby, describes her own education: "Personne ne s'est occupé de moi dans mon enfance, lorsqu'il eût été si facile de former mon coeur à la confiance et à l'affection. . . . Je renfermai donc en moi-même tout ce que j'éprouvais, j'acquis de bonne heure ainsi l'art de la dissimulation. . . . je déteste les moments que l'on destine à se tout dire" (2:41). Mme de Vernon's deathbed confession owes much to the marquise de Merteuil's long autobiography (L. 81) at the center of *Les Liaisons dangereuses*, just as the entire character of Mme de Vernon is reminiscent of Laclos's marquise. Never to write, never to confide, are Mme de Vernon's mottoes.

On the other hand, encouraging the *confiance* of others, particularly Delphine, is part of her strategy—not only encouraging these confidences, but discouraging those that could be made at ill-timed moments to foil her plans. Thus Sophie cuts Delphine off each time she tries to confess her growing and reciprocated love for Léonce, just as Merteuil stalls Cécile from confiding her love for Danceny until the marquise is ready to use that *confidence* (cf. *Liaisons*, Ll. 20, 38). As long as Delphine's and Léonce's love remains secret, Mme de Vernon can feign ignorance and proceed with the betrothal of her daughter Mathilde to Léonce. As we might expect of a woman of Merteuil's lineage, she plays her confidante role with studied, lockgate precision, releasing Delphine's effusions only at the right moment.

This moment occurs at the end of part 1, at a time when the generous Delphine has backed herself into an awkward corner by playing a confidante's role less successfully than Sophie de Vernon. Whereas Sophie has held off Delphine's confession, Delphine has listened all too sympathetically to the problems of her unhappily married friend Thérèse d'Ervins and has agreed to let Thérèse and her well-intentioned suitor Serbellane meet secretly in Delphine's house. When this meeting is discovered, Delphine sacrifices her own reputation to save Thérèse by letting society believe Serbellane was *her* suitor, not Thérèse's. She confides the truth, including her love for Léonce, to Sophie, entrusting her friend with the responsibility for disculpating her in Léonce's eyes. This time Sophie listens (Delphine notices that

Sophie "vint elle-même au-devant de la confiance que je voulais avoir en elle" [1:32]) and assures Delphine she has nothing to fear. Reluctant to disclose Thérèse's secret in a letter, Delphine entrusts Sophie with a note to Léonce instructing him to believe Sophie, in whom she has "confided" everything. As we might expect (although we cannot see it in an epistolary novel, which necessarily presents such events obliquely), Sophie uses this letter against Delphine; the heroine does not hear from Sophie again until the day of Léonce's marriage to Mathilde. The careful opposition of Mme de Vernon's and Delphine's characters in terms of "confiance" thus culminates at the end of part 1 in the first betrayal of Delphine's confidence.

Although the first letters of part 2 reveal that some of Delphine's former trust in Sophie is lost ("ma confiance n'est plus sans bornes" [2:3]), it is still strong enough for her to make another fatal confidence. When Léonce, repenting his hasty judgment, writes Delphine requesting an interview of explanation, she grants him an appointment, but Delphine at the same time makes the mistake of entrusting Mme de Vernon with a letter of safe-conduct for M. de Serbellane. Léonce does not show up for the interview. Thus at two crucial moments in parts 1 and 2 Sophie betrays her friend's *confiance* with the aid of letters Delphine has entrusted to her.

Delphine does not learn until Mme de Vernon's death, at the end of part 2, to what degree Sophie has abused her friendship and trust. When Mme de Vernon is dying, Delphine finally becomes her confidante and even more—her confessor. Sophie's daughter Mathilde and her priest try repeatedly to force Mme de Vernon to accept confession and the rites of extreme unction, but Sophie finds it impossible to "parler avec confiance à un homme que je ne connais point" (p. 228). Instead Sophie chooses Delphine as her bedside minister and her long letter to Delphine serves as her confession, Delphine being the only one who can, and does, absolve her. The thematics of confidence here is reinforced by an opposition of religious confession to secular confession, which we have already seen is the main motif of *Mademoiselle La Quintinie*.

Mme de Vernon is not the only foil for the "confiante" Delphine. The man she has recognized as her destined spiritual partner betrays Delphine's trust less villainously but no less frequently than Delphine's friend. Léonce's willingness to accept the opinion of third parties regarding Delphine's actions demonstrates a lack of trust that Delphine perceives immediately after his marriage (2:21). Whereas Mme de Vernon betrays Delphine's *confiance* by exploiting it, Léonce betrays it by failing to return it. Thus, even after he and Delphine establish the truth and resume a chaste lovers' relationship, Léonce will repeatedly take umbrage at certain of Delphine's or others' actions, close in upon himself, and refuse to confide in Delphine. Particularly salient are Léonce's parallel, mystifying silences after he and Delphine separately receive letters from M. de Lebensei justifying divorce (4:19) and the breaking of convent vows (6:12). In each case Léonce refuses to reveal his reaction to the possibility of overcoming the obstacles to their union, and Delphine must lament the erosion of "la plus douce de nos jouissances, la parfaite confiance déjà altérée!" (4:22). The contrast between their characters is nowhere more evident than in part 3, when Léonce's annoyance at the platonism of their relationship is translated in epistolary fashion by curtness and mystification. In this sequence of exchanges (3:20–23), Léonce's short notes contrast visibly on the printed page with Delphine's intervening long effusive letters. Léonce obediently agrees not to alter the chaste nature of their love, but his withdrawal, his refusal to confide in Delphine, has stifled some of her own *confiance*: "j'étais heureuse, je vous l'aurais dit; oh! que vous avez bien réprimé cette confiance imprudente!" (3:21).

Throughout Mme de Staël's novel, Delphine continues to find her *confiance* frustrated, betrayed, exploited. Even her rejected suitor, M. de Valorbe, responds to Delphine's generous concern when she visits him in prison by locking her up with him (Delphine: "c'est l'amitié que j'avais pour vous que vous punissez . . . c'est ma confiance en vous dont vous démontrez la folie" [5:24]). In each of the six sections of the novel Delphine's *confiance* is subjected to a major blow: 1—Léonce's and Mme de Vernon's betrayal, which leads to the marriage; 2—Léonce's second preference of Mme de Vernon's *confidences* to Delphine's; 3—Léonce's withdrawal of *confiance* because of sexual frustration; 4—Léonce's refusal to confide in Delphine after M. de Lebensei's letter on divorce; 5—Valorbe's betrayal of her trust; 6—Léonce's withdrawal after the second Lebensei letter.

Even those friends of Delphine who fill the more traditional confidant role—that is, the role of listener rather than protagonist in the plot—in some sense fail her. Delphine confides most regularly in her older sister-in-law Louise d'Albémar, but switches in part 4 to Mme de Lebensei, returning to Louise only in part 5; occasionally she confides in Mme d'Artenas, Mme de R., or Mme de Cerlèbe. As Delphine switches from one confidante to another, each appears inadequate; they either misunderstand her, disappear at crucial moments when she needs them, or try ineffectually to tear Delphine away from her amorous ties, thus appearing as weak rivals to Léonce and Mme de Vernon for Delphine's allegiance. Delphine's repeated failure to leave Paris to go live with Louise in the country demonstrates the weakness of traditional confidential ties in this novel.

If Delphine's confidantes disappear or can be discarded so easily, it may well be due to Mme de Staël's mechanics: they appear when epistolary exigencies require them and disappear when no longer needed. But even if technical necessities are the prime motive, an important thematic result is the creation of a vacuum of *confiance* around Delphine, as one after another of her chosen confidants fail her, either through exploitation of *confiance* (Sophie, Valorbe), nonreciprocation (Léonce), or ineffectuality (Louise, Mme d'Artenas, and others). For this heroine who is continually defined as "confiante," *confiance* is a total affair, involving a personal self-confidence independent of others' opinions and demanding relationships in which trust and sharing of innermost thoughts would be mutual and unlimited. The only people who reciprocate this *confiance* cannot hold Delphine; those who attract her cannot match her *confiance*. In part 5 Delphine cries out that "il vaut mieux mourir que de se livrer à un sentiment de confiance ou d'abandon qui ne serait pas entièrement partagé par ce qu'on aime" (5:25). Her tragic suicide is the necessary conclusion.

CONFIDENCE VERSUS COQUETRY:
## The Language of Friendship and the Language of Love

The thematics of *confiance/non-confiance* in *Delphine* and other works is integrally related to the thematics of *amitié/amour*. If we examine any epistolary work whose plot relies heavily on the winning or losing, existence or nonexistence, of *confiance* (*Les Liaisons dangereuses, Delphine, La Nouvelle Héloïse*, and countless others), we note a similar emphasis on the importance of *amitié* and a frequent opposition of *amitié* to *amour*, of *l'ami* to *l'amant*. Mme Riccoboni's novels provide a case in point, with their valorization of candor and trust in opposition to secrecy and feint. Here, as elsewhere, *confiance-confidence* appears the province of *amitié*; to receive or make confidences, even lovers must become friends. Typical is Juliette Catesby's statement to her former suitor who has finally confided in her: "sensible à votre confiance . . . je vous reverrai avec ce plaisir vif qu'on sent en retrouvant un ami" (*Lettres de Juliette Catesby*, L. 37). "Le charme de la confiance" that Mme Riccoboni's Fanni Butlerd repeatedly praises becomes so much the property of "l'amitié" that the two are fused into the cliché "le charme de la confiante amitié" of other epistolary fiction. Rousseau's Julie is very much in the tradition of Mme Riccoboni's heroines when she values "confiance" and "franchise" above "amour." The oath that Julie exacts from her lover is not an oath of "amour éternel," as Julie herself points out, but of "vérité, sincérité, franchise inviolable": "Jure-moi . . . que je ne cesserai jamais d'être la confidente de ton coeur" (1:35).

To the ties of "confiance," "amitié," and sincerity are usually opposed dissimulation, feint, and the desire to please. Fanni is constantly contrasting "le naturel et la vérité" of her own epistolary style with the studied art, and implied feint, of Milord Alfred, whose prime purpose is to "please." Merteuil writes Valmont that she is bound to him by "la confiante amitié: c'est elle qui fait que vous êtes toujours ce que j'aime le mieux; mais en vérité: le Chevalier est ce qui me plaît davantage" (L. 10). When Delphine opposes "confiance" to "coquetterie" (1:6), she sums up the essential difference between the two possible approaches to relationships and epistolary style.

It should be evident that we are dealing here with two separate, although related, aspects of epistolary *confiance*. On the one hand, in opposing *amitié* to *amour*, we are doing little more than distinguishing between the two principal slots into which almost all epistolary characters fit: the friend-confidant or the lover.[13] On the other hand, in opposing "confiance" and sincerity to coquetry or dissimulation, we are dealing with questions of style or tone.

This division would oppose two essential letter traditions: that of Crébillon and Laclos to that of Richardson, Mme Riccoboni, and Rousseau. The letter has been extolled by epistolary authors for its potential both as a faithful portrait and as a deceptive mask, as we can easily see by comparing the preface to *Fanni Butlerd* ("le naturel et la vérité . . . sont tout le mérite de ces Lettres") and Merteuil's advice to Cécile ("Vous voyez bien que, quand vous écrivez à quelqu'un, c'est pour lui et non pas pour vous: vous devez donc moins chercher à lui dire ce que vous pensez, que ce qui lui *plaît* davantage" [L. 105; italics mine]).

As might be expected, the relationship polarity (*amitié/amour* or confidant/lover) and the tone polarity (*confiance/coquetterie* or candor/dissimulation) frequently coincide. More often than not, letter writers restrain themselves with the lover (or mystify or deceive him) while revealing their real sentiments to the confidant. Thus Lovelace writes, "I never lied to man and hardly ever said truth to woman"; Valmont tells the présidente about his "pupitre" but reveals to his confidante Merteuil the true nature of this writing desk. But just as some of the most interesting plays are those that lie on the generic borderline between tragedy and comedy and therefore can play off our expectations of one against the conventions of the other, so some of the most intriguing epistolary works blur these distinctions between the associated pairs *confiance-amitié* and *coquetterie-amour*.

A common instance of blurring is that in which an epistolary character dissimulates with a friend (the duke in Dorat's *Les Malheurs de l'inconstance* closes almost every letter to Mirbelle with an allusion to their "amitié" yet deceives him about Syrcé and Sidley) or takes his lover for a confidant: almost all epistolary lovers are forced by the medium itself to write occasional *lettres-confidence* to each other. These cases are so common as to be uninteresting in and of themselves. It is only when a tension is created between the confidant and lover roles, between the options of *confiance* and *coquetterie*, so as to produce what Hans Wolpe would call "psychological ambiguity,"[14] that blurring merits closer attention.

For example, the bond between Delphine and Sophie de Vernon is one of friendship, but from the very beginning this bond is troubled by an equivocal element. Delphine's constrained "inquiétude" in her first letter to Sophie, her fear of having "displeased," her malaise at finding that Mathilde has come between them, contrast with the next, much longer letter to her sister-in-law, in which she speaks freely of everything, including her relationship with Sophie: "Il n'existe aucune borne à ma confiance en elle; mais, sans que j'y réfléchisse, je me trouve naturellement disposée à ne lui dire que ce qui peut l'intéresser; je renvoie toujours au lendemain pour lui parler des pensées qui m'occupent. . . . mon désir de lui *plaire* met dans mon amitié pour elle encore plus, pour ainsi dire de *coquetterie* que de *confiance*" (1:6; italics mine). This movement from constraint to effusion, from "coquetterie" (with Sophie) to real "confiance" (with Louise), mimes the conventional epistolary movement from lover to confidant. If we have not yet grasped this movement, Delphine's subsequent allusions to Mme de Vernon's "charme," to the "je ne sais quoi" that attracts her to Sophie, making her repeatedly forgive her aunt in spite of herself, and ultimately the violence of Delphine's disillusionment, impress upon us that the bond between the two is comparable in strength and nature only to that between Delphine and Léonce. The similarity between Sophie's and Léonce's hold over Delphine is reflected in her desire to *please* them regardless of how ill-matched her character is to theirs.

When Delphine discovers the full extent of Sophie's betrayal of her "tendre amitié," her vocabulary reveals both the strength and the ambiguity of the ties between them: "Je suis troublée, tremblante, irritée comme s'il s'agissait de Léonce. Ah! quand on a consacré tant de soins, tant de services, tant d'années à conquérir une amitié pour le reste de ses jours, quelle douleur on éprouve. . . . Je ne puis plus offrir à personne ce coeur qui se livrait sans réserve, et dont elle a possédé les premières affections" (2:31). The tension between words like "amitié" and "tendre," "amitié" and "conquérir," and the comparisons of Sophie to her lover that run counter to comparisons of Sophie and her regular confidante Louise, maintain the ambiguity of a relationship that is neither *amitié* for a confidante nor *amour* for a lover, but equivocally both.[15]

The "tendre amitié" that binds Delphine to Sophie has its obvious parallel in the relationship between the "inseparables" in

*La Nouvelle Héloïse.* Claire, like Mme de Vernon for Delphine, is much more than a confidante to Julie,[16] and occasionally the bonds between these two appear even stronger than those between Julie and Saint-Preux. How revealing, for instance, is the first line of the note in which Claire announces to Saint-Preux Julie's marriage: "votre amante n'est plus; mais j'ai retrouvé mon amie" (3:17).

If Claire and Julie are "inseparables," Julie and Saint-Preux are all too separable. The themes of separation and absence, which since the *Heroides* have been the special property of lovers' correspondence, are just as important, if not more stressed, in Julie's letters to Claire than in her correspondence with Saint-Preux. Whereas Julie on several occasions requests Saint-Preux's absence (Claire is even twice—in 1:64 and 3:1—the instrument of their separation), she laments the distance between herself and Claire more frequently than the various absences of her lover. Julie's first letter to Claire is punctuated by a "reviens" that will be the thematic refrain of most of her letters to her cousin. At first it would appear that Julie needs Claire's presence primarily as a confidante and chaperone to protect her virtue (1:6, 7, 28, 29), but by the time Julie opens part 4 with a letter to Claire, "Que tu tardes longtemps à revenir. . . . Pour moi, ton absence me paraît de jour en jour plus insupportable, et je ne puis plus vivre un instant sans toi," it is clear that her need for Claire is much deeper. Significantly enough, Rousseau's novel closes on the theme of the unmaintainable separation of the inseparables: "Confiance, amitié, vertus, plaisirs, folâtres jeux, la terre a tout englouti. [. . .] son cercueil ne la contient pas tout entière . . . il attend le reste de sa proie . . . il ne l'attendra pas longtemps." *Amitié* in *La Nouvelle Héloïse* thus constitutes in many ways a stronger bond than *amour* and even borrows some of the properties of the love relationship. When love is finally expunged from Saint-Preux's life, he and Edouard follow the example set by Julie and Claire and become "inseparable" themselves. As Saint-Preux vows to Edouard: "le règne de l'amour est passé, que celui de l'amitié commence; . . . je ne te quitte plus qu'à la mort" (4:3).

The relationships of the four principal characters in *La Nouvelle Héloïse* are marked by a certain interchangeability of the confidant and lover roles. Edouard enters the novel as Julie's suitor but is quickly transformed into an *ami-confident* by the letter in which Julie confides in him her love for Saint-Preux (1:58). At the end of the novel Claire is both confidante and potential spouse to Saint-Preux; an erotic element, moreover, has always been present in their relationship, which they stifle out of fear of destroying mutual *confiance*. But it is particularly in the Julie-Claire and Julie–Saint-Preux relationships that the tension between *amitié* and *amour* produces real psychological ambiguity. To this extent the equivocal relationship between Julie and Claire (or even occasionally between Claire and Saint-Preux) reflects the tension between the two central lover-friends, as Julie moves from *confidences* to mystification with Saint-Preux (her various "secrets") or, conversely, tries to purify her *amour* into *amitié*.

The kiss episode that prefigures the famous "baiser du bosquet" is an apt emblem of the ambiguous triangle formed by Julie, Saint-Preux, and Claire. Whereas the later kiss is exchanged by the two lovers in the presence of Claire, this first kiss is exchanged by the two cousins while the tutor watches:

> quelle extase, de voir deux beautés si touchantes s'embrasser tendrement, le visage de l'une se pencher sur le sein de l'autre, leurs douces larmes se confondre, et baigner ce sein charmant comme la rosée du ciel humecte un lis fraîchement éclos! J'étais jaloux d'une amitié si tendre; je lui trouvais je ne sais quoi de plus intéressant que l'amour même, et je me voulais une sorte de mal de ne pouvoir t'offrir des consolations aussi chères, sans les troubler par l'agitation de mes transports. . . . Ah! qu'en ce moment j'eusse été amoureux de cette cousine, si Julie n'eût pas existé! Mais non, c'était Julie elle-même qui répandait son charme invincible sur tout ce qui l'environnait. [1:38]

The uncertainty of Saint-Preux as to which cousin's charm highlights the other, his valuation of "amitié" above "amour," of "consolations" (the province of confidants) above "transports," in an account that betrays the very eroticism (or at the least his own erotic perception) of that *amitié*—all of these elements deepen the ambiguity of the entire triangle. *Amitié* will be preferred over *amour* throughout *La Nouvelle Héloïse*—every character will at some point acknowledge himself "plus ami(e) qu'amant(e)"—but not without borrowing from that repressed *amour* its voluptuous aspect and thus internalizing the *amitié-amour* tension within *amitié* itself.

In *Lettres de Fanni Butlerd*, on the other hand, the love-friendship dichotomy occurs within *amour* and is unilateral, in keeping with the unidirectional nature of this single-voice work. Whereas Fanni, like any Mme Riccoboni heroine and like Julie herself, would prefer *l'ami* to *l'amant*, her seducer, unlike Saint-Preux, would not appear to share her values. In repeatedly taking her would-be lover for her confidant, Fanni makes herself all the more vulnerable to seduction. Fanni's letters to Milord Alfred offer a striking contrast to Crébillon's nevertheless formally similar *Lettres de la marquise de M\*\*\* au comte de R\*\*\**. Whereas the sophisticated, flippant marquise mystifies both count and reader as to her true sentiments for a fifth of the novel, the open, candid Fanni makes hers clear from the very beginning: "Je vous ai dit que je vous aime, parce que je suis étourdie; je vous le répète, parce que je suis sincère" (L. 6, p. 9). Most of Fanni's letters to Alfred, unlike the marquise's, are as much letters to a confidant as letters to a lover.

If Fanni confides everything from her daily chagrins to her love itself in Alfred, it is because he at times appears to be her best friend. Her other friends refuse to listen to her: "Vous qui êtes mon ami, mon plus tendre ami, partagez donc ma peine; souffrez que je vous la confie. Ne faites pas comme Miss Betzi; écoutez-moi avec douceur" (L. 61). Fanni speaks *to* Alfred *about* Alfred, much as any epistolary character would write to a confidant about a lover: "Il m'aime, il m'a toujours aimée: il le dit, il le jure, et je le crois" (L. 110). Fanni's confidences to Alfred concerning Alfred himself are a function of her candor, the virtue for which she most prides herself. Her use of the third-person pronoun for the very person to whom she is writing, however, is not without its coquetry: "D'où vient donc qu'il ne donne pas des fleurs à sa maîtresse? il sait qu'elle les aime" (L. 20, Fanni to Alfred). Although Fanni never mystifies her lover, as Crébillon's marquise does constantly, she develops her own kind of coquettish language of which *confiance* and openness are paradoxically an integral part. By speaking *to* Alfred *of* Alfred, and by repeatedly making *confidences* to a lover who can take advantage of them, she adds an ambivalence to the conventional epistolary language of love.

The ambivalence of the epistolary character who is both lover and confidant is nowhere better exploited than in *Les Liaisons dangereuses*. Like *La Nouvelle Héloïse*, Laclos's novel presents four letter writers who relate to each other alternately and sometimes simultaneously as confidants and lovers. Thus Merteuil and Danceny, like Saint-Preux and Claire, begin on a confidential tone, but the erotic element soon interferes. If Julie and Edouard move from amorous ties (Edouard as Julie's suitor) to those of *confiance*, Valmont and Cécile move in the opposite direction. In both novels, moreover, the two central characters are bound together by both reciprocal *confiance* and an early amorous liaison. We might diagram these relationships in the following fashion:

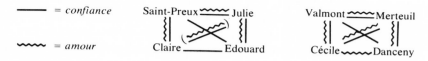

Here, as in Rousseau, *amour* that is taken for *amitié* and *amitié* that borders on love are important thematic elements. Cécile writes Danceny her hope that their "amitié" will last forever (L. 19). If the présidente de Tourvel decides to become Valmont's "friend" early in the novel, her *confiance* in him is ironically based on the fact that Valmont is Merteuil's "friend": "j'ai cru, jusqu'à la réception de votre Lettre, que ce qu'il [Valmont] appelait *amitié* entre eux deux était bien réellement de l'*amour*. . . . J'avoue que je ne regardais que comme *finesse*, ce qui était de sa part une honnête *sincérité*. Je ne sais; mais il me semble que celui qui est capable d'une amitié aussi suivie pour une femme aussi estimable, n'est pas un libertin sans retour" (L. 11; italics mine). The multiple ironies present in this situation where, on the word of her own friend-confidante (Mme de Volanges), a woman reverses a previous (correct) opinion regarding the nature of the relationship between two lover-confidants who are equally capable of destroying her, is typical of this novel, where *amour* is not any more "dangerous" a "liaison" than *amitié*.

Indeed, so intertwined are erotic and confidential bonds between characters that one can scarcely separate them. When Danceny writes the following to Merteuil, is he addressing a confidante or a mistress?

> Oui, je l'avoue, l'amour qu'elle [Cécile] m'inspire m'est devenu plus
> précieux encore, depuis que vous avez bien voulu en recevoir la
> confidence. J'aime tant à vous ouvrir mon coeur, à occuper le vôtre
> de mes sentiments, à les y déposer sans réserve . . . et puis, je vous
> regarde et je me dis: C'est en elle qu'est renfermé tout mon
> bonheur. . . .
>    Ah! revenez donc, mon adorable amie . . . ou apprenez-moi à
> vivre où vous n'êtes pas. [L. 118]

The kind of transferral that Danceny is revealing here, in which
the confidante, as "depositary" of love sentiments, actually
becomes identified with the loved one to the point of almost
replacing her, is of course the same situation that arises between
Saint-Preux and Claire. Merteuil's bond with Cécile, moreover,
has its erotic side; in one and the same letter, the marquise
suggests their lesbian activities and announces, "j'ai l'honneur
d'être sa confidente" (L. 38). Even Valmont's ties to Danceny are
not merely those of *confiance*; as Valmont jokingly remarks when
he begins to write Cécile's love letters to Danceny, "J'aurai été à
fois son ami, son confident, son rival et sa maîtresse!" (L. 115).
Laclos plays the ambiguity of these relationships (Valmont as
lover-confidant to both Cécile and Danceny) for all their ironic
and erotic worth when he has Cécile write a love letter "dictée par
Valmont" to Danceny: "Oh! vous avez là [in Valmont] un bien
bon ami, je vous assure! Il fait tout comme vous feriez vous-
même" (L. 117).

The most complicated and often puzzling relationship in *Les
Liaisons*, however, is that of the marquise and the vicomte. Held
together by bonds of libertine conspiracy, reciprocal *confiance*
based on possession of each other's secrets, a past love affair and a
potential future one, Merteuil and Valmont have every reason to
stick together, yet ultimately they declare a suicidal war on each
other. The seeds as well as the arms of conflict, however, are latent
in the bonds themselves and arise particularly from a kind of
interference between amorous interests and those of *confiance*.

From the beginning, the marquise and the vicomte speak an
ambivalent language to each other. Both address each other as
confidant: Valmont confides his progress with the présidente
while Merteuil relates episodes in her affair with Belleroche. Like
many other epistolary exchanges of *confidences*, this one is

marked by a spirit of comparison and competition.[17] Here, however, the rivalry is complicated by jealousy, for Valmont and the
marquise address each other not merely as friend-confidants but
as former and potential lovers. Thus every *confidence* concerning
a conquest has a double edge: it is designed to provoke not only
the admiration of the friend-confidant but the jealousy of the
potential lover. Merteuil's and Valmont's letters are equivocally
phrased in the language of both primary types of epistolary
relationship. The "revenez" motif that runs throughout the novel
epitomizes the ambivalent nature of their language. The plea to
return is of course an eminently epistolary motif, deriving from
the separation inherent to the correspondents' situation. We have
already noted its ambiguous use in letters from Julie to Claire and
from Danceny to Merteuil (see quotation from L. 118, above),
where "revenez," repeatedly addressed to a confidant, suggests a
sentiment much stronger than friendship. In the case of Valmont
and Merteuil, "revenez" is the first word pronounced between
them ("Revenez, mon cher Vicomte, revenez" [L. 2]) and is
already ambivalent. This imperative is one of "empire"; Merteuil
uses (L. 2), and Valmont accepts (L. 4), the image of the
"Chevalier-esclave" who takes orders from his sovereign lady "à
genoux."[18] But is this "empire" that of love or friendship?[19] It
would be foolish to choose, for in their letters coquetry is inseparable from *confidences*. The "revenez" that is traditionally
the language of epistolary lovers becomes the "revenez à vous" (L.
5), or the "Revenez donc, Vicomte, et ne sacrifiez pas votre
reputation à un caprice puéril" (L. 113) of Merteuil's "concerned
friendship" for Valmont. Yet so much emphasis on separation
sets up the expectation of an amorous reunion of the two ("peut-
être au bout de la carrière nous rencontrerons-nous encore"
[L. 4]). After Merteuil promises herself as a prize for Tourvel's first
postconquest letter, this expectation is maintained by Valmont's
frequent allusions to the lovers' night he and Merteuil will spend.
Valmont's progress reports seem at times a subordinate function
of his desire to win Merteuil back again as mistress, thus further
embroiling confidential and amorous motives for writing.

    In fact, we can measure the confidential and amorous power
play between Valmont and Merteuil by the way in which they

echo each other's pleas of "revenez." A curious reversal of positions is noticeable in three groups of successive letters in the Merteuil-Valmont correspondence (L. 113; Ll. 115 and 125; Ll. 127, 133, 138, and 144). In letter 113 Merteuil writes from Paris to Valmont in the country, informing him that his long absence is causing him to become the laughing stock of the city, suggesting that he return if he wants to salvage his reputation. At the same time, however, she announces that she herself is leaving for the country, to effect a rupture with Belleroche, because Belleroche has begun to claim "un droit exclusif," and the "insultante confiance qu'il prend en moi" is humiliating her.

In his reply (L. 115) the vicomte gloats over what is now Merteuil's provincial boredom in terms reminiscent of the marquise's previous letters, speaking of his "indulgence" toward her, threatening to withdraw his "confiance" to punish her for her lack of interest in his affairs, and mentioning the imminent renewal of their previous liaison as his "règne." He is speaking to her the same imperious language that she had used with him, in letters 2 and 5, in which she threatened withdrawal of confidence and demanded that he return to Paris. From the marquise's point of view, however, Valmont is beginning to assume the same kind of overconfidence she complained of in Belleroche. By the time he sends his next letter (L. 125), Valmont not only commends himself again for his indulgence but reminds her that in coming to claim his prize, "le nouvel Amant ne veut rien perdre des anciens droits de l'ami." This time it is Valmont who is in Paris, where he will remain until the end of the novel.

Though by this reversal in letters 115 and 125 Valmont appears to have gained the upper hand over the marquise, now stuck in the country, this ascendancy will be only momentary. It is soon the marquise's turn to refuse to return to Paris, and she does so even more stubbornly and viciously than Valmont: "vous voyez bien, qu'aussi éloignés l'un de l'autre par notre façon de penser, nous ne pouvons nous rapprocher d'aucune manière" (L. 127). Valmont's subsequent "revenez" (Ll. 133, 138, 144) are more pleading than Merteuil's imperatives ever were.

In the Valmont-Merteuil exchange at the end of Laclos's novel, the possibility of reunion of separated lovers (pleaded for by Valmont in his letters) is played off against the possibility of a rupture of confidants (threatened by Merteuil both in her letters and by her stubborn silences). Here, as in the case of Julie (*La Nouvelle Héloïse*) or Léonce (*Delphine*), the withdrawal of *confiance* or the refusal to reveal secrets—such an important thematic emphasis in letter fiction—is formally implemented by epistolary silence or curtness. The physical distance between Merteuil and Valmont, which has necessitated their epistolary communication all along, has become increasingly psychological. Just at the moment when it could be eliminated, the rift widens; the expected lovers' reunion becomes instead a suicidal separation, with each one betraying the other's confidential letters. A significant factor contributing to this rupture is the very tension inherent in an epistolary relationship based on both amorous and confidential bonds.

If we examine, for instance, the most immediate cause for rupture—Valmont's interruption of Danceny and Merteuil's tête-à-tête, which ironically constitutes the only meeting of the central characters in the novel—we notice that Valmont is more insulted by Merteuil's breach of confidential faith than by Danceny's presence. For the vicomte, who has repeatedly proclaimed the right of exclusivity for their "amitié" only (L. 15—they may have many lovers but only one inviolable friendship), a Danceny who has been Merteuil's unique confidant concerning her return to Paris (although she had promised to inform Valmont first) is an even greater irritation than a Danceny-lover.

Slightly different reasons underlie the marquise's *dépit*, which, unlike Valmont's, is not the reaction of a moment that can be checked and thus give way to pardon. Whereas Valmont resents, but is willing to forgive, a single breach of *confiance*, the marquise has been irritated all along by too many *confidences* on Valmont's part, by his all-too-sincere letters extolling the présidente. Most of her letters to Valmont abound in mockery of his effusive style; even after repeated correction by Merteuil, even after he has sacrificed Tourvel at the marquise's request, Valmont persists in slipping in an offensive "ange" or "femme sensible et belle, qui n'existait que pour moi, qui dans ce moment même meurt peut-être d'amour et de regret" (L. 151). Valmont's numerous, long *confidences* revealing his involvement with the présidente outweigh in Merteuil's mind the pro forma gallant remarks addressed to her at the end of his letters. Yet the marquise values gallantry highly; her last letter to Valmont is filled with lessons emphasizing the importance of "charme," being "aimable," and knowing how to please: "il faut plaire. . . . Le Valmont que j'aimais était charmant. . . . Redevenez donc aimable" (L. 152).

Whereas Valmont values "confiance" above all in his epistolary relationship with Merteuil, the marquise prefers gallantry. Throughout the novel Valmont needs the marquise more as admiring confidante, as someone to whom he can boast of his conquests, than as mistress. She, on the other hand, has less use for Valmont as a listener. Most of her letters (and she writes far fewer than Valmont) are sarcastic reprimands concerning Valmont's betrayal of the libertine code or persiflage directed against the présidente, whom she regards as her rival. Her tone with Valmont is one of irony, mystification, and coquetry—that of the "lettre galante" tradition—as opposed to the vicomte's faithful, candid accounts. In short, whereas Valmont addresses the marquise most frequently as a confidante and fellow genius in the art of corruption whose approval his ego requires, Merteuil assumes with Valmont the tone of an offended mistress whose ego requires the admirer's total submission to pleasing her.

The difficulty of course arises when Valmont tries to reassert his lover's rights without playing the lover's game, basing his claims on *amitié* rather than *amour*. What Valmont sees as the mere "confiance" of a "longue . . . amitié" Merteuil calls "présomption" (L. 129), just as Valmont regards what the marquise would call "l'art de plaire" as "insipide cajolerie." The marquise, who mocked Valmont for taking so much time with Tourvel, now asks Valmont, What's your hurry? To his "j'en appelle . . . à la longue et parfaite amitié, à l'entière confiance qui depuis ont resserré nos liens" (L. 129), she replies, "ne soyons qu'amis, et restons-en là" (L. 134). In short, when Valmont becomes involved with the présidente, he needs a confidante more than a mistress, so his relationship to Merteuil changes—his letters become confidential *bulletins* rather than gallant love letters. That change produces, however, the inverse change in Merteuil, who, regarded as a confidante, refuses to play anything else.

In Valmont's and Merteuil's case, *amitié* ultimately renders *amour* impossible. The vicomte has revealed too candidly and persistently to his confidante that on the level of *amour* she has a rival. To be more precise, Valmont has changed the nature of his *confidences* from part of their love-gallantry game to reflections of his love for someone else; in Jost's terms, his *lettres-drame* have become *lettres-confidence*. Valmont has moved from making love in order to be able to make *confidences* (in which case Merteuil holds the reins) to making *confidences* because he is in love (in which case Tourvel governs affairs). To maintain her power, Merteuil strikes Valmont at his vulnerable point—his *confiance*—and demonstrates first by equivocating and postponing, finally by lying, that she cannot be counted on, either as mistress or confidante. The Danceny whom she throws in Valmont's path as both rival confidant and lover is Merteuil's declaration of independence. When Valmont pursues his course of candor with his ultimatum (no more of Merteuil's "cajoleries" and "tergiversation"; "le moment de la franchise est arrivé" [L. 153]), offering a choice between *l'amour* and *la guerre*, the marquise can only choose the latter.

The tension between *amitié* and *amour* is hardly unique to epistolary narrative. Yet its frequent occurrence there seems to derive from the nature of the epistolary exchange itself, which sets up two essential categories of letter writers, lovers and friend-confidants, who speak two fundamental kinds of language: on the one hand that of candor and *confiance*, on the other that of coquetry, mystification, and dissimulation. In narrative that blurs these distinctions—by presenting characters who dissimulate with friends (*Delphine, Les Liaisons dangereuses, Les Malheurs de l'inconstance, Les Lettres de Vallière*), speak a lover's language to confidants (*La Nouvelle Héloïse, Delphine*, Rémy de Gourmont's *Le Songe d'une femme*), or are too candid with lovers (*Fanni Butlerd, Les Liaisons*)—the ambiguity of relationship is accompanied by a thematic emphasis on the compatibility or incompatibility of *amitié* and *amour*.[20]

Thus even lovers' correspondence is complicated by that epistolary necessity, the confidant, and by the *lettres-confidence* that the narrative medium requires at least occasionally. Likewise, though we can oppose in general the candid, "from the heart" style of Rousseau's correspondents to the artful ironic dissimulation of Laclos's, both kinds of narrative depend on moments of mystification (e.g., the various secrets of Julie or Mme Riccoboni's characters) and moments of candor (Valmont's inadvertent confessions and his crucial "moment de franchise," or Madame de Vernon's "moments que l'on destine à tout se dire"). Indeed, much of epistolary suspense is based on an alternation between these two tones.

A technical necessity, confidential letters and the confidant figure can become in the hands of many epistolary novelists an integral part of the structure and thematics of the narrative. Central to *Mademoiselle La Quintinie* is the opposition of confession to *confidence*, of the priest-confessor to the secular confidant. At the center of Mme de Staël's *Delphine* is a vacuum of *confiance*, as Delphine's successively chosen confidants fail her. The losing and gaining of *confiance*, as well as confessional letters, play a crucial structuring role in *La Nouvelle Héloïse*, while much of Claire's activity and importance derive from her role as confidante to both Julie and Saint-Preux. As depositary of Julie's feelings, Claire becomes almost an extension of Julie, acting occasionally as her delegate. As confidante to both Julie and Saint-Preux and at times mediator of their correspondence, Claire is also, so to speak, implicated in the "crossfire" of their affections, appearing sometimes as a love object to both.

Even the passive confidant who always remains external to the action can serve an auxiliary purpose by his mere ineffectuality (Anna Howe, Pierre in *Le Paysan perverti*, Louise in *Delphine*), by his inability to extricate or entice the hero or heroine from the locus of his trouble to the peaceful locus from which the confidant writes. The most complicated, best-integrated confidants, however, are obviously those who, like Claire, play a more active role. Part of the recognized brilliance of Laclos lies in his decision to make the confidants as such the most important agents in the plot. Very few *lettres-confidence* in *Les Liaisons* serve only as narrative vehicles; even Valmont's *lettres-bulletins* have at least two auxiliary functions: (1) to provoke admiration and (2) to destroy, unknown to Valmont, the very *confiance* on which they are based.

The active confidant derives power from mere possession of

letters. In a letter to her friend Juliette, in Mme Elie de Beaumont's *Lettres du marquis de Roselle*, Léonore warns against "le danger des confidents" (L. 69); ironically it is this letter, which Juliette ultimately sells, that will expose Léonore's conniving, just as one of the two publicized confidential letters of the marquise de Merteuil at the end of *Les Liaisons* is precisely the one (L. 81) in which she emphasizes that one must never write. *Confiance* in *Les Liaisons* is both the source of power over others for Merteuil and Valmont and the germ of their own downfall. It constitutes both a motive for their own correspondence and ultimately a seed of discord between them.

The confidential role, letter, tone, and relationship are necessary components of epistolary narrative. When authors develop the potential of these indispensable components—by multiplying and complicating the functions of the confidant; by playing off against each other *confiance* and *coquetterie*, confidant and lover; by marking key points in the narrative by confessional letters or a change in, or disappearance of, confidants—then the epistolary necessity becomes an instrument of literary complexity.

1. Both of these words have multiple denotations in French. *Confiance* signifies, according to context, either the trust one places in another, self-reliance, or a sense of security. *Confidence* can denote a confidential relationship ("les charmes de la confidence") but most regularly is a confidential communication. The confidential relationship is basic to most epistolary fiction, but the thematics of confidentiality are particularly visible in Romance literature, where it is reinforced by the language itself. The similarity between words of the *confier* family would not be as readily noticed in English translation, although the same psychological action (e.g., winning or loss of trust—*confiance*—or the need for a confidant) is portrayed in English letter novels. Here, as with the *amitié/amour* polarity that we shall examine in the second half of this chapter (cf. n. 15 below), linguistic phenomena would appear to encourage thematic emphases, as my use of French terms will demonstrate throughout this chapter.

2. Clifton C. Cherpack, "A New Look at *Les Liaisons dangereuses*," pp. 515, 520. Cherpack's linking of these two terms is hardly gratuitous, since both derive from the same Latin *confidentia* (contaminated, in the case of *confiance*, by the Old French for "foi," *fiance*).

3. Sophie often regrets retrospectively a "manque de confiance" in her relationships (pt. 1, L. 12). She is saddened to leave her friend Cécile without Cécile's having confided in her (pt. 1, L. 30), reproaches herself for her own

"défaut de confiance" (pt. 1, L. 35) in not telling Mme de Monglas about her love for the marquis de Germeuil. Only when she (mistakenly) thinks Germeuil is married does she rejoice not to have to "se reprocher la folle confiance" of a love declaration (pt. 1, L. 32). Throughout the second part of the novel, numerous times she is on the verge of confiding in Germeuil but leaves him with false notions about her sentiments. Even the long interpolated *récit* by her newfound friend Lindsay, concerning Sophie's parents (Henry and Emma Maubray), is full of the same emphasis on the tragedy of lack of trust in one's friends: Henry's repeated refusal to confide in his friend Lindsay leads to misunderstandings that bring about both his and Emma's death.

4. Aphra Behn, *Love-Letters between a Noble-Man and His Sister*, in Natascha Würzbach's anthology of short early English epistolary novels, *The Novel in Letters*, p. 243.

5. See Introduction for a summary of Jost's theory.

6. The confidant being primarily a figure in classical dramaturgy, most of my theatrical examples will be drawn from seventeenth-century plays. An excellent discussion of the development of the confidant's role in classical French theater can be found in Jacques Schérer, *La Dramaturgie classique en France*, pp. 39–50.

7. The analogue to the theatrical monologue in fiction is of course the diary novel. The diary novel is a close relative of the letter novel, however, as both its documentary nature and the "dear diary" formula suggest.

8. Contrast Claire in *La Nouvelle Héloïse*, who, like Dubois, often acts as her friend's agent. Claire, however, not only acts by delegated authority (as does Dubois); we also *see* Julie delegate this power to her by confidential letters exposing her inner feelings and asking Claire to interpret these feelings and act accordingly.

9. Racine's confidants are nonetheless much closer to their epistolary counterparts than are those of the comic theater or Corneille, and one could make a good argument for the importance of the *confiance-confidence* theme in his theater. Agrippine at the very beginning of *Britannicus* is upset because she has lost Néron's "confiance"; Britannicus makes the error of placing too much confidence in Narcisse; and the entire play is a power struggle between Agrippine, Burrhus, and Narcisse for the position of privy counselor to Néron. In *Phèdre* the theme of the "aveu" is all-important. *Phèdre* is perhaps the play one could most easily imagine translated into epistolary form. Dialogue exchanges are almost always between two interlocutors; the role of narrative and confession is preponderant enough to admit division into letters. The characters seek to avoid direct confrontation; in fact, Ovid, in his *Heroides*, had perceived quite early the effect that could be produced by having Phaedra confess her love to Hippolytus by letter. If the epistolary novel draws its inspiration from the theater, its closest affinities are with Racinian theater, where the mere act of speaking or not speaking, confessing or not confessing, weighs so heavily.

10. There is, for example, a difference between the theatrical "nurse" or "governor" who serves as an evil counselor and the stock epistolary character of the mentor-corruptor, who is chosen as a friend by the protagonist.

11. The clearest, most systematic statement of this "rule" governing the

actions of Laclos's characters can be found in Tzvetan Todorov, *Littérature et signification*, pp. 64–65.

12. H. Gfeller analyzes the theme and rhythm of confession in *La Nouvelle Héloïse* in his thesis, "Die Funktion der Geständisse in Rousseaus *La Nouvelle Héloïse*" (diss., University of Bonn, 1964). His distinction of seven main confessions implies their importance as narrative nodes.

13. This division is similar to Jost's distinction between *la lettre-confidence* and *la lettre-drame* (see Introduction). It must be remembered, however, that Jost's distinction concerns narrative technique (whether the action of the novel is narrated *by* the letters or proceeds *through* the letters), whereas in this chapter we are more concerned with the thematic emphases that are a function of that technique. Moreover, whereas Jost is interested in the classification of the work as a whole within a larger system of types (and classifies any given work as either *lettres-confidence* or *lettres-drame* in its entirety), we are concerned here primarily with transformations of relationships between characters within individual works (and are therefore more interested in the juxtaposition or superposition of *confidences* and *drame* within the same work).

14. Wolpe uses this term in his study of Claire's importance in "Psychological Ambiguity in *La Nouvelle Héloïse*."

15. The French verb *aimer* and noun *ami(e)* lend themselves to this kind of ambiguity, since they retain both senses of the Old French *amor*, which could denote either love or friendship. When Delphine writes, "j'aimais Mme de Vernon," when Valmont addresses Merteuil as his "belle amie," which relationship is being established?

16. See Wolpe for a more detailed analysis of Claire's dimensions.

17. In both Balzac's *Lettres de deux jeunes mariées* and Mme d'Epinay's *Histoire de Mme de Montbrillant*, for example, we find an exchange of letters between two girls who, after their marriages, compare their different kinds of conjugal situations—one a *mariage de raison* and the other a *mariage d'amour*.

18. Indeed the image of the sovereign lady and the knight distinguishes aptly between the different types of confidential ties linking these two. Whereas most of the vicomte's letters to the marquise are progress reports of knight to sovereign, confiding information and events to win her admiration, in the letters that flow in the opposite direction Merteuil confides instead projects for Valmont to implement. Their subtly differing use of the word *confier* in their first letters to each other is instructive: Merteuil—"il m'est venu une excellente idée, et je veux bien vous en confier l'exécution" (L. 2); as opposed to Valmont—"Dépositaire de tous les secrets de mon coeur, je vais vous confier le plus grand projet que j'aie jamais formé" (L. 4).

19. In *Fatalité du secret et fatalité du bavardage au XVIIIe siècle*, Georges Daniel makes a case for interpreting all of Merteuil's actions as emanating from her offended secret love for Valmont.

20. Rémy de Gourmont's *Le Songe d'une femme* (1899), composed uniquely of letters, provides a compendium of many of the themes and structures studied in this chapter. It consists essentially of exchanges between two sets of confidants—Anna and Claude (former convent friends), and Pierre and Paul—who form a *chassé-croisé* of relationships not unlike those of *Les Liaisons* and *La Nouvelle Héloïse*. Furthermore, the bond of *confiance* between Anna and

Claude is troubled by a number of secrets that the enigmatic Anna dangles enticingly in front of her friend. In this case lesbianism is obvious; Claude writes to Anna: "avant tes confidences, je ne savais pas. . . . Viens et je te parlerai avec une entière confiance. Quand j'écris, je suis si réservée. . . . je te parlerai comme à un confesseur que je voudrais faire trembler d'amour" (pp. 110–11). Secrets, *amour, amitié*, confession, *confiance,confidences,* lovers who become confidants, confidants who are lovers, ambiguous and conflicting "venez"—all are synthesized here.

# CHAPTER THREE

# THE WEIGHT OF THE READER

Underlying the previous two chapters is the assumed and obvious importance of that second party to every epistolary situation—the addressee of the letter. Chapter 1 dealt only indirectly with the addressee as the object of mediated communication, and chapter 2 focused more closely on his or her protean existence as confidant and lover, as receiver of confessions and influencer of epistolary language. It is time now to concentrate on this figure, whose presence alone distinguishes the letter from other first-person forms.

The "reader" has begun to assume such importance in critical discourse that some preliminary clarification of my approach in this chapter is in order. Particularly influential in recent years have been the contributions of rhetorical, psychoanalytic, and phenomenological theories that engage the issue of reader response and participation in a text. Wayne Booth, Wolfgang Iser, and Hans Jauss have identified the "implied reader." Stanley Fish, in calling for an "affective stylistics," and Michael Riffaterre, in his practice of structural stylistics, have insisted on the role of reading as process in the production of a text's meaning. Psychoanalytic critics like Norman Holland and David Bleich have explored the subjectivization of literature in the reader. Jacques Derrida, Roland Barthes, Geoffrey Hartman, and Harold Bloom have all addressed the problematic relationships of writing and reading, of the writer-as-reader, from different angles. Distinct from these approaches are the narratological typologies of Gerald Prince or Gérard Genette, who classify the theoretically possible readers or narratees that any narrative text constructs linguistically.

None of the above theories, of course, is genre-bound; all have relevance for the study of epistolary narrative and are potentially complementary approaches to the one that I will be taking in this chapter. For an inquiry into epistolarity, however, the simple distinction that I make below, between the internal and external reader of epistolary narrative, is the most crucial. In no other genre do readers figure so prominantly within the world of the narrative and in the generation of the text. Some survey and assessment of their role is necessary and indeed preliminary to any more thoroughgoing phenomenological, psychoanalytic, or narratological approach to the epistolary reader.

If first-person narrative lends itself to the writer's reflexive portrayal of the difficulties and mysteries surrounding the act of writing, the epistolary form is unique among first-person forms in its aptitude for portraying the experience of reading. In letter narrative we not only see correspondents struggle with pen, ink, and paper; we also see their messages being read and interpreted by their intended or unintended recipients. The epistolary form is unique in making the reader (narratee) almost as important an agent in the narrative as the writer (narrator). Even when the internal[1] reader's interpretation of the letter does not constitute part of the represented action of the epistolary work (we can know only indirectly, for example, what "reading" the recipient of unidirectional correspondence has given to the letters he receives), this reader is nonetheless a determinant of the letter's message. Indeed, at the very inception of the letter, he plays an instrumental generative role. If pure autobiography can be born of the mere desire to express oneself, without regard for the eventual reader, the letter is by definition never the product of such an "immaculate conception," but is rather the result of a union of writer and reader.[2]

The epistolary experience, as distinguished from the autobiographical, is a reciprocal one. The letter writer simultaneously seeks to affect his reader and is affected by him. Borderline cases, like Diderot's *La Religieuse* or Marivaux's *La Vie de Marianne*, which are primarily memoir novels, derive whatever epistolary characteristics they have from the presence of an influencing and influenceable reader. I have chosen to deal with these two hybrid novels first, not because they provide the best examples of the epistolary reader figure, but because here, as in other chapters, these borderline cases are interesting precisely because they help us define the outlines of the epistolary form.[3]

In contrast, it would be difficult, or at least uninteresting, to deal with Duclos's *Confessions du comte de* *** as an "epistolary" novel, even though the entire novel is in fact a letter addressed to a friend who has inquired why the count is living in solitude. Duclos uses the epistolary convention only to trigger memoirs, since the friend is not invoked after the beginning of the novel. Closer to the epistolary novel, in fact, are those diary novels written for specific readers within the world of the narrative—like Tanizaki's *The Key* or Mauriac's *Le Noeud de vipères*—where the desire to influence the reader is narrativized and figures prominently in the novel's action and thematics. What distinguishes epistolary narrative from these diary novels, however, is the desire for *exchange*. In epistolary writing the reader is called upon to respond as a writer and to contribute as such to the narrative.

I insist upon the fact that the reader is "called upon" to respond. Whether the novel is actually a *Briefwechselroman* (mul-ticorrespondent novel) obviously matters little, although the German noun (literally, "letter exchange novel") alerts us to that fundamental impulse behind all epistolary writing; if there is no desire for exchange, the writing does not differ significantly from a journal, even if it assumes the outer form of the letter. To a great extent, this is the epistolary pact—the call for response from a specific reader within the correspondent's world. Most of the other aspects of epistolary discourse that I focus on in this study can be seen to derive from this most basic parameter.

Let us look, then, at two particularly instructive hybrid cases, *La Religieuse* and *La Vie de Marianne*. Both Marianne and Diderot's nun, Suzanne, address their autobiographies to a single specific reader; Marianne writes eleven letter installments to a friend who has requested her story and whom she wants merely to amuse, whereas Suzanne sends her unsolicited narrative to a marquis whose assistance she desperately needs. The addressee is constantly present in the various asides—casual and playful in

*Marianne* ("voyez comment il va réagir"), more formal and rhetorical in *La Religieuse* ("Cependant, monsieur le marquis, ma situation présente est si déplorable . . . craignez qu'un fatal moment ne revienne" [p. 308]). Both are concerned to enlist their reader's help and input; whereas Suzanne seeks a protector, Marianne solicits advice concerning her style: "Comment fait-on pour en avoir un? . . . Celui de mes lettres vous paraît-il passable?" (p. 9).

The "qu'en pensez-vous?" that constantly concerns them, to the point of governing the act of writing itself, is nowhere more clearly articulated than by Suzanne toward the end of her novel: "lorsque les choses peuvent exciter votre estime ou accroître votre commisération, j'écris . . . avec une vitesse et une facilité incroyables. . . . Si je suis forcée au contraire de me montrer à vos yeux sous un aspect défavorable, je pense avec difficulté, l'expression se refuse, la plume va mal, le caractère même de mon écriture s'en ressent" (pp. 383–84). Not only *what* Suzanne writes but *how* she writes is shaped by her addressee. Similarly, Marianne worries about her reader's reaction, particularly to her numerous "réflexions"; and halfway through her novel, persuaded that her friend finds her letters overlong, Marianne vows to abandon these digressions.

Robert J. Ellrich has made a cogent analysis of *La Religieuse* in terms of forensic rhetoric, developing the trial motif into an image of the novel as legal brief, an extension of the *roman-mémoires* into a juridical *mémoire*. Suzanne is the lawyer and Croismare is the philosophe-judge: *"La Religieuse* is, in fact, a 'procès des couvents,' and the judge before whom the plea is being presented is the eighteenth-century *philosophe*, morally and intellectually, the highest tribunal of the land."[4] Suzanne's stance as a lawyer, her awareness of her audience, is not unlike Marianne's vanity, although the latter heroine aims merely at "pleasing" a worldly countess whereas the former seeks to persuade a powerful marquis. In each case the letter writer's consciousness of a specifically delineated reader appreciably alters the tone of a memoir novel.[5] Marianne's coquettish, interrogative "style badin" and Suzanne's forensic rhetoric are a function of their respective internal readers.

Significantly, the epistolary traits of both Diderot's and

Marivaux's novels are in part dictated by a real historical reader; each work had its genesis as letters written to an actual addressee. The letters of *La Religieuse* were part of the practical joke played by Diderot on the marquis de Croismare to prompt his return to Paris, whereas Marivaux coyly used letters as serial installments to test the popularity of his work among readers before continuing it. Both Marivaux and Diderot create a specific internal reader persona (Croismare, Marianne's "friend") who becomes increasingly dispersed into the vague "ceux qui liront ces mémoires" (*La Religieuse*, pp. 307–8) or the "friends" with whom Marianne's confidante shares the heroine's letters. In other words, the internal reader persona frequently loses his or her specificity to coincide with the external reader, who could be anyone. *Marianne* recaptures some of the specificity of the reader by internalizing the reactions of the external readers, making these reactions part of the novel itself, as at the beginning of part 6 where she allows the readers' critique of previous letter installments to influence subsequent letters. Most importantly for our discussion of epistolarity, neither novel is perceived as complete without the reader response. "La réponse de M. le marquis de Croismare," writes Suzanne, "me fournira les premières lignes de ce récit." This desire to incorporate a specific reader response within the world of the narrative distinguishes epistolary from autobiographical writing. The epistolary reader is empowered to intervene, to correct style, to give shape to the story, often to become an agent and narrator in his own right.

Being borderline cases, *Marianne* and *La Religieuse* provide us with a simple example of how awareness of a specific second-person addressee can alter the character and experience of the first-person writing itself. In purer epistolary narrative we find countless examples of this influential reader presence. We have only to examine any *bulletin* from Valmont to Merteuil to recognize how radically even his reporting of dialogue differs from simple first-person reporting: "Aussi me précipitant à ses genoux, et *du ton dramatique que vous me connaissez:* 'Ah! cruelle,' me suis-je écrié" (L. 125; italics mine). Even more a poser than Suzanne or Marianne, Valmont never lets us forget to whom he is addressing his accounts, and his superior tone derives in part from the fact that he is regarding his victim with the eyes of

Merteuil, to whom he wants to appear a "vainqueur couronné."
Thus epistolary writing, as distinguished from simple first-person
writing, refracts events through not one but two prisms—that of
reader as well as that of writer. We as external readers must
always interpret a given letter in the light of its intended recipient.

If writing is partially shaped by potential reading in letter
narrative, it is not surprising that the act of reading should itself
be an important narrative event. Epistolary novels are filled with
portrayed readings, rereadings, and even proofreading. Restif de
la Bretonne, who seems almost obsessed by the act of reading,
considers it worth the attention of a voyeurlike observer. In *La
Malédiction paternelle* Dulis constantly spies through a crack in
the wall on the Englishwoman he adores while she reads the
letters he has slipped to her through the same crack; as he tells us,
he delights in reading his reader: "J'ai l'art de lire dans l'âme par
les mouvements des yeux et du visage" (L. 123).

The letter is a prime instrument of revelation and discovery, so
that the act of reading in epistolary fiction often corresponds to
the classical moment of recognition (Aristotle's *anagnorisis*), be it
through a rereading of one's own letters or a close scrutiny of the
letters of others. Through the letters they stumble across, Edmée-
Colette in Restif's *Le Paysan perverti* discovers that her marriage
is incestuous, and Adélaïde de Sancerre in Mme Riccoboni's
*Lettres de Sancerre* learns of her husband's infidelity. Such facile
chance discoveries, however, are so common in all types of fiction
that they merit little attention. What is more striking in epistolary
narrative is its emphatic portrayal of the art of close reading, the
art of analysis and explication.

Rereading one's own letter entails a switch in perspective—
from writer to reader—and a consequent distancing that may lead
to self-discovery. Upon rereading, Dorat's Mirbelle perceives a
personal weakness he had tried to hide in his letter to the duke:
"toute ma lettre décèle les combats d'un homme honnête
qui . . . se dissimule sa faiblesse" (*Les Malheurs de l'inconstance*, pt. 1, L. 10). No character is more skilled at the careful
reading of her own letters than Crébillon's duchess (*Lettres de la
duchesse*), whose analyses of her previous letters often constitute
the subject matter of subsequent ones.

The careful epistolary reader is sensitive to messages of all kinds within the letter he decodes. A sleuth like Valmont learns all he needs to know about the présidente's sentiments from tearstains on a letter and the evidence that she has pieced together in private a letter that she had torn up in public. Colette's Mitsou discerns Robert's hidden feelings by the length of his last letter to her, rather than through what he writes. The work of this internal reader-interpreter bears such close resemblance to that of the literary or textual critic that narrative where the reader plays such a predominant role seems to contain within itself the explication of its own text. Internal reading may be so important that the decoding of a message becomes part of a new message; the critique is incorporated into the work. In his letter of 9 July, Lovelace depicts for Belford a communal reading of one of Clarissa's letters, in which sentences from the original letter alternate with running commentary on them; this letter could be called Lovelace's "Annotated Clarissa." In Mme d'Epinay's *Histoire de Mme de Montbrillant*, Emilie sends her confidante a copy of one of M. de Montbrillant's letters, inserting her own glosses in parentheses between the lines of his letter (vol. 1, p. 28).

Valmont and Merteuil constantly engage in such explications de texte for each other's benefit. Terser than Richardsonian characters, the marquise and the vicomte tend to omit copying letters for the other to read and limit themselves instead to incisive summaries.[6] Typical is Valmont's brief analysis of a letter from the présidente: "Je viens de recevoir un second billet, toujours bien rigoureux, et qui confirme l'éternelle rupture, comme cela devrait être; mais dont le ton n'est pourtant plus le même. Surtout, on ne veut plus me voir: ce parti pris y est annoncé quatre fois de la manière la plus irrévocable. J'en ai conclu qu'il n'y avait pas un moment à perdre pour me présenter" (L. 138). Merteuil provides a no less penetrating critique when she points out the parallels between two letters she has received from Cécile and Mme de Volanges shortly after betraying the former to the latter: "A mon réveil, je trouvai deux billets, un de la mère et un de la fille; et je ne pus m'empêcher de rire, en trouvant dans tous deux littéralement cette même phrase: *C'est de vous seule que j'attends quelque consolation.* N'est-il pas plaisant, en effet, de consoler pour et contre, et d'être le seul agent de deux intérêts directement contraires? Me voilà comme la Divinité, recevant les voeux opposés des aveugles mortels" (L. 63).

The creation of a "Divinité" of the type described by Merteuil, a kind of Super Reader,[7] who reads, interprets, and censors the letters of most of the other characters, is one of the hallmarks of epistolary fiction. Lovelace, once he gains control of the Anna Howe–Clarissa correspondence, assumes this role briefly. The letters that flow between the many correspondents of Restif de la Bretonne's *Le Paysan perverti* (1775) are collected by Edmond's brother Pierrot, who stays on the farm and persists in the virtuous path while Edmond is corrupted by the city. Not only is Pierrot Edmond's chief confidant and therefore the recipient of the bulk of the letters, but many of the letters not addressed to him are forwarded to him for a variety of reasons.[8] Pierrot's overview of the situation. enables him to serve from the beginning as a kind of editor of the novel, footnoting and supplying rhetorical "arguments" that precede some of the letters (e.g., "Celle-ci est un piège qu'il nous tendait" [L. 35]).

Restif uses the reader-judge figure also in *Le Nouvel Abélard* (1778), where the role of overseeing all correspondence is assumed by four parents. As the preface explains, after betrothing their children Heloise and Abelard to each other at birth, two couples conceived the idea of having the children "faire l'amour par lettres" without knowing each other's identity, "en sorte que leurs âmes se connussent, et que leurs corps ne se vissent pas" (vol. 1, pp. 31–32). Although the parents write very few letters, they read, censor, and footnote those of the children, in addition to authoring many of the lessons and model stories that Abelard sends to Heloise as her epistolary tutor. These "modèles" often foreshadow what will later happen to Heloise and Abelard; the ignorance of the children contrasts with the superior knowledge of the parents (revealed in the stories and the footnotes), who appear increasingly as puppeteers controlling the actions of their children.

In an ironic final interpolated story ("Le petit Abélard"), which Heloise's father sends Abelard in a letter, he finally points out explicitly to the boy the parallels between Abelard and the hero of this "modèle," whose parents had likewise imposed the "bridle of the pen" on him:

> Et voilà que le Babouin écrivait . . . tout-comme toi. Ça était plaisant! Et le Père de la petite Personne, bon réjoui, tiens, tout-comme toi, riait de tout son coeur, de voir mon petit Vaurien bridé, qui rongeait son frein, tant bien que mal, et qui écrivait, écrivait. . . . Et la petite Personne répondit à mon bon sujet, tantôt en petite sainte-nitouche, tantôt avec un peu plus d'intérêt; par-ci par-là elle aurait bien voulu lui marquer certaines choses; mais on y mettait bon ordre. [L. 85].

Continuing in the same vein, the father's letter is an ironic reading of the letters by one of the characters who, by their censoring and analytic powers, have controlled their shape all along.

Laclos's marquise and vicomte provide us with an even more fascinating example of the Super Reader. Like the parents of *Le Nouvel Abélard*, these two read, analyze, censor, and even occasionally write the correspondence between the younger couple in *Les Liaisons*, Cécile and Danceny, thus playing the same puppeteering role vis-à-vis their ignorant tutees as Restif's parents. Because Laclos's novel is so much more complex than Restif's—in terms of sheer multiplicity of points of view, plots, and correspondents—and because Laclos's main characters participate in a veritable "mythology of intelligence,"[9] their role as lucid readers of letters is correspondingly more complex.

Very few letters in *Les Liaisons* are read by their intended recipients only. The Cécile-Danceny correspondence is conducted under Merteuil's surveillance in Paris, under Valmont's in the country. Valmont forwards many of the letters from his exchange with the présidente to Merteuil for her to read and comment upon ("lisez et jugez" [L. 25]). The vicomte intercepts letters that pass between Tourvel and Volanges and, later in the novel, between Tourvel and Rosemonde. A letter such as Danceny's apology to Mme de Volanges (L. 64) is read by both Valmont and Merteuil before being sent to its original addressee. Knowledge—the key to power for Valmont and Merteuil—is acquired by reading, by gaining access to the correspondence of others.

As we read *Les Liaisons*, we develop the illusion that we are

reading a novel in the process of being written. Merteuil and
Valmont speak self-consciously of themselves as creators of their
own novel, as "historiens," playwrights, and directors. "C'est de
vos soins que va dépendre le dénouement de cette intrigue,"
Merteuil writes Valmont. "Jugez du moment où il faudra réunir
les acteurs" (L. 63). As we have just seen, we the external readers
are not the only readers of this novel in the making, for the
vicomte and the marquise themselves gradually become privy to
almost as many letters as we. Indeed, part of our own reading is
determined by the fact that we share their vision. When we read
Valmont's celebrated letter to the présidente (forwarded to
Merteuil) in which he speaks of his "pupitre" (actually the back of
the prostitute Emilie), our appreciation of the multiple ironies
generated by the situation comes from our stereoptic reading
through Merteuil's as well as the présidente's eyes. The Super
Reader dimension assumed by Valmont and Merteuil is the
epistolary role that most closely approximates that of the omniscient narrator in third-person fiction. Because we so often
share this omniscient viewpoint of Laclos's two principal
characters, we are drawn into their conspiracy and participate in
their ironic stance.

Creators and readers of their own novel, the marquise and the
vicomte acquire power not merely through access to the correspondence of others but through their highly developed science
of reading. Although the letters of simple-minded souls like
Danceny and Cécile pose no problems, the more complex psychology and restraint of the présidente's letters offer a greater
challenge. Valmont scrutinizes every line of the présidente's
letters for signs of weakness; his responses reflect his close reading
in their point-by-point rebuttal of Tourvel's arguments, including
those that she has not explicitly formulated.

Even the archdecoders Valmont and Merteuil do not always
concur on the interpretation of the présidente's letters. Whereas
Valmont early in the novel is certain the présidente has revealed
her vulnerability, Merteuil disagrees: "elle vous bat dans sa Lettre" (L. 33). Often Merteuil's position as observer rather than
participant in the action makes her a better reader than Valmont.
Valmont, moreover, frequently defers to the marquise's superior
interpretive powers. In letter 59 he forwards Danceny's letter 60

to Merteuil for an explication: "Apprenez-moi, si vous savez, ce que signifie ce radotage de Danceny." Likewise, in letter 76 Valmont admits to being baffled by one of Merteuil's letters and asks for an interpretation: "J'ai beau vous lire et vous relire, je n'en suis pas plus avancé. . . . Qu'avez-vous donc voulu dire?" Such queries contribute to our feeling that, though Valmont *writes* more letters than Merteuil, the marquise is the central *reader* and decoder of this novel. Indeed, toward the end of *Les Liaisons,* as the Merteuil-Valmont correspondence becomes the crucial one, much of Valmont's frustration hinges on his inability to understand what reading Merteuil is giving to his letters. Merteuil begins to resort to one of her favorite techniques, using quotations from her correspondent's letters to reveal the correspondent to himself.

The marquise has already used this approach with Cécile in letter 105, where Merteuil selects from Cécile's previous letter passages such as "ce trouble . . . qui vous faisait trouver *si difficile de se défendre*," in order to prove to Cécile that she took more pleasure in Valmont's rape-seduction than she realized or was willing to admit. Similarly, Merteuil holds up to Danceny quotations from his letters in order to force the chevalier both to the recognition that he is in love with her and to a choice between her and Cécile; she does this so indirectly and coquettishly, however, as to preserve her own reputation:

> Vous ne trouverez donc dans ma lettre que ce qui manque à la vôtre, franchise et simplesse. Je vous dirai bien, par exemple, que j'aurais grand plaisir à vous voir . . . mais vous, cette même phrase, vous la traduisez ainsi: *apprenez-moi à vivre où vous n'êtes pas*; en sorte que quand vous serez, je suppose, auprès de votre maîtresse, vous ne sauriez pas y vivre que je n'y sois en tiers. Quelle pitié! et ces femmes, *à qui il manque toujours d'être moi*, vous trouverez peut-être aussi que cela manque à *votre* Cécile? [L. 121]

Merteuil uses her various readings of letters as mirrors, which she holds up so that others can recognize themselves in the image that their own words have created.

As Valmont begins to pressure Merteuil to award him his promised "prize" toward the end of the novel, Merteuil responds (as she had done with Danceny and Cécile) with quotations from his own letters: "Quand, par example, vous voudrez vous distraire un moment de *ce charme inconnu* que *l'adorable*, la *céleste* Madame de Tourvel vous a fait seule éprouver . . . " (L. 127). In Merteuil's mirror Valmont now can finally "read" his own letters as she has read them all along, for though he has gallantly paid hommage to the marquise, the images by which he has described Tourvel have been more forceful. To defend himself, Valmont accuses Merteuil of being a bad reader, because "ces mots [those quoted by Merteuil], plus souvent pris au hasard que par réflexion, expriment moins le cas que l'on fait de la personne que la situation dans laquelle on se trouve quand on en parle" (L. 129). Here, however, it would appear that it is Valmont who is the bad reader, for even if he has forgotten the marquise's earlier admonition ("Vous voilà donc vous conduisant sans principes, et donnant tout au hasard" [L. 10]) or her formulation of her own rigid code ("mes principes . . . ne sont pas . . . donnés au hasard . . . ils sont le fruit de mes profondes réflexions" [L. 81]), he is overlooking how much this attribution of his word choice to "le hasard" condemns him. By letting "le hasard" play a role, Valmont is betraying his own and the marquise's code of intelligence and calculation. Furthermore, one need not wait for Freud to know that unconscious language is often more revealing than conscious language, as the subsequent exchanges between Valmont and Merteuil demonstrate.

In letter 134 Merteuil again singles out passages to criticize from Valmont's previous letter: "En effet, ce n'est plus l'adorable, la céleste Madame de Tourvel, mais c'est *une femme étonnante, une femme délicate et sensible*, et cela, à l'exclusion de toutes les autres; *une femme rare enfin*, et *telle qu'on n'en rencontrerait pas une seconde*." The incorrigible Valmont makes the same error again and again, as Merteuil points out to him in subsequent letters: "Encore dans votre dernière Lettre, si vous ne m'y parlez pas de cette femme uniquement, c'est que vous ne voulez m'y rien dire de vos *grandes affaires*; elles vous semblent si importantes que le silence que vous gardez à ce sujet vous semble une punition pour moi" (L. 141). Yet in these letters that Merteuil so mockingly quotes, Valmont has included many a cajolery directed at Merteuil. It is as if Merteuil, by continually asking Valmont to go home and correct his paper, were forcing him to play a schoolboy's role, just as they had together made pupils of

Danceny and Cécile. Each time Valmont appears to bring his new paper back with words erased and complimentary addenda on Merteuil; yet each time Merteuil reads closely enough to discover the new references to the présidente that have slipped in: "C'est ainsi qu'en remarquant votre politesse, qui vous a fait supprimer soigneusement tous les mots que vous vous êtes imaginé m'avoir déplu, j'ai vu cependant que, peut-être sans vous en apercevoir, vous n'en conserviez pas moins les mêmes idées" (L. 134).

In her capacity as reader-judge of the letters of others Merteuil appears, even more than the vicomte, to be at the central switchboard for all the lines of communication in the novel. To decode letters Valmont himself defers occasionally to this central intelligence agency. There are many reasons why we sense Merteuil to be Laclos's superior character, as Seylaz and so many others have remarked.[10] Not the least of these, however, is her function as Laclos's Super Reader.

If we turn now to three other novels where portrayed readings and readers play a significant role, we will find many of the observations made in the first part of this chapter still operative— the moment of reading as a moment of *anagnorisis* or discovery, the tendency of epistolary decoders to pore over specific words and shape new letters around quotations from old ones, the presence of dominating reader figures who excel in the art of explication de texte. All of these factors are present in *La Nouvelle Héloïse*, where even many years after their initial writing, letters are subject to many readings and rereadings.

Emotional though they may be when reading each other's letters, Julie and Saint-Preux are nonetheless attentive to logical matters and occasionally indulge in the same kind of close analysis that we have seen in *Les Liaisons*. In part 1, letter 9, Julie catches a subtle contradiction on Saint-Preux's part: "en sorte que, dans la même lettre, vous vous plaignez de ce que vous avez trop de peine, et de ce que vous n'en avez pas assez." Julie and Claire together formulate a critique of Saint-Preux's letters from Paris (2:15), mocking his wordly style by quoting his absurd metaphors. A careful reading of Saint-Preux's letters enables Julie to deduce from his style the company he is keeping and the kinds of frivolous, even dangerous, activities into which he may be drawn (2:27).

It is Claire, however, more than any other character, who engages in the most significant analyses of the novel. When Julie is faced with her crucial decision (2:9)—whether to accept Milord Edouard's offer of a haven for the two lovers in England—she lays the burden of choice in Claire's hands, sending to Claire both Edouard's letter (2:3) and her own efforts to articulate her emotions (2:4). Julie begs Claire to "read" both Edouard's letter and Julie's heart. In her long response Claire verbalizes equally complex and divided emotions, affirming the uniqueness of Julie's destiny and Claire's willingness to follow Julie wherever she goes, even if it means abandoning her own fiancé. Although Claire ostensibly leaves the decision to Julie, Julie reads in Claire's letter the advice she was seeking ("Je t'entends, amie incomparable et je te remercie") and in her next letter (2:6 to Edouard) declines the Englishman's offer.

An even more curious exchange in which Claire "reads Julie's heart" through her letter occurs in part 4. Both letter 7, in which Julie describes her feelings for Saint-Preux upon seeing him for the first time in over four years, and letter 8, in which Claire interprets Julie's letter 7, are fascinating witnesses to the weight of the reader in the epistolary exchange. For Julie's letter is written as if Wolmar were not to read it, though in fact she expects him to read it. Claire's commentary is double; Claire tells Julie both how Wolmar would have read his wife's letter and how she, Claire, reads it.

Julie's letter actually contains two radically different sections: the body proper, which is a straightforward description of Saint-Preux and her reactions to his return, and a postscript, in which Julie reveals to Claire her resolution to write each letter "comme s'il [Wolmar] ne la devait point voir, et de la lui montrer ensuite." In the postscript, which is almost as long as the body of the letter, Julie reports Wolmar's refusal to read the letter when she brought it to him, his almost clairvoyant knowledge of its contents ("Avouez, m'a-t-il dit, que dans cette lettre vous avez moins parlé de moi qu'à l'ordinaire"), and the complete trust in his wife that inspires his respect for confidentiality between her and Claire. The perceptive Wolmar teaches his wife that it is impossible to communicate intimately with two readers simultaneously through the same letter: "Il y a mille secrets que trois amis doivent savoir, et qu'ils ne peuvent se dire que deux à deux. Vous communiquez bien les mêmes choses à votre amie et à votre époux, mais non pas de la même manière; et si vous voulez tout confondre, il arrivera que vos lettres seront écrites plus à moi qu'à elle, et que vous ne serez à votre aise ni avec l'un ni avec l'autre." Julie's letter itself bears witness to this wise observation, for in spite of her effort to be totally candid, to speak from her soul, she has decorously denied herself the pleasure of praising her husband in a letter he would see. Her double reader-consciousness, in this case awareness of a second addressee, has given her writing a different turn from that of her usual confidences to Claire.

Claire totally approves of Wolmar's decision not to read Julie's letter; in her compensatory double commentary Claire systematically contrasts her own reading with the reading Wolmar would have given the letter:

> M. de Wolmar aurait d'abord remarqué que ta lettre entière est employée à parler de notre ami, et n'aurait point vu l'apostille où tu n'en dis pas un mot. Si tu avais écrit cette apostille, il y a dix ans, mon enfant, je ne sais comment tu aurais fait, mais l'ami y serait toujours rentré par quelque coin, d'autant plus que le mari ne la devait point voir. . . .
> Enfin il s'imaginerait que tous ces changements que tu as observés seraient échappés à une autre; et moi j'ai bien peur au contraire d'en trouver qui te seront échappés. Quelque différent que ton hôte soit de ce qu'il était, il changerait davantage encore, que, si ton coeur n'avait point changé, tu le verrais toujours le même.

Claire's dual analysis enables us to delve into a complex psychology, to explore many of the nuances of Julie's feelings for Saint-Preux and the progress Julie has made over ten years, by observing the long-awaited scene of the lovers' reunion from multiple reader perspectives—including those offered by hypothesis and memory.

The way in which Claire measures this progress is not only to compare her own reading with the hypothetical reading of a Wolmar but to compare Julie's letter with a letter Julie might have written ten years ago. Claire's measurement of Julie's progress is a measurement of change. In a novel where the theme of change over time is so important, we might well expect to see letters of "ten years ago" contrasted with those of the present, and rereadings of old letters give rise to memories of irretrievable past happiness.

Both Julie and Saint-Preux make a "recueil" of their letters. Nowhere more than in *La Nouvelle Héloïse* are individual letters more subject to later resurrection as mementos and as edifying "manuels"(Saint-Preux's term in 2:13) to be reread privately in the future. Frequent specific allusions are made to letters written in the distant past; even Edouard and Claire show an extraordinary familiarity with Saint-Preux and Julie's correspondence as they cite letters long after the lovers had written them. When offering Julie asylum in England (2:3), Edouard alludes to the letter in which Saint-Preux described the Valais country (1:23); Edouard writes Julie that in his idyllic English province "vous pourrez accomplir ensemble tous les tendres souhaits par où finit la lettre dont je parle." This technique of citation and allusive cross-referencing suggests a community of rereaders who have the entire text of their past correspondence at their fingertips. It draws attention, moreover, to the letter as a privileged physical trace of temporal experience. In part 3, letter 7, Claire reminds Saint-Preux of his letter 55 of part 1, which Claire had read and which was proof of the condensability of a lifetime into one year; Claire tries to console him with the thought that the letter itself, in its rereadability, is a souvenir preferable to a slow decline in love.

Letters in *La Nouvelle Héloïse* mark points in time and by so doing participate in Rousseau's complex mythology of change and the irreversibility of time. To reread an old letter is to measure one's own change against a point perceived as fixed in the past. To compare today's letter with yesterday's is to discover the distance traveled between two temporal moments. Saint-Preux's last letter in the novel opens with a reading of Julie's first letter to him in seven years, a letter that he cannot refrain from juxtaposing with the earlier ones. Every physical aspect—"la forme, le pli, le cachet, l'adresse, tout dans cette lettre m'en rappelle de trop différentes. . . . Ah! deviez-vous employer la même écriture pour tracer d'autres sentiments?" (6:7). Such a strong preoccupation with "anciennes lettres" is no cause for alarm, however, Saint-Preux writes Julie, for it helps him realize and accept the fact that the Julie and Saint-Preux of the present are no longer and can never be the lovers of the past. As in other novels, the act of reading in *La Nouvelle Héloïse* is linked with acts of discovery—recognition of change, deepening understanding of complex emotions. Rousseau's characters attempt to read each other's souls by reading letters as the changing reflections of these souls.

For Crébillon's duchesse de *** writing *is* reading. Although we never directly see the letters of the duke who courts her from a distance, the duchess's published responses are filled with quotations from his letters, which she scrutinizes and explicates. Indeed, most of her letters are based on examination and analysis of her own language and that of the duke; many of them revolve around the interpretation of a single word. Rarely does the duchess take the duke's words at face value. Most of her conclusions about his character are inferences drawn from attentive reading, as when she deduces that in spite of what he has written, he does not believe her denial that she loves another (L. 4), or when she repeatedly sees through her seducer's techniques. So carefully does the duchess measure her own words, so analytical is her style, that we sense that her refusal to become the duke's mistress is not the formal "no" of an epistolary heroine who will eventually surrender. Yet the duchess's emotions are perceptible. They are evident in her indirect statements and her constant use of the conditional, the same "if I loved you" that Mme de Tourvel begins to use with Valmont in letter 50 of *Les Liaisons*. "Si j'avais le malheur de vous aimer," the duchess writes, "je ne vous le dirais que le plus tard qu'il me serait possible. Mais si cela était, auriez-vous besoin que je vous le disse?" (L. 47) The duke, however, would appear to need a more explicit statement, since he opts for an easier affair with the disreputable Mme de L. . . , thereby proving that he has not mended his ways for the duchess, as he had claimed and she had doubted. If the duke and the duchess never get together, it is because she has been too clever a reader of his letters and he not a perceptive or persistent enough interpreter of hers.

In the game of love, close reading may prevent a union of lovers (the case of the duke and duchess, of Merteuil and Valmont), or it may facilitate it (Mme Riccoboni's *Comtesse de Sancerre*—where a curious mirror reading of letters catalyzes recognition of love).[11]

*Pamela* would fall into the latter category of novels, for the marriage of Pamela and Mr. B and the entire denouement are largely determined by a reading of letters.

Although one can often question whether Pamela's letters to her parents are really letters and not merely a personal diary, particularly during her imprisonment by B, Pamela repeatedly emphasizes that she writes her letters to be read and reread: "as I know you keep my letters, and read them over and over . . . and as it may be some little pleasure to me, perhaps, to read them myself, when I am come to you, to remind me of what I have gone through . . . (which, I hope, will further strengthen my good resolutions, that I may not hereafter, from my bad conduct, have reason to condemn myself from my own hand as it were)" (L. 20). The letter thus becomes a symbol of virtue for Pamela, and her reader-consciousness is none other than consciousness of a moral monitor, be it future self or parents, who shape her writing to the extent that they influence the actions that she writes about. That B recognizes this symbolic value of the letter for Pamela is evidenced by his constant efforts to prevent her from writing, even early in the novel (cf. L1. 12, 27), just as he will later make attempts upon her virtue.

The readers for whom Pamela intends her letters (her parents and her future self) are not the ones who actually read all of them. As the editor tells us in the interpolated section between the first episodes and the Lincolnshire section, B has contrived quite early to intercept Pamela's letters to her parents and even retains three of them, which Pamela's parents never see. B has intimated as much in a conversation with Pamela: "I have seen more of your letters than you imagine . . . and am quite overcome with your charming manner of writing . . . and all put together makes me, as I tell you, love you to extravagance" (L. 30). When B becomes the reader of Pamela's letters, Richardson is providing us with an interesting variation on the theme of the letter as a means of seduction, for Pamela's letters win, without her knowing it, her master's love.

In fact, the turning point in the novel occurs when, after a long period at Lincolnshire during which he has not been able to discover where Pamela hides her letters, B finally succeeds in stealing a group Pamela had intended to smuggle to her parents.

After perusing these letters, B demands that Pamela show him the rest of her writings: "I long to see the particulars of your plot, and your disappointment, where your papers leave off: for you have so beautiful a manner, that it is partly that, and partly my love for you, that has made me desirous of reading all you write. . . . Besides, said he, there is such a pretty air of romance, as you relate them, in *your* plots, and *my* plots, that I shall be better directed in what manner to wind up the catastrophe of the pretty novel" (p. 242). B's consciousness of Pamela's letters as her "novel," *their* novel—which he reads and yet is an agent in—resembles Valmont's and Merteuil's awareness of themselves as creators and readers of their own story. Here, as in *Les Liaisons*, it is B's reading of the "novel" he is a part of that influences the action portrayed in the novel.

Pamela finally surrenders her letters to B and, having no choice, agrees to show him her subsequent letters, though not without complaining about the difficulty of writing for two different readers: "how can I write with any face, what must be for your perusal, and not for those I intend to read my melancholy stories?" (p. 251). Soon B is the first to read all of Pamela's letters. When B becomes Pamela's primary reader, the seduction vector changes direction. Witnesses to Pamela's moral and literary virtue, the letters convince B simultaneously that Pamela's character is disinterested and that his jealousy of Pamela's friend Williams is unfounded.[12] B's decision to free Pamela and to propose marriage to her is the immediate result of his reading of her entire correspondence.[13]

The novel does not end here, however (although many critics think it should have). Even after marriage to B, Pamela must undergo the trials of being presented to a society that is dubious about her social station and her motives for marrying B. To interpret the second part of *Pamela* it is instructive to refer again to the reader motif. If, in the first half, B is Pamela's principal reader, in the second half her audience multiplies. First B's sister, Lady Davers, then Lady Davers's friends read her letters; ultimately the letters are circulated among an even wider public. This "publication" of Pamela's story is consonant with B's general efforts to make a spectacle of Pamela in other ways—by having her tell stories in salons and even reciting himself one of her

poems before a group of guests. Pamela's letters again become the
instruments of conversion, of an entire society this time—
including the proud Lady Davers—who soften upon reading
about her virtuous resistance and even ask Pamela to continue
writing letters "that this wondrous story be perfect, and we, your
friends, may read and admire you more and more" (p. 317).
Artificial though this reason for Pamela's continued "scribbling"
may be, it nonetheless reinforces the role of letter reading in the
novel and the characters' own consciousness of Pamela's writing
as a story that must be completed as a rhetorical unity.

The movement from the first half to the second half of
Richardson's novel is the movement from the privacy of the
prison and the tête-à-tête to the world of society and the salon, the
movement from private reading to publication. By a curious
reversal, the "very things that I [Pamela] most dreaded his seeing,
the contents of my papers" become "the means to promote my
happiness" (p. 326). If Pamela's story must become public, it is
because Pamela must serve as an example. In a sense she becomes
public property at the end, as it becomes imperative that she keep
society apprised of all events in her story. The letters hidden and
regarded as criminal in the first half of the story become documents for public edification in the last half. If B's reading of
Pamela's papers puts an end to her first period of trials, the
reading by B's society puts an end to her second period, and it is
only fitting that the reading by that wider circle—the external
public—should put an end to Richardson's novel.

The movement from private to public reading is not unique to
*Pamela*. We have already seen the tendency of the single reader to
multiply in *La Religieuse* and in *Marianne*, where letters written
for one addressee are shared by him with other readers. In fact,
any moment when letters begin to circulate among several readers
marks their passage from a private to a more public domain. This
occurs in Restif's *Le Paysan perverti*, where the characters
increasingly forward copies of letters to each other so that by the
end of the novel Pierrot is able to piece together Edmond's story
and we understand better why he has served as editor of the
published collection.[14] Within Clarissa's fictional universe, Jack
Belford assumes a role approximating that of the editor. Just
before Clarissa's death Belford furnishes her the letters from

Lovelace to Belford, which, together with the letters Clarissa requests from Anna Howe, enable Belford and Clarissa to reconstruct the heroine's story. Her will, moreover, names Belford as compiler of the collection and gives him jurisdiction over a copy of it.

The internally portrayed collector-publisher figure appears briefly in Mme de Genlis's *Adèle et Théodore, ou Lettres sur l'éducation*. At the close of this multicorrespondent novel, when Adèle is married, her wedding gift from her mother (one of the chief correspondents in the novel) is none other than the collection *Lettres sur l'éducation*. Mme de Genlis does not bother, however, to show us how Adèle's mother collected these letters.

A much more narratively integrated collecting of letters occurs at the end of *Les Liaisons*, when Mme de Rosemonde gradually assembles most of the novel's correspondence. If Valmont, and particularly Merteuil, have been the central confidant and reader figures of the first part of the novel, Rosemonde replaces them in the denouement; all the letters begin to flow toward her, sent by people who now entrust her (*confier* is again the key word) with their documents, just as Cécile and Danceny earlier entrusted their letters to the marquise and Valmont for safekeeping. A footnote informs us that the published edition was compiled from the letters Rosemonde assembled. Rosemonde's collection and subsequent publication of this correspondence would not have been possible if Valmont had not been a letter collector himself. When she inherits Valmont's pile of papers, Rosemonde gains access not only to Valmont's correspondence (letters to him from Tourvel and her priest, from Danceny, Merteuil, Cécile, his chasseur, as well as rough drafts of Valmont's letters to them) but also to all the letters that Cécile received in the country and that Valmont kept. Through Danceny Rosemonde acquires the Danceny-Cécile correspondence; she inherits the dying présidente's letters; and she of course already has her own correspondence with the présidente and Mme de Volanges. Yet curiously enough, in this novel where every end is tied, where each phenomenon is so highly motivated and integrated into the rest, Laclos does not account in any way for Rosemonde's access to the other letters. If we could assume that Danceny's letters to Cécile, and Cécile's to Sophie, were acquired through Rosemonde's friendship with Mme de Volanges, how can we account for her possession of the letters sent to the marquise de Merteuil? Here, as in Restif's *Paysan perverti*, it is merely the illusion of acquisition that has been created by so much portrayed collecting.

A significant difference between Laclos's and Restif's novels, however, lies in the motivation for collecting letters. Rarely in *Le Paysan perverti* are letters forwarded to second recipients for any reason other than a vague desire to communicate ("I thought you might like to see this letter") or preserved for any motive other than to constitute a story that can be reread. In *Les Liaisons*, on the other hand, where letters are stockpiled as weapons, the collecting and passing on of correspondence is a major element in the plot, and the events whereby the letters wind up in Rosemonde's hands are the principal episodes of the denouement.[15] Fatally wounded by Danceny in a duel, Valmont bequeathes to him a package of letters, which Danceny circulates among the Parisian public to avenge their mutual betrayal by Merteuil. Rosemonde acquires the letters that Valmont had given Danceny only because Danceny sends them to her to vindicate himself and to prevent her from prosecuting him as Valmont's murderer. Her acquisition of Tourvel's and Danceny's letters is likewise well motivated. Rosemonde urges Danceny to send her Cécile's letters (as a kind of "safety deposit") in order to protect Cécile from exposure; Rosemonde argues that since Danceny no longer is interested in Cécile and yet has been partially responsible for her corruption, his honor requires him to surrender her letters. The respectful Danceny can only comply. The présidente entrusts Rosemonde with her cassette of letters for what must be the same reason: in order to bury her affair in "le silence et l'oubli" (L. 171).

Letters in *Les Liaisons* are thus collected for two contradictory reasons: either to expose others publicly or to bury an affair in oblivion. In other words, letters are collected either to prevent further reading or to extend the circle of readers. In fact, the entire novel moves between these two poles of secrecy and publication, between the need for privacy and the need for publicity. Merteuil and Valmont distinguish between private and public versions of the same story; Merteuil sends Valmont an account of the Prévan episode written for private reading but writes her letter to Volanges for a "lecture publique" (L. 85). The vicomte and the marquise conduct their affairs in secret, yet each needs the other as an audience for approbation; indeed, even this restricted need for a public will lead to their ultimate destruction.

The denouement constitutes an acceleration of the oscillation between the private and public poles. Ironically, it is precisely Merteuil's private version of the Prévan episode (L. 85, to Valmont) that will be subjected to a "lecture publique" at the end. The marquise, Valmont, and Danceny all use exposure of letters to a wider audience as a means of vengeance.[16] Yet after the initial rapid-fire publication of letters, the pendulum swings back to secrecy; Danceny, Volanges, and the présidente hasten to "deposit" (the image most frequently used) letters with Mme de Rosemonde so that all may remain "à jamais ignoré de tout le monde" (L. 174). The novel whose principal characters have emphasized acquisition of knowledge through reading of letters, and public exposure of others through collection of letters, ends on the note of silence and deliberate ignorance. "Il ne reste qu'à pleurer et se taire," Mme de Rosemonde advises Danceny. "Se taire" is precisely what Rosemonde does in response to Volanges's request for enlightenment on her daughter's motives for retiring to a convent.

And yet the fact remains that this story has not been buried in silence; the very existence of the novel belies such a myth of oblivion. A footnote to letter 169 explicitly informs us that an unidentifiable "on" has formed the present "recueil" from Mme de Rosemonde's collection. The existence of this work is a monument to the letter's potential for publication. As a tangible document, even when intended for a single addressee, the letter is always subject to circulation among a larger group of readers. It passes freely from the private to the public domain and even back again.

Mme Riccoboni's *Lettres de Fanni Butlerd* offers a different example of the same movement in epistolary narrative. Since this novel follows the love affair of a woman through her letters to her lover, the correspondence is of the most intimate nature, yet the final letter, in which Fanni finally renounces the man who has betrayed her, is addressed to him in "les papiers publics." Fanni chooses this public rather than private means of communication in order to seal symbolically the fact that their affair is no longer intimate; she stresses the significance of print over handwriting: "Vous me reconnaîtrez: un style qui vous fut si familier . . . mais vos yeux ne reverront jamais ces caractères que vous nommiez sacrés, que vous baisiez avec tant d'ardeur, qui vous étaient *si chers*, et que vous m'avez fait remettre avec tant d'exactitude" (L. 116). Furthermore, Fanni chooses to publish equally anonymously her entire half of the correspondence in order to immortalize her passion, blaming her suffering on the lover rather than on the love. Her preface to this collection is an unusual variation on the typical "au lecteur," in that it is addressed to a single specific reader: "Miss Fanni, à un seul lecteur." The first lines make the identity of this reader clear: "Si le naturel et la vérité, qui font tout le mérite de ces Lettres, leur attirent l'approbation du Public; si le hasard vous les fait lire; si vous reconnaissez les expressions d'un coeur qui fut à vous . . ." Just as Fanni had transformed an intimate letter into a public one by publishing it in the newspaper, in her preface she converts a traditionally public form into a personal letter by restoring the specificity of the reader. By being both the first letter of the volume and the last letter Fanni writes, the preface seals the novel's circle, which moves from the original intimate correspondence to a final public letter whose purpose is to annul the previous intimacy. Her final letter thus points back to the other public act, the preface, in which Fanni paradoxically addresses herself anew to her original reader, who may now reread the correspondence in published form. In other words the cycle of reading may begin again, since the original private sequence is now subject to both a private rereading and a public first reading.

Each novel that we have examined—*La Religieuse, Marianne, Pamela, Le Paysan perverti, Clarissa, Adèle et Théodore, Les Liaisons dangereuses, Fanni Butlerd*—has its own way of motivating and rendering explicit the movement from private to public reading. Yet all share the same tendency not only to dramatize the act of writing but also to tell the story of their own publication, either by the presence of a reader-editor figure whose collecting of letters is part of the action of the narrative (as in *Le Paysan perverti, Clarissa, Les Liaisons, Adèle et Théodore*) or by the internal representation of letter circulation among a wide public (as in *Marianne, Fanni Butlerd, Les Liaisons, Pamela*).

The effect of such an internal publication, within the world of the narrative, is to blur the distinction between external and internal reader. Between the internal addressee and the external eavesdropper lie the internal eavesdroppers. The path from internal private reader to internal public to external public appears a continuous unbroken one. We pass almost imperceptibly from the fictional to the real, historical world in narrative that portrays the story of its own publication.

The concern to account for publication of private documents is of course primarily an eighteenth-century preoccupation.[17] This fact alone may explain why the majority of the texts in this chapter are eighteenth-century novels. To justify the claim to authenticity, the real publisher of an eighteenth-century novel naturally had to account for his possession of "private" letters. Such clichés as discovery in an old trunk or inheritance of letters were weak justifications and could not be applied at all to multicorrespondent works. Such ploys, furthermore, necessitated the introduction of an editor figure removed from the world of the narrative, whereas what is interesting about the texts that we have just examined is precisely their internalization of the publisher figure. Even a unicorrespondent novel like *Fanni Butlerd* offers the originality, for reasons integral to the story, of making the publisher the letter writer herself.

The internal reader's role in shaping epistolary narrative cannot be overestimated. Addressee-consciousness informs the act of writing itself, and acts of reading constitute consequential narrative events. Epistolary mythology tends to locate power with the reader, as its regular creation of a Super Reader figure reveals. The external reader's experience is partially governed by the presence of his internal counterpart; we read any given letter from at least three points of view—that of the intended or actual recipient as well as that of the writer and our own. Even when only implied, the interpretation that the addressee would give to a letter enters into our own reading: we are drawn to read the présidente's letters from Valmont's point of view, having been sensitized to watch, like him, for signs of weakness. When portrayed, on the other hand, the internal reader's decoding of a message becomes part of a new message (Lovelace's annotations, Merteuil's analyses). For the external reader, reading an epistolary novel is very much like reading over the shoulder of another character whose own readings—and misreadings—must enter into our experience of the work. In fact, the epistolary novel's tendency to narrativize reading, integrating the act of reading into the fiction at all levels (from a correspondent's proofreading of his own letters to publication and public reading of the entire letter collection), constitutes an internalizing action that blurs the very distinctions that we make between the internal and external reader. I shall have more to say about this phenomenon in the Conclusion.

1. Throughout this chapter a simple distinction will be made between the *internal* reader (a specific character represented within the world of the narrative, whose reading of the letters can influence the writing of the letters) and the *external* reader (we, the general public, who read the work as a finished product and have no effect on the writing of individual letters). In his "Discours du récit," published in *Figures III*, pp. 265–66, Gérard Genette makes a similar distinction, valid for all forms of narrative discourse, between the "intradiegetic narratee" (our internal reader) and the "extradiegetic narratee" (our external reader). In his "Introduction à l'étude du narrataire," Gerald Prince systematically examines the role of the implied addressee in narrative in general.

2. I am not suggesting, by these distinctions, that writers of autobiography or memoir novels have no real or implied readers, or that they never address a reader directly. My notion of "pure autobiography" is a theoretical model, emphasizing that the autobiographer's primary relations are with *self* and the *act of self-expression*, whereas in the truly epistolary novel writing is governed by a desire for *exchange* with an *addressee* who is specifically *other*. This distinction is implicitly supported by studies of other first-person forms: namely, Philippe Lejeune's work on a corpus that he carefully defines as "autobiography" (*L'Autobiographie en France* [1971] and *Le Pacte autobiographique* [1975]), Philip Stewart's analysis of the role of the reader in the memoir novel (pp. 141–68 of *Imitation and Illusion in the French Memoir Novel* [1969]), Patricia M. Spacks's study of autobiography and novel in eighteenth-century England (*Imaging a Self* [1976]), and Gerald Prince's article "The Diary Novel: Notes for the Definition of a Sub-genre" (1972). The autobiographer's reader, if acknowledged, is nonspecific (typically an anonymous public or posterity, Rousseau's "qui que vous soyez"), whereas the letter writer's language is shaped by the specificity of his reader. If invoked, the autobiographer's reader is typically called upon to read and judge a total account of a life, not to influence that life or account.

3. Jost, in his classification of epistolary narrative (discussed earlier, in the Introduction), considers *Marianne* and *La Religieuse* as epistolary in genre; the "type-Marianne" constitutes, in fact, one of Jost's six major divisions. By displacing the emphasis from classification to definition, I intend to use these novels to help define epistolarity itself, while offering further evidence of the specific aspects that can justify dealing with them as "epistolary" novels.

4. Robert J. Ellrich, "The Rhetoric of *La Religieuse* and Eighteenth-Century Forensic Rhetoric," p. 138.

5. For other perspectives on the hybrid generic affiliations of *La Religieuse* and their relation to the novel's well-known "mistakes" (*bévues*) see Georges May, *Diderot et "La Religieuse*," pp. 199–218; Jacques Rustin, "*La Religieuse* de Diderot: mémoires ou journal intime?"; and Emile Lizé, "*La Religieuse*, un roman épistolaire?" For *Marianne* a comparison with Marivaux's more formally conventional memoir novel, *Le Paysan parvenu*, is instructive; Marianne engages in much more discourse with her reader than the narrator of *Le Paysan* and maintains a clearer distinction between her style as narrator and her style as character. What Rousset has called Marivaux's "double register" figures far less in *Le Paysan* (see Conclusion, note 21).

6. We notice the same tendency in reporting dialogue: instead of faithfully registering and reproducing dialogue in their letters, as would a Pamela or a Clarissa, Valmont and Merteuil offer concise analyses. Here, for example is a passage in which the marquise quickly and cleverly reduces an entire conversation to its component parts: "Je ne vous rendrai donc pas notre conversation que vous suppléerez aisément. Observez seulement que, dans ma feinte défense, je l'aidais de tout mon pouvoir: embarras, pour lui donner le temps de parler, mauvaises raisons, pour être combattues . . . et ce refrain perpétuel de sa part, *je ne vous demande qu'un mot*; et ce silence de la mienne . . . au travers de tout cela, une main cent fois prise, qui se retire toujours et ne se refuse jamais" (L. 85). The entire dialogue is condensed into its salient elements and filtered through the marquise's interpreting intelligence.

7. This epithet has nothing to do with Michael Riffaterre's "Super-Reader" (*Archilecteur*), a construct defined as a sum of readings for purposes of stylistic analysis, in his *Essais de stylistique structurale*.

8. See, for example, letters 72, 172, 249, and especially 232, where Pierrot is heir to a large volume of letters. In his recently published study *Rétif de la Bretonne et la création littéraire* (1977), Pierre Testud likewise notes the extent to which Restif emphasizes his characters' function as readers. Although Testud examines the role of the reader in a chapter devoted to Restif's epistolary novels (pp. 366–400), he offers examples and conclusions quite different from mine. Since his arguments bear upon many of the same works that we shall be discussing in this chapter and the next (Restif's *Malédiction paternelle, Paysan perverti, Nouvel Abélard*, and *Posthumes*), it is worth clarifying the extent to which they complement or diverge from the readings I offer. After a sensitive analysis of all of the technical resources of the epistolary form that Restif did *not* exploit, Testud concludes that Restif chose the letter form because it reproduces "l'image de la communication entre l'écrivain et son lecteur" (p. 391). The instances that Testud cites, however, are all cases in which the letter writer forwards a *récit* (interpolated story) to his correspondent. Testud points out in particular the frequency with which Restif's letter writers send each other copies of Restif's already published works and comment upon them; such a ploy allows Restif to create his own public and orient the reading of his own work (pp. 394–95). A second phenomenon that Testud points out is the frequency with which the letter prolongs or gives rise to an oral communication; whenever a letter either transcribes an orally delivered story or is itself read orally, it testifies to Restif's view of the letter as a privileged form for establishing a direct relationship between a narrator and a public (p. 400). Testud's findings intersect with mine in demonstrating Restif's preoccupation with reader response.

However, since Testud deals only with the communication of *récits* that are exterior to the world of the correspondents, the readership that he studies bears more pertinently upon Restif's view of literary reception in general than upon his use of the epistolary form in particular. I would argue—through the examples I offer in chapters 3 and 4—that although Restif is hardly an outstanding technician, his use of the epistolary form is more subtle than is usually acknowledged. For in Restif's *epistolary* novels, correspondents do not read only interpolated stories. They also read letters, and in so doing become implicated in superimposed narrational levels and multiple perspectives on the very letters that compose their own story.

9. The expression comes from André Malraux's often reprinted article "Laclos et *Les Liaisons dangereuses*," in his *Le Triangle noir: Laclos, Goya, Saint-Just* (Paris: Gallimard, 1970), pp. 23–51, which first appeared in 1939. J.-L. Seylaz, in *"Les Liaisons dangereuses" et la création romanesque chez Laclos*, also analyzes the novel as "une mythologie de l'intelligence."

10. See Seylaz, pp. 112–16, for a discussion of Merteuil's superiority.

11. In Mme Riccoboni's *Adélaïde, comtesse de Sancerre*, Adélaïde's friend Nancé forces her to acknowledge her love for the marquis de Montalais by mirroring revealing juxtapositions from her letters in his own letters. It is only by reading between the lines of Nance's letters (which reflect Adélaïde's), rather than her own, that Adélaïde recognizes the nature of her emotions.

12. Wolmar similarly calls the Julie–Saint-Preux correspondence, which he has read without Julie's knowledge, "les fondements de ma sécurité" (4:12), since the letters bear witness to the fundamental virtue of both Julie and the man she chose as a girl.

13. Fielding in his parody *Shamela* of course questions whether Pamela was not trying to seduce B for his money all along!

14. Restif does not account for Pierrot's access to all of these letters, however. We do not actually see him collect all of the letters but merely enough of them that the illusion that he has access to them is created.

15. Tzvetan Todorov was the first to point out that the denouement of *Les Liaisons* tell the story of its own creation. For his perceptive analysis see his *Littérature et signification*, pp. 47–49.

16. *Les Liaisons* in this respect seems an inversion of *Pamela*. If *Pamela* is the novel of "virtue rewarded," *Les Liaisons* is the novel of "vice punished." In both cases it is through a publication of letters that justice occurs. The publication of Merteuil's letters brings about her punishment, whereas Pamela's "rewards" are due in part to B's reading of her letters: "I still wish to see them [her letters] too . . . to have before me the whole series of your sufferings, that I may learn what degree of kindness may be sufficient to recompense you for them" (pp. 284–85). *Les Liaisons* and *Pamela* thus offer interesting epistolary approaches to the eighteenth century's preoccupation with verisimilitude and moral justification. Internal publication of letters brings about reward and punishment in addition to accounting for how such documents as letters might have passed into an editor's hands.

17. The incorporation of the publication process into the fiction is not, however, limited to the eighteenth century. Jacques Derrida's *Envois* plays as fully as any eighteenth-century narrative upon the epistolary potential to move between the historical and fictional worlds, between private and public readings.

(See in particular pp. 191 ff., where the game of authenticity [are these real or fictional letters?] begins with the writer's stated plan to burn part and publish the rest of the correspondence we have been reading.) The author and principal correspondent of *Envois* (who both *is* and *is not* Jacques Derrida) even reports on negotiations with his publisher, Flammarion, thereby fictionalizing the "real" publisher of the book. After publication, however, the writer plans to continue the intimate private correspondence destined for the fire, thereby rehistoricizing the fictional correspondence. With Derrida the letter's potential to oscillate between private and public readings becomes emblematic of a general "crise de la destination": to whom, for whom, does one write?

# CHAPTER FOUR

# EPISTOLARY DISCOURSE

The language of the letter belongs to the larger linguistic system of "discourse," that is, utterances that suppose a speaker or writer (*I*) and a hearer or reader (*you*).[1] Epistolary discourse is distinguishable from other types of discourse—such as the memoir, diary, rhetoric, or theater—by certain basic pronominal and predicative traits. No one of these traits alone defines epistolarity, and none is applicable only to the letter, but taken together they constitute what is unique to its language. This chapter will explore in detail each of the following characteristics of epistolary discourse:

1. *Particularity of the I-you*, the *I* of epistolary discourse always having as its (implicit or explicit) partner a specific *you* who stands in unique relationship to the *I*. (Epistolary narrative is thus distinguished from both memoir and diary narrative, where there is no reified addressee, or from rhetorical works, where the addressee is anonymous and could be anyone.) In letter language, moreover, the addressee plays a role; he is able, and is expected, to initiate his own utterance. Such reciprocality whereby the original *you* becomes the *I* of a new utterance is essential to the maintenance of the epistolary exchange.

2. *A present tense*, which figures prominently as a pivot for past and future. Like the diary writer, the letter writer is anchored in a present time from which he looks toward both

past and future events. The relationship of both temporal
aspects to the present is important in the unfolding of letter
narrative.

3. *Temporal polyvalence.* The temporal aspect of any given
   epistolary statement is relative to innumerable moments:
   the actual time that an act described is performed; the
   moment when it is written down; the respective times that
   the letter is dispatched, received, read, or reread. (Such time
   lags distinguish epistolary from theatrical dialogue.)

In the concluding section of this chapter we shall further examine
the effect that time lags have on the epistolary exchange in terms
of the relationship between written dialogue and its oral model.

PRONOMINAL RELATIVITY: Particularity of the *I-You*

Perhaps the most distinctive aspect of epistolary language is the
extent to which it is colored by not one but two persons and by the
specific relationship existing between them. As we have already
seen in the chapters on mediation, the confidant, and the reader,
the interpersonal bond basic to the very language of the letter (*I-
you*) necessarily structures meaning in letter narrative. Those
works that we perceive as being the most "epistolary," as cultivat-
ing the letter form most fully, are those in which the *I-you*
relationship shapes the language used, and in which *I* becomes
defined relative to the *you* whom he addresses. Thus in a work like
*Les Liaisons* we must distinguish between the Merteuil who
writes Mme de Volanges, the Merteuil who writes Valmont, the
Merteuil who writes Cécile, and the Merteuil who writes Danceny.

If the addressee is an eminently necessary reference point for
interpreting any letter in *Les Liaisons*, Senancour's *Oberman*
provides an instructive example of a minimal epistolary use of the
*you*. Although the bulk of Oberman's writing, like that of his
forerunner *Werther*, resembles diary entries more than letters (so
heavy is the weight of the *je* and so undeveloped the personality of
the *vous*), Senancour nevertheless makes it clear that his hero is
not merely writing for the sake of writing, but in order to be read
and to be written to by a specific reader. When his confidant goes
abroad, Oberman gives up writing: "je n'écrirai pas jusqu'à votre

retour; je n'aime pas ces lettres aventurées qui ne sauraient rencontrer que par hasard celui qui les attend; et dont la réponse, qui ne peut venir qu'au bout de trois mois, peut ne venir qu'au bout d'un an. Pour moi, qui ne remuerai pas d'ici, j'espère en recevoir avant votre retour" (L. 73). Oberman's "[je] ne remuerai pas d'ici" is a key to the most important function of the *vous* in this novel. For Oberman letter sending is always connected with fixity: "J'attendais pour vous écrire que j'eusse un séjour fixe" (L. 5). It is obvious that the epistolary exchange is facilitated if both partners are easily reachable by the postman; the addressee cannot assume much importance if he does not have an address. In *Oberman*, however, where the hero wanders from place to place seeking an end to his ennui and a meaning to his life, the postal theme acquires a value beyond the simple mechanics of sending and receiving letters. The theme of fixity and stability is a major one in the narrative; Senancour's wanderer seeks to attach himself to something permanent, to come to rest somewhere, to acquire weight instead of floating. For this reason he attributes a great deal of importance to place (the word *lieu* figures prominently), hopping from one location to another (a fact accentuated by the postmarks) and becoming successively disenchanted with each. He buys several properties and abandons them one by one; "Quel lieu me faudra-t-il donc?" (L. 4). The only fixed point in the novel is the friend, the *vous*: "N'avez-vous pas été jusqu'à présent ma seule habitude? . . . Vous êtes le point où j'aime à me reposer dans l'inquiétude qui m'égare, où j'aime à revenir lorsque j'ai parcouru toutes choses" (L. 4). The friend provides a stable reference point against which Oberman measures his own instability.

The *I* of epistolary discourse always situates himself vis-à-vis another; his locus, his "address," is always relative to that of his addressee. To write a letter is to map one's coordinates—temporal, spatial, emotional, intellectual—in order to tell someone else where one is located at a particular time and how far one has traveled since the last writing. Reference points on that map are particular to the shared world of writer and addressee: underlying the epistolary dialogue are common memories and often common experiences that take place between the letters. Thus Oberman will allude to places and people that only he and his friend know ("J'ai été jusqu'à Blammont, chez le chirurgien qui a remis si adroitement le bras de cet officier tombé de cheval en revenant de Chassel" [L. 38]).

Pushed to its logical extreme, epistolary discourse would be so relative to its *I-you* that it would be unintelligible to an outside reader. In analyzing a real correspondence—that of Mme de Sévigné and her daughter Mme de Grignan—Roger Duchêne observes, "Plus la lettre est réussie en tant que lettre, c'est-à-dire profondément adaptée à la personnalité d'un destinataire complice de celui qui l'écrit dans la complexité d'un contexte vécu, plus elle est, en définitive, illisible à autrui."[2] In fictional letters, where there is no historical "contexte vécu" as in a real correspondence, the illusion that something is going on between the letters or preceding the letters must be created without having the characters tell each other things they already know; this is usually accomplished by editorial footnotes, by shorthand allusions within the letters to memories or intervening events, by enigmatic statements that are part of the complicity of the *I* and *you* but exclude the outside reader. The creator of fictional letter narrative must produce an impression of authenticity without hopelessly losing his outside reader. To do so he not only establishes a code that is particular to the *I-you* messages but also ultimately makes this code accessible to others—either because what remains obscure appears minor (as when characters' allusions to shadowy common experiences are less important than their communication of their reactions to these experiences) or because accumulation of fragmented esoteric messages makes the total code clear.[3] Epistolary discourse is thus a coded—although not necessarily an obscure—language, whose code is determined by the specific relationship of the *I-you.*

The *I-you* relationship that governs epistolary discourse also governs our perception of which characters are to be the principal narrative agents. It is not necessarily the voice that pronounces "I" who captures our attention, as the opening letter of *Clarissa* teaches us. Anna Howe's first letter, like her subsequent ones, is so *you*-oriented that it establishes Clarissa once and for all as the chief protagonist in the narrative. Such *you*-oriented letters provided us with second-person narrative long before Butor's *La Modification.*

The status of epistolary discourse as both first-person and second-person narrative derives from the reversibility of the *I-you* pronouns. The *you* of any *I-you* statement can, and is expected to, become the *I* of a new text. In Mme de Graffigny's *Lettres d'une Péruvienne*, where epistolary communication takes place via reusable knotted *quipos*, even though the addressee never responds to the Peruvian heroine's letters, the image of epistolary discourse as a reversible medium is nonetheless tangibly visible; Zilia writes Aza, "Les mêmes noeuds qui t'apprendront mon existence, en changeant de forme entre tes mains, m'instruiront de ton sort" (L. 1).

*Lettres portugaises* reveals how well the notion of epistolary exchange is adapted to the idea of reciprocality in love. Mariane writes at first because she believes that both her letters and her love will elicit a reciprocal response in her lover. She feels that the "excess" of her own love should guarantee her an extraordinary measure of fidelity on her lover's part (L. 2). As Mariane begins to face the knowledge that loving and being loved are not necessarily interdependent, she opts for independence, continuing both to love and to express her passion in spite of its unidirectionality: "mon amour ne dépend plus de la manière dont vous me traiterez" (L. 2). Her last letter, however, acknowledges the impossibility of prolonging a correspondence that is not a real dialogue, concurrently with her bitter recognition that "l'amour tout seul ne donne point de l'amour" (L. 5). Loving is no more a guarantee or substitute for being loved than writing is for receiving letters.

Because the notion of reciprocality is such a crucial one in epistolary narrative, the moment of reception of letters is as important and as self-consciously portrayed as the act of writing. The hastily torn-open envelope makes as frequent an appearance as the pen and ink. In no other form of dialogue does the speaker await a reply so breathlessly; in no other type of verbal exchange does the mere fact of receiving or not receiving a response carry such meaning. Roger Duchêne has analyzed the Sévigné-Grignan correspondence in terms of the role the letter played in working out the problems of the mother-daughter relationship. Cold in person, Françoise-Marguerite de Grignan was better able to demonstrate her affection for her mother in letters and through her very assiduity in responding: "C'est que le thème de la récep-

tion des lettres ne peut être dissocié de celui des sentiments de
Mme de Sévigné. . . . "Adieu, ma bonne, continuez à m'écrire
et à m'aimer," prie-t-elle en achevant; comme l'insinue la coor-
dination des verbes, l'assiduité épistolaire est une preuve
d'amour."[4] Love narratives do not have a monopoly on the theme
of reciprocality, as a quick glance at the first line of *La Religieuse*
reminds us: "La réponse de M. le marquis de Croismare, s'il m'en
fait une, me fournira les premières lignes de ce récit." It is the
hallmark of epistolary language in general to make statements in
order to elicit a response from a specific addressee. To write a
letter is not only to define oneself in relationship to a particular
*you*; it is also an attempt to draw that *you* into becoming the *I* of a
new statement.

TEMPORAL RELATIVITY: The Pivotal and Impossible Present

Caught up in the particularity of its writer-reader relationship,
epistolary discourse is also governed by its moment of enunciation. The letter writer is highly conscious of writing in a specific
present against which past and future are plotted: "Je vous aime
plus que je ne vous aimais il y a un moment; et dans un moment je
vous aimerai plus encore que je ne vous aime" (Boursault, *Treize
lettres amoureuses*, L. 8). Epistolary characters constantly engage
in such ritual acts of stocktaking, communicating their "état
présent" in terms of what they have already done, where they are
now, and what they fear, hope, or plan for the future. Thus Julie
entreats Saint-Preux: "Mon ami, songez à vous, à moi, à ce que
nous fûmes, à ce que nous sommes, à ce que nous devons être"
(6:6).

In Julie's statement the past tense ("ce que nous fûmes") is
opposed to the present ("ce que nous sommes"), which is the
pivotal tense from which all else radiates. Whether the epistolary
preterite refers to a distant past (as in Julie's statement) or merely
relates actions that have occurred in the interval since the last
letter, its meaning is always relative to the present that is the
writer's reference point. Here we note a significant difference
between memoir and epistolary narrative. Whereas in the latter
the present is the pivotal tense, in the former the preterite is the
central and most immediate tense; the reader of the memoir novel
is transported to the world of a distant past, experiencing as his

new present scenes from the life of the actor in the story rather than experiencing the present of the narrator telling the story. Even when the voice of the narrator interrupts momentarily our involvement in a past-become-present, as occurs so frequently in Marivaux,[5] the present of the memoir narrator intervenes only to shed light on the past that interests us, to add the illuminating perspective of *now*'s reflections to the obscurity of *then*'s actions. In epistolary narrative, on the other hand, the past is the interloper, intervening to shed light on the present. Even interpolated autobiographies within epistolary narrative (from the long notebooks of Mme Riccoboni's characters to Merteuil's comparatively succinct letter 81), which may appear to be interpolated memoirs, have as their function to illuminate the present, to provide background explaining why a character has become what he is. In short, whereas in the memoir the present is subordinate to the past, in the letter the past is always relative to the present.

But of what present are we speaking when we discuss epistolary discourse? In any first-person narrative it is useful to distinguish between time of narration (*Erzählzeit*) and time of narrated action (*erzählte Zeit*). Obviously in the simple memoir form, where the time of narration does not begin until all the events narrated have been completed, the entire *Erzählzeit* relates to *erzählte Zeit* as present to past; but in the diary or the letter the situation is more complex. At any given point in the time of narration, narrated time may relate to time of narration as past to present, present to present ("just now . . . "), or future to present ("I will . . . ").

The pivotal time in epistolary discourse is therefore the present, and the pivotal tense is the present of narration (*Erzählzeit*). No matter how interesting the narrated events are in and of themselves, they always depend upon, and are partially defined by, the time when they are narrated. This axiomatic statement bears investigation, since its ramifications are numerous and varied. First of all, we might consider the reporting of events by a Valmont in his "bulletins," where even the vicomte's rendering of past dialogue is colored by an equally important present one: the ongoing dialogue with Merteuil. Richardsonian narrative illustrates yet another way in which a stress on present *Erzählzeit* affects the reader's perception of the events narrated. "Writing to the moment" creates a sense of immediacy and spontaneity that plunges the reader in medias res, so that he feels tuned in to the hotline of events narrated as they occur by the person experiencing them.[6] This sense of immediacy is also essential to Richardsonian suspense: Pamela and Clarissa write under the constant threat of danger, they fear both bodily injury and discovery of the fact that they are writing. Their much-portrayed time of narration (frequent mention of the writing instruments, highly self-conscious picking up and laying down of the pen, running to the window at a noise or to the door to check that it is locked) serves to emphasize the instability of their present, the imminent danger that threatens to interrupt the writing totally. Similarly, Soeur Suzanne's fragments at the end of *La Religieuse*, which are contemporary with the action she narrates, make her plea for help more pressing by driving home the insecurity of her present position. Hence, the importance—in Richardson and his imitators—of the letter as a cry for help, not just a recording of past dangers.

This sense of immediacy, of a present that is precarious, can only exist in a world where the future is unknown. The present of epistolary discourse is vibrant with future-orientation. Interrogatives, imperatives, and future tenses—rarer in other types of narrative—are the vehicles for expression of promises, threats, hopes, apprehensions, anticipation, intention, uncertainty, prediction. Letter writers are bound in a present preoccupied with the future.

In *Delphine* futurity is a crucial component of epistolarity. Perhaps the central question in Mme de Staël's novel is whether statements made in the present can bind the future, whether today's verb is valid tomorrow. The entire narrative is structured around two issues raised by the French Revolution: divorce and the revocability of religious vows. The events of the plot lead up to and away from two foci of the same ellipse, Léonce's forced marriage to a woman he does not love and Delphine's convent vows made under pressure. The only two long philosophical letters in the novel punctuate this structure: in part 4, letter 17, M. de Lebensei writes to Delphine on divorce and in part 6, letter 12, to Léonce on the breaking of monastic vows.

As the most pro-Revolutionary, antitraditional voice in the novel, M. de Lebensei is very future-oriented. He defends the French Revolution by its future establishment of liberty: "cette révolution . . . sera jugée dans la postérité par la liberté qu'elle assurera à la France" (6:12). Similarly, his arguments in favor of both divorce and revocability of convent vows are based on prospective rather than retrospective vision. To the "moralistes qui ont écrit contre le divorce, en s'appuyant de l'intérêt des enfants," he responds that children should also be considered as "époux futurs" who should also have a right to divorce (4:17). Monastic vows are an "esclavage complet de tout notre avenir" that deprives us of the innate human right to hope; these vows constitute a slavery whereby "l'homme d'un jour enchaînerait l'homme de toute la vie" (6:12).

M. de Lebensei's thematic emphasis on futurity is echoed by the language of the letters. Almost all of the letters in *Delphine* close on verbs in the future tense. The action of the narrative is continually projected into a future that obsesses the characters, who at one and the same time try to control it and acknowledge it as uncontrollable. We have only to examine any sequence of letters to discovery the variety and importance of future tense usage in *Delphine*:

[3:1, Léonce to Delphine]
Oh! ma Delphine, je te verrai, je te verrai sans cesse. Demain . . . j'irai chez vous. . . .

[3:2, Delphine to Léonce]
Léonce, . . . quand je me sentirai prête à mourir, j'aurai encore un moment de bonheur qui vaut tout ce qui m'attend, je me permettrai de t'appeler auprès de moi. . . .

[3:3, Léonce to Delphine]
Sais-tu ce que j'appelle le bonheur? c'est une heure, une heure d'entretien avec toi. . . . Delphine, une heure! et tu pourras après. . . .

Dialogue in *Delphine* is, to paraphrase Valéry, "un dialogue toujours futur."

Just as individual letters close on the future tense, each of the six parts of the novel terminates on an oath binding a character's future (1—Léonce's marriage vows; 2—Delphine's oath to the

dying Mme de Vernon to protect Mathilde; 3—Thérèse's
religious vows, followed by Léonce's effort to get Delphine to
swear on the same altar to belong to him; 4—Delphine's letter
promising Mathilde to leave Paris, followed by a letter to Thérèse
in which she contemplates taking religious vows; 5—Delphine's
convent vows; 6—Léonce's second attempt to force Delphine to
swear to be his, ending in two oaths of separation). The structuring of *Delphine* around such vows, coupled with the future-
oriented language of the letters, makes futurity a central question.
*Delphine* is about the necessity and yet impossibility of engaging
one's future. Each letter halts us in a present time where the future
is uncertain and yet where the characters have attempted to
control that future by threats or vows. Mme de Lebensei's "Que
vont devenir Léonce et Delphine?" which closes her letter 42 of
part 2 to Louise, epitomizes the attitude of any character at any
given point—an explicitly expressed anxiety about the future,
shared by the reader. Yet M. de Lebensei's remarks to the lovers
epitomize the other possible stance vis-à-vis the future. In paint-
ing a vivid picture of the life Delphine and Léonce would share
("Heureux . . . vous oublierez les hommes que vous ne verrez
pas" [6:12]), Lebensei affirms the power of man to possess, to
change, his future.

The future-orientation of the characters propels the novel
suspensefully forward to its conclusion, in which the central
characters reject the future offered them. Responding to
Lebensei's letter Léonce uses the future ironically: "Delphine a
donné son consentement à votre proposition, je l'accepte; elle
change mon sort, elle change le sien. Nous vivrons, et nous
vivrons ensemble; quel avenir inattendu! Demain devait être mon
dernier jour, il sera le premier d'une existence nouvelle. Delphine
enfin sera heureuse! Adieu . . ." (note included in 6:12). The fact
is that Léonce has become so death-oriented as to lose his concern
for the future. Delphine's and Léonce's suicidal deaths at the end
constitute the ultimate reversal; the narrative that has turned on
speculation about, and preoccupation with, the future is brought
to a halt by the main characters' decision to refuse that future
completely.

*La Nouvelle Héloïse*, long before *Delphine*, had raised the
same question about the possibility of engaging tomorrow today.

Julie points out repeatedly that one can make statements about the past and present, but the same verbs are less valid in the future: "Nous réglons l'avenir sur ce qui nous convient aujourd'hui, sans savoir s'il nous conviendra demain; nous jugeons de nous comme étant toujours les mêmes, et nous changeons tous les jours. Qui sait si nous aimerons ce que nous aimons, si nous voudrons ce que nous voulons, si nous serons ce que nous sommes" (6:6). Such preoccupation with the future is intrinsic to the epistolary form, where each letter arrests the writer in a present whose future is unknown.

So oriented toward the future is the epistolary present that deadlines, dreaded days, and hoped-for days assume great importance. Letters, with their date lines, provide a built-in means of marking time between the writer's present and the moment he anticipates. In *Clarissa* Richardson indulges in many such countdowns toward dreaded days: the Tuesday that Clarissa has agreed to confront Solmes, the Wednesday on which she fears she will be forced to marry Solmes, the Thursday that Lovelace projects as their wedding day. Saint-Preux looks forward to the secret rendezvous Julie has given him with impatience: "Quoi! trois jours d'attente! trois jours encore!" (1:38).

If the present of epistolary discourse is charged with anticipation and speculation about the future, it is no less oriented toward the past. Janus-like, epistolary language is grounded in a present that looks out toward past and future. "Now" defines itself relative to a retrospective or anticipated "then." The epistolary present is caught up in the impossibility of seizing itself, since the narrative present must necessarily postdate or anticipate the events narrated. For this reason epistolary narrative is particularly adapted to the schemer or calculator figure, who plots future events and analyzes past ones. On the other hand, the epistolary medium is also well adapted to Rousseauist nostalgia. Because the narrative present cannot be perfectly simultaneous with the event narrated, Saint-Preux can capture the euphoria of a night spent with Julie only by anticipatory and retrospective letters (1:54, 55). In Rousseau, happiness is unseizable, always past or future; in Rousseau, Rimbaud's "La vraie vie est absente" takes epistolary form.

For the letter writer *is* "absent"—removed, however slightly, from his addressee and from the events to which he refers. The present is as impossible to him as "presence." Yet paradoxically, epistolary discourse has many ways of creating this impossible present. In writing to the moment, the oscillations between immediate future (e.g., "I'll go now to see . . . ") and immediate past (e.g., "I have just come back . . . ") are so frequent as to create the illusion of a narrative present simultaneous with the events narrated. Writing to the moment in Richardson, however, is significantly different from what we might call writing to the moment in a work like *Lettres portugaises*. In Richardson important events take place independently of the writing; by closing the gap between *Erzählzeit* and *erzählte Zeit*, the Richardsonian writer creates a sense of immediacy, of tension about the events themselves. In *Lettres portugaises* (or any similar letter narrative from one lover to an absent lover), on the other hand, the oscillation is between memory and hope; separation leaves the writer with only memories of past union and hope of a future one or fear of permanent separation. The switch from past tenses (e.g., "Je vous ai vu souvent passer en ce lieu avec un air qui me charmait" [*Portugaises*, L. 4]) to future ones ("ne paraîtrez-vous pas agréable à d'autres yeux? . . . Je vois bien que vous demeurerez en France" [L. 4]) is the oscillation between memory and hope (or fear) that poisons the present of the writer. Here it is not events that are highlighted. Far more significant than past or future events are the emotions of the writer herself; the memory is less important than the experience of remembering. If in Richardson the approximation of *Erzählzeit* to *erzählte Zeit* heightens tension about the narrated events (*erzählte Zeit*), in narrative of the *Portugaises* type, the tension is created at the level of *Erzählzeit*; indeed, the action is so exclusively psychological that it becomes difficult to speak of an independent *erzählte Zeit*.

   In the *Portugaises* type the "event" is the writing. Whereas in Richardson vicissitudes are external to the writer but are reflected immediately in the changing emotions of the writer-seismograph, in the *Portugaises* the vicissitudes are internal and may often result from the experience of writing itself. Mere expression of a sentiment can cause the emotional pendulum to swing in the opposite direction: "Adieu, je voudrais bien ne vous avoir jamais vu. Ah! je sens vivement la fausseté de ce sentiment, et je connais, dans le moment que je vous écris, que j'aime bien mieux être malheureuse en vous aimant, que de ne vous avoir jamais vu" (*Portugaises*, L. 3). So important has the narrative present become that all action takes place on that level, yet even this present of narration is precarious and unseizable.

Epistolary discourse is the language of the pivotal yet impossible present. The *now* of narration is its central reference point, to which the *then* of anticipation and retrospection are relative. Yet *now* is unseizable, and its unseizability haunts epistolary language. The epistolary present is caught up in three impossibilities:

1. The impossibility of the narrative's being simultaneous with the event (when the event is not part of the writing itself); hence a time of narration that must always be out of phase with the time of the event narrated. That is, the letter writer can only say "I have just done" or "I will soon do."

2. The impossibility of the written present's remaining valid (especially when the important events are the writing itself— e.g., the expression of sentiments); the unseizability and precariousness of *now* is constantly reflected in the epistolary seismogram, wherein one moment's sentiment is contradicted or modified by the next. That is, though the letter writer can say, "I feel, I believe, I am writing . . . ," his present is valid only for that moment, as subsequent moments demonstrate.

3. Since the present of the letter writer is never the present of his addressee, epistolary discourse is caught up in the impossibility of a dialogue in the present. That is, "I feel" cannot be interpreted by the addressee as "you feel" but rather as "you felt when you wrote this letter . . . "

Epistolary narrative plays constantly on the disparities between these various times, as we shall see in our next section.

TEMPORAL POLYVALENCE

The meaning of any epistolary statement is determined by many moments: the actual time that an act described is performed, the moment when it is written down, the respective times that the letter is mailed, received, read, and reread. Time intervals and intervening events are of crucial importance. Thus in *La Nouvelle Héloïse* a letter reread several years later will have a significantly different effect from that of the first reading. In *Les Liaisons* the letter from Mme de Rosemonde to the présidente congratulating her on her courageous resistance has a different meaning from the intended one when it arrives after Tourvel's fall. In both cases the novelist is playing on the disparity between two or more moments, between the time of the writer and the time of the reader, between the time of the first reading and the time of the rereading. Meaning is relative not to one time but to two or more.

An interesting passage from *La Nouvelle Héloïse* illustrates the way in which epistolary statements depend on multiple temporal levels. Saint-Preux gives an account to Claire of a moment of weakness, in which there is a curious interplay between the time of the event narrated and the time it is written down:

> En entrant dans la chambre qui m'était destinée, je la reconnus pour la même que j'avais occupée autrefois en allant à Sion. A cet aspect je sentis une impression que j'aurais peine à vous rendre. J'en fus si vivement frappé, que je crus redevenir à l'instant tout ce que j'étais alors; dix années s'effacèrent de ma vie, et tous mes malheurs furent oubliés. Hélas! cette erreur fut courte, et le second instant me rendit plus accablant le poids de toutes mes anciennes peines. Quelles tristes réflexions succédèrent à ce premier enchantement! Quelles comparaisons douloureuses s'offrirent à mon esprit! Charmes de la première jeunesse, délices des premières amours, pourquoi vous retracer encore à ce coeur accablé d'ennuis et surchargé de lui-même! O temps, temps heureux, tu n'es plus! J'aimais, j'étais aimé. Je me livrais dans la paix de l'innocence aux transports d'un amour partagé. Je savourais à longs traits le délicieux sentiment qui me faisait vivre. [5:9]

We are dealing with three distinct times here: the time (distant past) of Saint-Preux and Julie's first love, the time (immediate past) of Saint-Preux's recent stay in his old room, and third, the time that he writes all this to Claire. When Saint-Preux enters into his apostrophic "Charmes de la première jeunesse," however, we enter with him into a confusion of times. Is his apostrophic lament simply a reporting in indirect discourse of his sentiments that night in his old room, or is it the expression of his feelings at the time of writing? Similarly, do the sentences beginning "Je me

livrais dans la paix de l'innocence . . ." and "Je savourais
. . . " refer to the distant or the recent past? Since a crucial issue at this point in Rousseau's novel is whether or not
Saint-Preux is "cured" of his love, these are not irrelevant
questions. A rigid answer to them is both impossible and less
important than the mere fact that confusion of times raises
such questions. The temporal ambiguity of the apostrophe
"Charmes . . . O temps" indicates that at the very least the act
of recording such past sentiments makes Saint-Preux relive them
once again, just as for a brief moment in his room he had relived
the distant past. Saint-Preux's effort to transcend his moment of
weakness by confessing it to Claire is paradoxically also one in
which he can savor that moment again.

Confusion of past and present is Saint-Preux's chronic
problem, as Wolmar writes to Claire:

> L'erreur qui l'abuse et le trouble est de confondre les temps et de se
> reprocher souvent comme un sentiment actuel ce qui n'est que l'effet
> d'un souvenir trop tendre.
>
> Il l'aime dans le temps passé: voilà le vrai mot de l'énigme. Otez-lui la
> mémoire, il n'aura plus d'amour. [4:14]

The power of memory to blur temporal distinctions is inherent to
epistolary narrative where lovers are separated, since memory is
all one has left in absence. Memory, imagination, and hope make
of past and future the only living present for the letter writer
separated from the lover, visible in the very oscillation between
past and future tenses: "je serais bien ingrate si je ne vous aimais
avec les mêmes emportements que ma passion me donnait, quand
je jouissais de témoignages de la vôtre. . . . Je ne puis vous
oublier, et je n'oublie pas aussi que vous m'avez fait espérer que
vous viendriez passer quelque temps avec moi" (*Lettres portugaises*, L. 1). The moment of separation fixes a permanent
image that makes the past persist into the present with all the
illusion of reality, when no real present comes to reveal the past as
past: "Le temps où vous séparâtes ces deux amants fut celui où
leur passion était à son plus haut point de véhémence. Peut-être
s'ils fussent restés plus longtemps ensemble, se seraient-ils peu à
peu refroidis; mais leur imagination vivement émue les a sans
cesse offerts l'un à l'autre tels qu'ils étaient à l'instant de leur
séparation" (Wolmar to Claire, 4:14).

The epistolary situation, in which both time lags and absence play such a large role, lends itself to the temporal ambiguity whereby past is taken for present. The only possible present is the most immediate past—be it the last contact or the last letter. In narrative whose action is the recovery from unrequited love, the lover will continue to "love in the past tense" until a more immediate present effaces that past. Thus for Saint-Preux the image of Julie d'Etanges can be effaced only by prolonged contact with the present Julie—Madame de Wolmar. After a stay at Clarens he is on his way toward a cure when he can say that "pour la première fois, j'ai vu Julie en son absence, non telle qu'elle fut pour moi . . . mais telle qu'elle se montre à mes yeux tous les jours . . . si chaste et si vertueuse, au milieu de . . . ses trois aimables enfants" (4:11). The Portuguese nun, who never actually sees again the man she had loved, confronts a more immediate image of him in the form of his last two cold, indifferent letters. In returning all of his other letters, she keeps these two to remind her of his indifference, to efface a past image with a more recent one.

The time gap between writer and addressee makes of any epistolary verb a potentially polyvalent one. In his statement the *I* can address only a *you* who is an image persisting from the past; likewise, the *you* who receives the message exists in yet another time, which was future to the *I* sending the message. Restif de la Bretonne's *Lettres posthumes* presents a curious exercise in such temporal polyvalence. De Fontlhète, fatally ill, writes letters for one year to his wife Hortense, to be mailed to her during the first year after his death and reread in succeeding years. The wife, not knowing that De Fontlhète has died but believing him on a trip, thinks that these letters are being written during the same year that she is reading them. To encourage this illusion, De Fontlhète had provided for a secretary to forge *postscriptum* replies to specific queries in his wife's letters after his death. As a result the novel, which consists of both the husband's letters and the wife's responses, does not read as a total "dialogue des sourds," although the time lag in such a dialogue between a dead man and his wife generates numerous ambiguities and ironies. For example, when De Fontlhète describes his plan in his first letter—"Tous les jours vous écrire une Lettre . . . que vous lirez peut-être, quand je ne serai plus"—the "lirez," which the wife must interpret as "reread," is meant quite literally by De Fontlhète, since the first time Hortense reads his letters he is already dead without her knowing it. In one of her letters Hortense complains of her husband's long absence but consoles herself with the knowledge that it is "forced."

Restif further complicates the interval between time of writing and time of reading by introducing new temporal levels. In each letter De Fontlhète describes not only his thoughts and the events of the day of the writing but those of the corresponding day of the previous two years as well. Since his wife is supposed to reread the letters on the anniversary of each day in succeeding years, he is taking a "five-year diary" approach to both writing and reading.[7] To De Fontlhète such an approach approximates immortality, since Hortense "réunira, dans un seul instant, quatre années, les deux passées, dont je décrirai chaque jour; celle qui s'écoule, et dans laquelle j'écris, et celle où elle me lira. Ainsi je prolonge mon existence, je la quadruple, et je sens à cet instant le bonheur" (L. 2). De Fontlhète's letters constitute not only a proto-Proustian effort to redeem time by superimposing various temporal levels, but also an attempt to project the past into the future by adding to the life of the word-when-written the life of the word-when-read.[8]

The time-lag aspect of epistolary discourse is the foundation on which Restif could build a novel like *Les Posthumes*. If such a time interval is exaggerated in Restif (one year between writing and reading) or in *Lettres persanes* (where delays in communication undermine Usbek's authority in the harem), even when shorter this interval plays a role. Just as De Fontlhète may no longer be alive when his wife receives his letter, so any statement made in the present by a letter writer may no longer be valid when his message is received. Saint-Preux is painfully aware of this time lag when he writes, upon receiving a letter from Julie, "Enfin je respire, je vis, tu te portes bien, tu m'aimes: ou plutôt il y a dix jours que tout cela était vrai; mais qui me répondra d'aujourd'hui? O absence! ô tourment! ô bizarre et funeste état où l'on ne peut jouir que du moment passé, et où le présent n'est point encore!" (2:16). And yet in similar circumstances Mme de Sévigné can write, upon receiving a letter, "Je vis défaire la petite malle devant moi, et en même temps, *frast, frast*, je démêle le mien [my bundle of letters] et je trouve enfin, ma bonne, que vous vous portez bien"

(13 December 1671). In the light of Saint-Preux's comment, Mme de Sévigné's use of the present tense is erroneous, yet it testifies to another prerogative of epistolary discourse. Depending on the correspondents, the time lag can be ignored or emphasized. Although epistolary discourse is characterized by time lags and a resulting temporal polyvalence or ambiguity, too much emphasis on such time lags would destroy the possibility of dialogue.

THE EPISTOLARY DIALOGUE

Epistolary discourse is inscribed within the larger domain of verbal exchange between two parties, each of whom alternately assumes the role of speaker or hearer. A brief comparison of the epistolary exchange with some other types of dialogue will help us keep in mind the traits particular to letter dialogue.

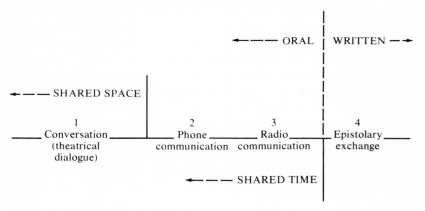

1. Communication between two or more parties who share the same time and space is extraverbal as well as verbal; tones and gestures play a role.
2. When space is no longer shared, tones still play a part in communication, but gestures are lost. Phone conversations already involve that sense of absence inherent to the letter exchange.
3. The comparison with shortwave radio communication is instructive. Here we have a situation parallel to phone communication (shared time, different space, tones are still important) but a significant difference that makes radio communication more akin to the epistolary exchange. The

participants in a radio conversation cannot interrupt each other; each speaker completes his speech as a discrete unit and signs off before the other begins. The radio message, like the letter, may be highly structured—with a beginning, middle, and end; its mode of existence has an independence, a separateness, that allies it with the monologue.

4. The letter is an even more discrete unit than the radio message. Writer and reader share neither time nor space. The discontiguity of the space and time is reflected in the discontinuity of the exchange, a dialogue composed of more separate, monologuelike units than the component units of the oral dialogue. The written exchange not only introduces the time lag between message transmission and message reception; it also widens the interval between message reception and response. The writer has more time to meditate, to measure and correct his words, to polish his style. The status of the letter as a written, tangible document, moreover, enables epistolary discourse to introduce its own extraverbal signs equivalent to tones and gestures in oral discourse. Tears, handwriting, punctuation, and even spelling may be part of the message. Finally, letters are both permanent words and losable words. They can complicate communication by crossing each other in the mail or getting lost or stolen; they make the epistolary dialogue one that can be scrambled, so that the order in which words are read is not necessarily the order in which they were written.

As written dialogue, epistolary discourse is obsessed with its oral model. No sooner is the writer aware of the gap that separates him from his reader than he tries to bridge that gap. The cliché "Il me semble que je vous parle quand je vous écris, et que vous m'êtes un peu plus présent" (*Portugaises*, L. 4) is an essential epistolary statement; epistolary language is preoccupied with immediacy, with presence, because it is a product of absence. Since both the temporal and the spatial hiatus are so much a part of epistolary discourse, the word *present* in the letter is charged with both its temporal and its spatial meanings; it signifies "now" as opposed to the "then" of past and future events or contact, and it means "here" as opposed to the "there" where the addressee always is. The letter writer is engaged in the impossible task of making his reader present; the epistolary dialogue attempts to approximate the conversation of the "here" and the "now."

Thus although the epistolary situation involves a wider hiatus between thought and expression than the oral one, we can note a self-conscious tendency among letter novelists to close this gap. Writing to the moment aims at bridging the interval between event and expression.[9] Likewise, the technique of invoking the postman or messenger who is pressing one to finish reduces the time of reflection and gives written language the unerasable qualities of spoken language: "Pourquoi n'ai-je pas la force d'effacer tout ce que je me reproche? . . . Sans Dupré, qui s'impatiente dans ma chambre, et qui ne me donnerait pas, sans doute, le temps de recommencer, je m'épargnerais la honte de tant de folies" (*Lettres de la marquise*, L. 27). In both writing to the moment and writing under postal pressure, the rhythm of writing is dictated by external forces that give the epistolary utterance the spontaneity of the oral one.

Occasionally the exchange of notes may be so rapid that even the spatiotemporal distance between correspondents seems to disappear. In the sequence of notes between Saint-Preux and Julie at the beginning of *La Nouvelle Héloïse*, the two lovers could be speaking rather than writing to each other:

### I.   Billet de Julie

N'emportez pas l'opinion d'avoir rendu votre éloignement nécessaire. Un coeur vertueux saurait se vaincre ou se taire, et deviendrait peut-être à craindre. Mais vous . . . vous pouvez rester.

### Réponse

Je me suis tu longtemps; votre froideur m'a fait parler à la fin. Si l'on peut se vaincre pour la vertu, l'on ne supporte point le mépris de ce qu'on aime. Il faut partir.

### II.   Billet de Julie

Non, monsieur, après ce que vous avez paru sentir, après ce que vous m'avez osé dire, un homme tel que vous avez feint d'être ne part point; il fait plus.

### Réponse

Je n'ai rien feint qu'une passion modérée dans un coeur au désespoir. Demain vous serez contente, et, quoi que vous en puissiez dire, j'aurai moins fait que de partir.

### III.   Billet de Julie

Insensé! si mes jours te sont chers, crains d'attenter aux tiens. Je suis obsédée, et ne puis ni vous parler ni vous écrire jusqu'à demain. Attendez.

The rapid alternation between "restez" and "je pars" produces a dramatic effect comparable to the most intense dialogues in the theater. Like stichomythia, such an exchange must be reserved for rare moments, as in the following example from Laclos:

### [Valmont's Letter 153]

J'ajoute que le moindre obstacle mis de votre part sera pris de la mienne pour une véritable déclaration de guerre: vous voyez donc que la réponse que je vous demande n'exige ni longues ni belles phrases. Deux mots suffisent.

REPONSE de la marquise de Merteuil écrite en bas de la même lettre.

Hé bien! la guerre.

The brevity of the ultimatum and the curtness of the response, the intensity of the emotion expressed "en deux mots"—all add to the violence of the collision: the ultimate clash between two superior minds whose words are brought together for the first time here on a piece of paper, but whose interests are henceforth in conflict. This brief dialogue is the culminating point of the narrative; the entire denouement will spring from this short exchange of words.

The collision of Valmont and Merteuil on a piece of paper is an epistolary coup on Laclos's part. Much less intense approximations of a conversation in the here and now occur throughout letter narrative. The act of picking up the pen to write even a leisurely letter becomes an almost magical ritual whereby one evokes the presence of the addressee. For this reason, what we might call "interior dialogue" or "pseudodialogue" is a fundamental occurrence in epistolary discourse.

When Zilia knots her *quipos* (the Peruvian equivalent of writing), "la sorte de ressemblance que j'imagine qu'ils ont avec les paroles, me fait une illusion qui trompe ma douleur: je crois te parler . . . " (*Lettres d'une Péruvienne*, L. 4). For the letter writer, to write someone is to speak to him, but in order for this illusion to be maintained in a lengthy letter, the other person's voice must somehow be heard. A common technique for making the partner "present" is one we have already examined in chapter 3—that of quotation and paraphrase of his remarks. The partner is *re*presented through his own words. In novels where we are given only one-half of the dialogue (usually that of the woman in novels that trace the development and decline of love), this is a common means of letting the outside reader glimpse the other half of the conversation: "*Je ne vous connais point assez?* qui vous l'a dit? *Je ne douterais jamais un instant de la sincérité, de l'ardeur, de la vérité* . . . Oh! va te promener avec tes plaintes" (*Fanni Butlerd*, L. 67). Werther conducts an interior debate with Wilhelm, reproducing Wilhelm's voice within his letter through paraphrase:

> Entweder, sagst Du, hast du Hoffnung auf Lotten, oder du hast keine. Gut, im ersten Fall suche sie durchzutreiben, suche die Er-füllung deiner Wüsche zu umfassen; im anderen Fall ermanne dich und suche einer elenden Empfindung los zu werden, die alle deine Kräfte verzehren muss. —Bester! das ist wohl gesagt und—bald gesagt.

> Either, you say, you have some hope of winning Lotte, or you have none. Very well, in the first case try to realize your hopes, try to seize the fulfillment of your wishes; in the other case take hold of yourself and try to get rid of a miserable sentiment that must ultimately consume all your strength. —Dear friend! your advice is well expressed—but so easy to give. [*Werther*, 8 August 1771; translation mine]

Thus within a letter written by a single correspondent we often hear several voices, different points of view, which transform the monologue into a dialogue.

Interior dialogue in which the addressee's words are quoted differs from that in which his voice is imagined. The technique of citation and paraphrase serves one of two purposes: (1) it is either a somewhat artificial device for letting us glimpse the other half of the conversation in novels that present only one correspondent's letters,[10] or (2) it is an integral part of the psychological action of the narrative, presenting the writer as reader-decoder (see chapter 3). In either case the partner's voice is his real, though past, one, heard upon replay because the letter writer has before him the partner's letter. Past stimulus (the partner's letter) is incorporated into present response (*re*presented—made present again).

In the imaginary dialogue, however, no letter stimulus is needed; or rather, the stimulus is the mere act of picking up the pen,
which can conjure up the addressee. Fanni Butlerd writes to her
lover as if he were in the room with her: "Adieu, Milord.
. . . Vous faites la mine. . . . Adieu mon ami. . . . Vous
boudez encore. . . . Eh bien! adieu, mon cher Alfred" (L. 10).
Merteuil engages in a pseudodialogue with Valmont in which she
symptomatically assigns him the lines of a dullard: "Mme de
Volanges marie sa fille. . . . Et qui croyez-vous qu'elle ait choisi
pour gendre? Le comte de Gercourt. . . . J'en suis dans une
fureur. . . . Eh bien! vous ne devinez pas encore? oh! l'esprit
lourd! Lui avez-vous donc pardonné l'affaire de l'intendante? Et
moi, n'ai-je pas encore à me plaindre de lui, monstre que vous
êtes?" (L. 2).[11] In Montherlant's quartet of novels, *Les Jeunes
Filles*, Andrée Hacquebaut pushes the epistolary one-person
dialogue to its psychotic extreme. After sending numerous unanswered, unopened love letters to the writer Pierre Costals, the
provincial spinster writes him, "Toute seule! Oui, oui, venez vite.
Je vous ouvre la porte. Oh! comme vous avez froid! Vous sentez
bon l'hiver, la gelée. Il faut que je vous réchauffe. . . . Sor-
tons. . . . Quelle robe me conseillez-vous? . . . Marchons
longtemps, jusqu'à ce que je demande grâce. Moi, froid? Toute
chaude de vous, oui" (*Les Lépreuses*, L. 7). Andrée's letter illustrates an extreme that is latent in the epistolary situation. In
the absence of the real addressee, one creates an image of a
present addressee, with whom one can converse comfortably.
Imagination substitutes what reality cannot supply. The world of
the lonely person, or of the person separated from lover or friend,
becomes so peopled with images that when he picks up the pen, it
is natural that he should engage in an immediate conversation
with the image conjured up by the act of writing.

The imagined dialogue, moreover, has an advantage over the
real conversation: one can manipulate one's partner. The
presence evoked by the sorcerer's pen can speak only the words
that the sorcerer assigns him. The fantasy dialogue thus reveals
more about the ventriloquist than the puppet. We have only to
reexamine the above-quoted passages to note how much of
Fanni's naive, childlike personality, Merteuil's superiority, and
Andrée's frustration are revealed. Likewise, Lovelace's frequent

pseudodialogues with Belford are more an occasion for Lovelace to exercise his wit than to confront any real moral objections on Belford's part:

> And now, Belford, what dost think? I shall be very sick tomorrow.
> Sick! Why sick? What a-devil shouldst thou be sick for?
> For more good reasons than one, Jack.
> I should be glad to hear but one. Of all thy roguish inventions I should not have thought of this.
> Perhaps thou thinkest my view to be, to draw the lady to my bedside: that's a trick of three or four thousand years old, and I should find it much more to my purpose, if I could get to hers. [Lovelace to Belford, 26 May]

Interior dialogue is haunted by an air of falseness. When the partner's words are imagined, the letter writer is addressing a manipulated pseudopresence; when they are quoted, the dialogue borders on artifice. Interior dialogue is an attempt to approximate a conversation of the here and now, which both grows out of and is doomed by the epistolary situation.

Epistolary discourse is a discourse marked by hiatuses of all sorts: time lags between event and recording, between message transmission and reception; spatial separation between writer and addressee; blank spaces and lacunae in the manuscript. Yet it is also a language of gap closing, of writing to the moment, of speaking to the addressee as if he were present. Epistolary discourse is the language of the "as if" present. In ordinary conversation language affirms a physical presence; it is an extension of the roll-call ritual—"Are you here?"—"Present." In the theater, which imitates a present action, dialogue traditionally affirms presence in the act of performance. The actors who speak stand corporeally before one another and the audience. The performance of a play, as the Latin languages indicate, is conceived as a *repraesentatio*, a "making present" by physical "presences." Epistolary language, which is the language of absence, makes present by make-believe. The particular *you* whose constant appearance distinguishes letter discourse from other written discourse (memoir, diary, rhetoric) is an image of the addressee who is elsewhere. Memory and expectation keep the addressee present to the imagination of the writer, whose narrative (*erzählte Zeit*) and narration (*Erzählzeit*), through a frequent oscillation between past and future, likewise seize the present through illusion.

1. I am following Emile Benveniste's well-known distinction between two fundamental linguistic subsystems: (1) the personal, or "discourse," characterized by the use of *I-you*, and (2) the nonpersonal, or "récit historique," characterized by the use of *il* (*Problèmes de linguistique générale* [I]). Harald Weinrich makes a similar distinction between "erzählte Welt" and "besprochene Welt" in his linguistic analysis of time in literary texts, *Tempus*. Weinrich's two systems are grounded primarily in distribution of verb tenses, whereas Benveniste uses both tense repartition and the notion of *deixis* (demonstrative function) developed by K. Brugmann (1904), Karl Bühler (*Sprachtheorie* [1934]), and R. Jakobson (*Essais de linguistique générale*, chap. 9 [1963]). Benveniste's *histoire/discours* distinction has been widely discussed and applied in linguistics and narrative theory. In the 1975 Benveniste festschrift (*Langue, discours, société*, ed. Julia Kristéva et al.), Jenny Simonin-Grumbach redefines the basic distinction and introduces some interesting nuances ("Pour une typologie des discours," pp. 85–120).

2. Roger Duchêne, *Réalité vécue et art épistolaire*, vol. 1, *Madame de Sévigné et la lettre d'amour*, p. 114. Duchêne's sensitive analysis of the Sévigné-Grignan correspondence as "le meilleur roman épistolaire et le plus beau roman d'amour" (p. 264) is based on the thesis that what distinguishes Mme de Sévigné's letters radically from those of the *secrétaires*, the greco-latin tradition, and the *galante* tradition is the particularity of the *I-you* relationship that shapes them and the role that "réalité vécue" plays.

3. At the beginning of *Humphry Clinker*, for instance, any one of the first letters taken singly would mystify the outside reader, but all of them together make clear the relationships between the various people mentioned and what activity the correspondents are engaged in.

4. Duchêne, p. 310.

5. Cf. Jean Rousset's analysis "Marivaux ou la structure du double registre," in *Forme et signification* (Paris: Corti, 1964), pp. 45–54.

6. "Writing to the moment" is the term coined by Richardson in his preface to *Sir Charles Grandison* to describe the simultaneity of writing with the event or emotion described: "The nature of familiar letters, written, as it were, to the *moment*, while the heart is agitated by hopes and fears, or events undecided, must plead an excuse for the bulk of a collection of this kind."

7. I refer only half facetiously to the commercially sold five-year diary, in which each page contains space for five consecutive years' entries for the same day (e.g., 1 January 1981, 1982, 1983, 1984, 1985). In fact, a regular preoccupation with superimposable anniversaries appears elsewhere in Restif's writing. In *Monsieur Nicolas* Restif tells about how he kept from 1752 to 1754 a series of notebooks of anniversary inscriptions; he habitually reread each inscription on the corresponding day in subsequent years and added marginal annotations. Michel Baude has located and studied this curious structure in Restif's diary

writing in his article "Une Structure insolite: les anniversaires dans le journal intime."

8. Restif writes similarly in *Les Nuits de Paris*, "Je vis quatre fois dans un seul instant, au moment actuel et les trois années précédentes. . . . Je compare le tableau et cette comparaison me fait revivre le temps passé comme dans le moment présent. Elle empêche, renouvelée, la perte des années écoulées, et qu'au bout d'un temps je ne me sois étranger à moi-même" (London, 1788, 6:2506). For Michel Baude, who finds the same mystic conception of time in Restif's journal *Mes Inscriptions* (see note 7 above), Restif's cult of anniversaries enables him to accede to an eternal present. In fact, as it works out in *Les Posthumes*, the multiplication of temporal levels in an epistolary context creates not only a sensation of Bergsonian *durée* but also an ironic gap between writer and reader that makes more apparent a play of Derridean *différance* (difference, deferring, postponement).

9. Gail B. Mensher has analyzed a striking stylistic trait in Mme de Sévigné's correspondence, which she calls "writing to the future." Mme de Sévigné's desire to live in her daughter's, rather than her own, spatiotemporal zone often led her to attempt to fantasize the situation in which her letter would arrive and be received. Whereas Richardsonian writing to the moment attempts to draw the reader into the writer's present, writing to the future involves an imaginative attempt to approximate a dialogue in the reader's present. See Gail Mensher, "Problems of Time and Existence in the Letters of Madame de Sévigné," Ph.D. dissertation, University of Iowa, 1977.

10. A comparison of Crébillon's *Duchesse* and *Marquise* with Mme Riccoboni's univoice novels reveals that Mme Riccoboni overuses quotation, whereas Crébillon employs it sparingly, relying more on paraphrase and allusion to keep alive his duke's and count's voices.

11. Merteuil's guessing game is reminiscent of a more elaborate and famous one—Mme de Sévigné's letter announcing the engagement of the Grande Mademoiselle to Lauzun (15 December 1670).

# CHAPTER FIVE

# THE DYNAMICS OF
# EPISTOLARY CLOSURE

The readings that I have proposed in the preceding chapters are based largely on the relationship of internal writer to internal reader that marks the epistolary situation. For this reason many of the remarks in these chapters are as valid in analyzing single letters as in approaching an entire novel. It is time now, however, to turn primarily to the analysis of the epistolary work as a whole. In this chapter we shall consider the relationship of internal writer to internal reader only insofar as it affects the structure of the entire correspondence—a structure that becomes particularly evident in the dynamics of epistolary closure.

Several recent studies concerned with the signifying process in poetic and narrative fictions have chosen, in one way or another, to "begin with the end." In her illuminating analysis of the architectonic principles underlying poetic closure, Barbara Herrnstein Smith has effectively transformed the question of "how poems mean" into the question of "how poems end":

> Closure occurs when the concluding portion of a poem creates in the reader a sense of appropriate cessation. It announces and justifies the absence of further development; it reinforces the feeling of finality, completion, and composure which we value in all works of art; and it gives ultimate unity and coherence to the reader's experience of the poem by providing a point from which all the preceding elements may be viewed comprehensively and their relations grasped as part of a specific design.[1]

In *Fable's End: Completeness and Closure in Rhetorical Fiction*, David H. Richter complements Smith's work on the lyric by focusing on closural strategies in one type of novel. Both Smith and Richter are attentive to reader expectation and response; both illustrate the way in which narrative and poetic forms satisfy, or frustrate, what Frank Kermode emphasized as man's deep-rooted metaphysical and psychological desire for "intelligible Ends": "We project ourselves . . . past the End, so as to see the structure whole."[2]

Other studies, particularly those that emphasize the modernity of the fictions they deal with or of their own approach, concentrate on the "open form." R. M. Adams, Alan Friedman, and Beverly Gross, among others, study open-endedness, unresolved conflict, and anticonclusion in the modern novel as emanating from a modern sensibility that conceives that life itself is open.[3] When Umberto Eco writes about open forms (*Opera aperta*, 1962), he likewise evokes an epistemology of indeterminacy. Eco is, however, the most radical and thorough of the apologists for openness (in both literature and literary criticism), for he chooses modern forms—musical, sculptural, literary—that not only lend themselves to multiple interpretations but demand the interpreter's collaboration in order to be created and completed.

The question of openness and closure has thus become a focal point for discussion of fundamental literary, psychological, and philosophical questions: the relationship of art to life, of literary structure to experience. "Men, like poets," writes Frank Kermode, "rush 'into the middest,' *in medias res*, when they are born; they also die *in mediis rebus*, and to make sense of their span they need fictive concords with origins and ends, such as give meaning to lives and to poems. The End they imagine will reflect their irreducibly intermediary preoccupations."[4] As a literary form, letter narrative imposes the ritual of closing upon both the individual correspondents and the novelist who creates them. Throughout this chapter we shall examine how letter writers end their fictions. The individual sign-off as well as the denouement of the work as a whole can "reflect their irreducibly intermediary preoccupations," can occasion an effort to "make sense of [the] span" covered by the narrative. Most importantly, to ask how narrative ends is to ask what makes it proceed; a close look at the

dynamics of epistolary closure should reveal many of the forces
that generate letter narrative in the first place.

In the subdivisions of any work of literature (scene or act in the
theater, chapter in the novel, stanza in poetry), the closing lines
can be a privileged moment for emphasis, summary, retrospective
illumination, or simply a playful punch line. Letter narrative
multiplies the number of such privileged positions, and in so
doing runs the risk of devaluation. Some novelists have
nevertheless made interesting use of the individual sign-off. The
two lovers who correspond in Edme Boursault's *Lettres à Babet*
(composed of letters both "à Babet" and "de Babet") close their
letters most frequently with "tout à toi," yet this formula is almost
always cleverly incorporated into the body of the letter:

> Vous verrez, par la différence de nos services [that of the writer and
> his rivals], que, n'étant pas si bête qu'eux, je suis plus digne d'être
> Tout à vous. [L. 4]

One can always measure the mood of the entire letter and the
degree of intimacy of the two lovers by its closing; the following
signature highlights a moment of coquettish retreat on the part of
Babet, who transforms her closing "tout" accordingly:

> Et si je m'avise de t'écrire, et après t'avoir commandé tout ce qui
> m'aura plu, tu croiras que ma lettre doive finir par la protestation que
> j'ai coutume de te faire, d'être à toi toute ma vie:
> Point du tout. [L. 16]

In fact, a cursory glance at the closing lines of all the *Babet* letters
would provide a summary of the action of the novel, from the
beginning of the courtship through all its vicissitudes to Babet's
final letter:

> Adieu, mon cher, je t'embrasse de toute mon âme avant que d'entrer
> en religion, et te proteste que je n'en sortirai de ma vie que pour être
> A toi.

Boursault continually invests the signature with the power to
summarize the narrative span of the individual letter.

*Babet*'s "tout à toi" is a brief formula that Boursault cleverly
reformulates. The more usual French closings of the type "j'ai
l'honneur d'être . . . ," however, are so cumbersome that most

letter novelists simply omit them. English epistolary style, being less restricted than the French by long conventional closing formulas, lends itself more easily to the incorporation of signatures into the narrative. Such integrated signatures are a hallmark of Richardson's style.[5] The act of terminating a letter seems to encourage the Richardsonian character to situate himself on an emotional map, to summarize his present psychological state and attitude toward the person to whom he is writing:

> and what is all this wild incoherence for? It is only to beg to know how you have been . . . by a line directed for Mrs. Rachel Clark . . . which . . . will reach the hands of *your unhappy*—but that's not enough—
>
> > Your miserable
> > Clarissa Harlowe [28 June]

Signatures in Richardson must be read; otherwise we fail to appreciate the ambiguity of a letter to Clarissa signed simply "A.H.," a letter so scolding in tone as to make Clarissa think it is from her shrewish sister Arabella Harlowe rather than from her beloved Anna Howe (5 and 6 July).

The ritual of opening and closing a letter imposes upon the writer a gesture of self-definition vis-à-vis the addressee. The five personal letters exchanged by Heloise and Abelard, years after Abelard's castration and their retirement into separate convents, offer the most interesting trace of this problematic activity. In the standard editions Abelard's salutations define both himself and Heloise in relation to Christ:

> Heloisae, dilectissimae sorori suae in Christo, Abaelardus, frater eius in ipso. [L. 2]
> To Heloise, his dearly beloved sister in Christ, Abelard her brother in the same.
> Sponsae Christi servus eiusdem. [L. 4]
> To the bride of Christ, his servant.

Abelard speaks from a relatively stable position; by his syntax he makes it clear that Christ is the ground for his own and Heloise's identity. Outside of Christ there is no relationship between Abelard and Heloise. Heloise's salutations, however, reveal a more troubled and fluctuating thought:

Domino suo immo patri, coniugi suo immo fratri, ancilla sua immo filia, ipsius uxor immo soror, Abaelardo Heloisa. [L. 1]

To her master, or rather father, her husband, or rather brother; his servant, or rather daughter, his wife, or rather sister; to Abelard, Heloise.

In this first letter Heloise's first impulse is always to speak in terms of the previous relationships, tutorial and conjugal ("master," "husband"). Her second gesture—that of erasure or correction—dramatizes her efforts to transform the relationship into acceptable ecclesiastical ones (Abelard becomes priestly "father" or "brother"). Yet the very movement to "father" and "brother" from "master" and "husband" suggests that the ground for relationship in Heloise's mind remains personal and familial; Abelard is not her brother "in Christ" but her "brother." Letter 3, beginning, "unico suo post Christum unica sua in Christo" ("To her only one after Christ, she who is his alone in Christ"), adds Christ seemingly as the ground for relationship but actually as afterthought and effectively as obstacle: without Christ, Abelard would be "her only one" and she "his alone." Heloise is attempting the impossible, to speak a language of *exclusive* love that would *include* both Abelard and Christ. The cryptic salutation of Heloise's final personal letter, "Domino specialiter, sua singulariter"—alternately translated as either "God's own in species, his own as individual" or "To him who is especially her lord, she who is uniquely his"—does not solve the dilemma but offers further evidence of its complexity. As a nun addressing her former husband and present convent counselor, Heloise wrestles most visibly and subtly with the problems of self-definition in the problematic moment of framing the letter.

Few writers investigate the depths implied by the gesture of closure as thoroughly as Heloise or Guilleragues's Portuguese nun (whose closings we shall discuss later in this chapter).[6] Most writers, like Boursault and Richardson, treat signatures playfully (and a more recent letter novelist, Rémy de Gourmont, even reproduces the handwritten signatures of the various correspondents of *Le Songe d'une femme* on the printed page). Many, however, use the closing for more serious emphases. Goethe's hero Werther reserves his most morbid thoughts for the final lines of his letters, which frequently close on death wishes or metaphors of annihilation (e.g., 16 July, 26 July, 10 August, 18 August, 30 August), just as his novel will be brought to a close by his suicide. Foscolo's *Ultime lettere di Jacopo Ortis*, very much influenced by *Werther*, adds to the Wertherian suicide motif a perennial Italian concern: despair over the state of the fatherland. (Foscolo's particular concern, in the final version of the novel [1802], is the concession of Venice to the Austrians in the treaty of Campo Formio.) Jacopo's letters abound in two kinds of death imagery: (1) personal death wishes that often revolve around a preoccupation with his own tomb (words such as *sepolcro, fossa, sepoltura,* and *seppellire* are dear to the poet of *I Sepolcri*), and (2) images of a larger-scale "Distruzione" in which he envisions the past and future destruction of nations in apocalyptic terms (in particular 10 January, 13 March, 21 May, 25 May, 28 May 1798; 19 February, 5 March 1799). The two visions of annihilation that often terminate his letters—personal and political—reinforce one another and propel the novel toward its ultimate Wertherian conclusion.

That "ultimate" conclusion, the point where the narrative work as a whole actually comes to a stop, is the moment that interests us most in this chapter, for the closural force of that ultimate ending depends on a dynamics particular to the epistolary form. Epistolary endings move between two contradictory possibilities: (1) the potential finality of any letter—given its conventional mechanism for closing, for "signing off," and (2) the open-endedness of the form—in which the letter writer is always in dialogue with a possible respondent, and in which any letter appears as part of a potentially ongoing sequence. The typical seduction novel (*Lettres de la marquise*, or the présidente-Valmont plot of *Les Liaisons*) plays on this dual possibility when it chains together a series of letters from the seducer's victim, each of which closes with an oath that she will not write again. Each letter's "adieu" threatens to bring the novel to a halt, yet the response to such a farewell letter gives the narrative new momentum, since the seducer's art lies in his very ability to keep the dialogue going.

Epistolary narrative, in keeping with the dual potential of the letter, falls into two major categories of closure: (1) those novels that come to a motivated state of arrest and equilibrium, producing a strong sense of closure, and (2) those novels that are open-ended, whose lack of resolution is due often to an enigmatic silence on the part of one of the writers. It is the former, more numerous group that we shall examine first.

All epistolary narrative ultimately drops off into silence, yet in some works this silence is more motivated than in others. An obvious cause for cessation of writing—the death of the principal correspondent—brings many a letter novel to a close.[7] Such a denouement differs from a simple tragic conclusion by its epistolary subtext: in works such as Crébillon's *Lettres de la marquise*, Restif's *Les Posthumes*, or those of the *Werther* strain, the act of writing becomes so identified with life and the life force throughout the narrative that the mere cessation of letters from the protagonist is synonymous with his death. Voltaire plays on this synonymity of *écrire = vivre* in his short *Lettres d'Amabed*. It is through the act of writing that Amabed, after a long silence, finally reveals that he has survived the Inquisition; his first letter following an abrupt halt in his correspondence begins: "Je suis donc au nombre des vivants! C'est donc moi qui t'écris, divin Shastasid!" (p. 443). Underlying Amabed's curious double syllogism (I write, therefore I live; I live, therefore I write) lies an equation that invests the act of writing with vital significance for both the writer and the receiver of the letter (to write is to live, when the letter is literally the only sign of life). Both for real letter writers and for readers of epistolary fictions there is doubtless a profoundly felt truth in the ostensibly specious argument that correspondents exist only in their letters.

In *Lettres de la marquise* the letter functions doubly as a symbol of life. At the end of Crébillon's novel, as in *Werther*, the continuation of correspondence by the dying marquise indicates that she has not yet expired; its interruption confirms her death. Whereas in theater, film, and opera the life force conventionally expresses itself metonymically through the breath that gives voice to speech or song (and death is communicated as that moment when breath = speech breaks off), in epistolary literature ink is regularly metaphorized—explicitly or implicitly—as life's blood. Furthermore, in *Lettres de la marquise* the metaphorical equation *écrire = vivre* is reinforced by the identities *écrire = aimer* and *vivre = aimer*. Throughout Crébillon's novel it is clear that writing and loving are equated as one and the same act; it is by corresponding with the count that the marquise comes to love him ("A force de vous écrire que je ne vous aimais pas, je vins enfin à vous écrire que je vous aimais" [L. 40]), or is it perhaps rather because she loves him that she agrees to write to him in the first place? The marquise likewise associates letters with life; after the count's cruel betrayal she announces: "J'ai brûlé vos lettres, et c'est par ce sacrifice que j'ai commencé à me détacher de la vie" (L. 69). In this novel love, letter, and life are so inextricably bound up together that when one ceases, the others must follow suit.

Thus tragic closure in epistolary narrative is regularly grounded in metaphorical structures that subtend the entire novel with the equation of writing to living. Comic closure, however, tends to produce resolution more ornamentally, as a more limited final cadence. Both types of closure, however, develop along predictably epistolary lines: if the tragic resolution of the epistolary work occurs when the letter writer can no longer write, we might say that in the comic denouement the letter writer no longer has anyone to whom to write. Typically, in those novels that end with a marriage of protagonists, there is no reason to continue writing the confidants, for the latter come to join the wedding party. Thus *Pamela* ends when the heroine's parents come to live with the newlyweds, and *Lettres de Juliette Catesby* closes on Juliette's wedding invitation to her confidante Henriette.[8] At the end of Mme Riccoboni's *Juliette Catesby*, moreover, for the first time in the novel new voices (other than Juliette's) are heard. Letters from Mylord d'Ossery, Mylady d'Ossery (Juliette), and Mylady d'Ormond follow each other in rapid succession, each inviting Henriette to join them for the wedding festivities. This sudden proliferation of letter writers resembles the final scene in classical comedy, where all the characters are brought together on stage to celebrate the lovers' marriage. An actress herself, Mme Riccoboni simply translated the conventional theatrical denouement into epistolary form to create the same sense of closure. Seen together, however, both comic and tragic closure in epistolary fiction point once again to those polar limits—total presence (reunion) and total absence (death)—that constitute the conditions obviating the letter.

What we have called comic closure (letters cease because of

addressee's arrival) and tragic closure (letters cease because of writer's decease) are not the only types of resolution possible in epistolary narrative, although they are the most traditional and conventional. An equally strong sense of closure can be produced by any motivated discontinuation of a correspondence. *Herzog* provides a simple illustration. Throughout Bellow's work, letter writing has become such a symptom of Herzog's manic state that his decision to give up message sending constitutes not only his most significant step toward a cure, but an appropriate conclusion to the novel: "Perhaps he'd stop writing letters. Yes, that was what was coming in fact. The knowledge that he was done with these letters. Whatever had come over him during these last months, the spell, really seemed to be passing, really going. . . . In a few minutes he would call down to her [the cleaning woman], 'Damp it down, Mrs. Tuttle. There's water in the sink.' But not just yet. At this time he had no messages for anyone. Nothing. Not a single word." Bellow's emphatic final lines leave us with the feeling that when Herzog gives up message sending there really is no more to say. Silence—the return of calm after Herzog's frantic scriptomania—puts an end to both Herzog's neurosis and Bellow's novel.

Motivated renunciation of writing provides the conclusion to *Lettres portugaises*. Only five letters long, this work by Guilleragues nonetheless shows a psychological development and unity of structure that make it worthy of treatment here. Mariane, the Portuguese nun responsible for the five letters, is an Ovidian heroine, abandoned by the lover to whom she desperately writes. Each of her first four letters terminates on a note of powerlessness: "Adieu, je n'en puis plus" (L. 1); "Mariane n'en peut plus, elle s'évanouit en finissant cette lettre" (L. 2). Overwhelmed by her uncontrollable emotions, Mariane is forced to break off abruptly: "Adieu, ma passion s'augmente à chaque moment" (L. 3); "Adieu, pardonnez-moi! Je n'ose plus vous prier de m'aimer; voyez où mon destin m'a réduite! Adieu" (L. 4). Although she always evokes the impossibility of continuing the letter in question, Mariane never renounces writing in these four letters. On the contrary, her closing includes a promise to take up the pen again: "Ah! que j'ai de choses à vous dire!" (L. 3). It is only in the fifth letter that Mariane renounces writing ("Je vous écris pour la dernière fois"), after she has recognized the total lack of dialogue between herself and her lover: "Vous ne m'écrivez point. . . . vous ne la lirez point [my letter]. . . . j'écris plus pour moi que pour vous" (L. 4). This moment of recognition occurs at the end of the fourth letter and prepares the denouement of the fifth. If the first four letters have broken off on a note of powerlessness, the fifth ends on a note of strength, of independence: "souvenez-vous que je me suis promis un état plus paisible, et que j'y parviendrai, ou que je prendrai contre moi quelque résolution extrême, que vous apprendrez sans beaucoup de déplaisir, mais je ne veux plus rien de vous, je suis une folle de redire les mêmes choses si souvent, il faut vous quitter et ne penser plus à vous, je crois même que je ne vous écrirai plus; suis-je obligée de vous rendre un compte exact de tous mes divers mouvements?" (L. 5). The very fact that this *is* Mariane's final letter, that no others follow, constitutes evidence that the resolution that she merely articulates here (silence and return to a peaceful state—through either self-control or suicide) has been actualized. The letters being an outward manifestation of inner turmoil, they cease when the turmoil ceases or is controlled.

In this instance it seems probable that closure is being pur-chased at the expense of repression. In renouncing letter writing Mariane is doubly renouncing her lover, for the two have become synonymous, with letter writing replacing the lover. In her very first letter, Mariane establishes the letter's quality as erotic metonymy for the person: "Adieu, je ne puis quitter ce papier, il tombera entre vos mains, je voudrais bien avoir le même bonheur." The first four letters stress her desire to have more frequent and longer letters from him and to prolong the moments when she writes him, as if the letter were the lover himself and writing an erotic experience. It is only in the last letter that she asks him not to write, resolves not to write herself, and returns his letters. Mariane would now be tempted to do to her lover's person exactly what she has almost done with his letters: "je me sens, depuis quelques jours, en état de brûler et de déchirer ces gages de votre amour. . . . si quelque hasard vous ramenait en ce pays, je vous déclare que je vous livrerai à la vengeance de mes parents." (L. 5). So complete is the identification of letter and lover that the end of the love affair and the end of the letter narrative cut the same thread in a single act of castration, as Mariane symbolically annihilates—or represses—lover, passion, and writing.

A radical shift in writing dynamics likewise closes Crébillon's *Lettres de la duchesse*. The duchess's final letter (L. 56) is even more distinct from the preceding narrative than Mariane's. Much longer than the preceding letters (forty-two pages) it is written two years after them. These forty pages serve as a key to the rest of the novel; in them the duchess summarizes and puts into perspective the events that the earlier correspondence had merely punctuated, providing us with a retrospective illumination of the feelings and motives behind her previously mysterious actions. It is here that we learn that the duchess's love for the duke preceded the beginning of their correspondence, that her sarcasm and indifference throughout have been feigned. For the first time, in this letter, she pronounces the word *aimer*; yet significantly enough, it is in the past tense: "je vous aimais." Even the conditionals that occasionally suggested her emotions in earlier letters ("if I loved you, I would . . . ") are now in the past: "vous auriez exigé de moi un aveu positif: je ne dois pas douter que vous ne l'eussiez obtenu. . . . il n'y a rien, peut-être, à quoi avec le temps vous ne m'eussiez conduite." Since the duke had chosen not to make time his ally, abandoning his courtship at an early point, the duchess invokes time as her bulwark: "le temps qui s'est écoulé entre votre lettre, et ma réponse, doit vous être une preuve que je n'ai rien donné au premier mouvement." The interval between letters sets this final letter apart, just as its retrospective tone (summary and illumination of the past, confession of love in the past tense) distinguishes it from the earlier letters. Such a movement backward in time, as compared with the earlier future-oriented correspondence, constitutes a significant braking action. Even the duchess's confession of love is a dead-end confession, not only because it is in the past tense, but also because it appears as a fulfillment of her earlier statement, "Si j'avais le malheur de vous aimer, je ne vous le dirais que le plus tard qu'il me serait possible" (L. 47). It remains only for the closing lines to bring the novel to its final state of arrest: "je vous préviens que je ne répondrai à aucune des lettres que vous pourrez m'écrire. . . . Adieu, Monsieur, quelqu'amertume que vous ayez répandue sur ma vie, c'est bien sincèrement que je désire que la vôtre soit heureuse." Since this letter is indeed the last one, we must assume that the duchess kept her resolution.

Epistolary narrative thus adds to the usual dynamics of closure (resolution of conflict, restoration of order, marriage, death) a dynamics of its own. Because the letter is not merely the narrative medium but frequently acquires a symbolic value as well, the very continuation or cessation of the writing constitutes a message that is often appropriate closure material:

| SYMBOLIC VALUE | CESSATION | EXAMPLE |
|---|---|---|
| sign of life | death | *Werther, Jacopo Ortis* |
| sign of love | renunciation of love | *Marquise, Duchesse, Portugaises* |
| neurosis | cure | *Herzog* |
| separation of friends | reunion | *Humphry Clinker, Juliette Catesby* |

In *Pamela* the letter becomes so much identified as a moral monitor and means to protect Pamela's virtue (see above, chap. 3) that the heroine cannot cease writing until she has convinced both B and B's society of that virtue (by the very fact that she writes, as well as by the events narrated within the letters). In *Les Liaisons*, where letters are stockpiled as secret weapons, the arms race easily explodes into total warfare, which destroys both of the warring parties. After the holocaust the survivors inherit the correspondence; as soon as all the secret weapons have been confiscated, the collection is complete, as is the novel.

The movement from private reading to public reading discussed in chapter 3 above is thus another example of the dynamics of epistolary closure. The novel that tells the story of its own publication (*Les Liaisons, Pamela, Fanni Butlerd, Adèle et Théodore*) is also telling of its own completion. The *finis* and the *imprimatur* in these novels are almost synonymous and are both contained within the narrative itself.

Thus far we have dealt only with narrative whose ultimate halt is motivated, leaving us with the impression of completion, of resolution. We feel that there is nothing more to say, either because there is no one left to say it, no one to whom to say it, or no longer any motivation for writing. Although such a strong sense of closure characterizes the majority of epistolary works, the letter form lends itself just as easily to open-endedness. Whenever we find ourselves wondering what the letter writer would have communicated in his next letter or asking why there is no response to the final letter, we are testifying to a particular potential for continuation implicit in any letter sequence.

If we compare the end of *Les Liaisons* with that of *La Nouvelle Héloïse*, for example, we are in each case faced with a silence: the silence of Mme de Rosemonde, that of Saint-Preux. Whereas Rosemonde's refusal to reply to Mme de Volanges is explicable and constitutes a message in itself (Rosemonde prefers not to reveal the full horror of what has happened to Cécile), Saint-Preux's silence is more enigmatic. He who opened the novel with a series of three aggressive letters has become a mere passive receiver of the six letters that close the novel (6:8–13). Saint-Preux never articulates his reaction to Julie's death or to her final letter. Instead it is Claire whose brief lament closes the novel. Saint-Preux's enigmatic silence, coupled with Wolmar's, Julie's, and Claire's final lines, terminate the action on an atmosphere of "attente," of waiting and suspension: "les larmes ne coulent pas encore: on vous attend pour en répandre" (6:11, from Wolmar); "Non, je ne te quitte pas, je vais t'attendre" (6:12, from Julie); "Son cercueil . . . attend le reste de sa proie . . . il ne l'attendra pas longtemps" (6:13, from Claire). Reunion or separation? Terrestrial or celestial? The suspension of writing opens a number of possibilities. Just as Saint-Preux's muteness is more appropriate to a grief that is ineffable than a letter would be, so the entire novel seems to trail off naturally into the void left by Julie's eclipse.[9] There *is* more to say, but what?

The unanswered letter, which leaves the narrative in suspension, is Montesquieu's choice for ending *Lettres persanes*. In Montesquieu's novel, as in Rousseau's, the hero is the passive receiver of the last six letters (L1. 156–61).[10] The final letter, from the dying Roxane, contains a revelation that is the inverse of Julie's (Roxane has appeared faithful but has been unfaithful all along), yet Usbek remains as silent in the face of this revelation as Saint-Preux is in response to Julie's confession.

Usbek's silence is even more significant than that of Saint-Preux. As Roger Laufer has pointed out, throughout *Lettres persanes* Usbek unconsciously leads a double life: in France that of the enlightened philosopher who believes in natural law and liberty, and at home that of the cruel despot.[11] Roxane's revelations should constitute a moment of *anagnorisis*, of recognition for Usbek. Her emphatic statement "j'ai toujours été libre; j'ai reformé tes lois sur celles de la nature" should make it clear to him how inconsistent his own tyranny has been with his philosophical observations: "Nouvel Oedipe, Usbek reconnaîtrait enfin sa mauvaise foi et sa misère, condamnerait la contradiction de ses pensées et de ses actes. . . . Mais le livre s'arrête brusquement. Montesquieu n'a pas osé, ou pu, tirer la leçon de son expérience. Usbek se tait, Usbek n'a probablement pas compris. Usbek n'est pas Oedipe."[12] If we examine the novel further, we discover that Usbek is not merely silent on the questions that Roxane raises. In a letter preceding Roxane's in order of presentation but actually postdating it by six months (in other words, a letter likely to have been written *after* Usbek received Roxane's, the usual mailing interval being five months), Usbek makes statements that reveal the full extent of his blindness. The letter in question (L. 146) is a scathing condemnation of a bad minister, presumably John Law, which begins, "Il y a longtemps que l'on dit que la bonne foi était l'âme d'un grand ministère." Usbek proceeds to describe in apocalyptic terms the ruin, chaos, and corruption that can be produced by "le mauvais exemple" of a single ministry:

> J'y ai vu une nation, naturellement généreuse, pervertie en un instant. . . . J'y ai vu tout un peuple . . . devenir tout à coup le dernier des peuples. . . .
> J'ai vu la foi des contrats bannie, les plus saintes conventions anéanties.

If the repetition of "J'ai vu . . . j'ai vu" throughout this letter testifies to Usbek's vision where European affairs are concerned, it only highlights ironically his extraordinary blindness where governance of his own harem is involved. In this letter Usbek does not even mention the recent harem events, yet these events have created a state of disorder at the very least equal to the conditions in Law's France. Both "final" letters of *Lettres persanes* (Roxane's presentationally final L. 161 to Usbek, Usbek's chronologically final L. 146 to Rhédi) break off inconclusively, leaving us with an Usbek who has not drawn the logical conclusion from the events he has witnessed.

The unanswered last letter of *Lettres persanes* or *La Nouvelle Héloïse* gives the impression of having been flung into the vacuum of blank space that follows. Montesquieu and Rousseau use the silence of the addressee for two completely different purposes: Rousseau to suspend us over the inexpressible grief of Saint-Preux and the uncertain future of the community at Clarens, Montesquieu to point an ironic finger at the tyrant-philosophe who is unable to draw from Roxane's letter the obvious conclusion about his own bad faith. In *Poor People* Dostoyevsky makes yet another use of this final letter tossed into a void.

*Poor People (Bednye lyudi)*, Dostoyevsky's first published novel (1846), is composed of letters exchanged between Makar Alexsyevich Dyevushkin, a timid, impoverished, older government clerk, and Varvara Alexsyevna Dobroselov, a poverty-stricken young girl who lives in the building across from him. Dostoyevsky carefully motivates the correspondence. Because Dyevushkin fears that the other boarders in his building will talk about his friendship with a girl so much younger than he, the older man limits himself to a very few visits, preferring the discretion of a correspondence, which will moreover help him "to improve his style" as an aspiring writer. In their poignantly simple language the two suggest tremendous depth of feeling and daily suffering. Dyevushkin's letters, full of self-deprecation, develop a character who occasionally borders on the ludicrous yet is redeemed by his constant efforts to help those around him. He gradually reveals (though never explicitly) that his paternal concern for Varvara's well-being is a reflection of his love for her. Although Varvara is appreciative, her much shorter letters (always interrupted to return to work) suggest that her attachment is not as strong. Dyevushkin's self-sacrificing efforts to save Varvara from poverty and protect her from her lecherous persecutor Bykov are to no avail; Varvara realizes that her situation is ruining them both and chooses the only way out—marriage to the wealthy Bykov, whom she despises.

In announcing her irrevocable decision, Varvara expresses a fear of the unknown into which she is stepping and only hints at the grief that leaving Dyevushkin will cause her, before breaking off her letter: "Bykov has come, I leave this letter unfinished. I wanted to tell you a great deal more. Bykov is here already!" (23 September). Dyevushkin receives a number of such incomplete notes. As Bykov is about to carry her away to his estate in the steppe country, Varvara bequeaths to Dyevushkin her last unfinished letter: "How will you do left alone here? To whom am I leaving you, my kind, precious only friend! I leave you the book, the embroidery frame, the unfinished letter, when you look at those first words, you must read in your thoughts all that you would like to hear or read from me, all that I should have written to you; and what I could not write now!" (30 September). "Unfinished" is the motif that echoes throughout this correspondence; Varvara's interrupted letters leave unexpressed her feelings for Dyevushkin, uncertain her future with Bykov. She promises to write, but "God alone knows what may happen" (30 September). If Varvara's letters are interrupted, cut short by her work and later by Bykov ("Mr. Bykov is calling me"), Dyevushkin's letters are a desperate attempt to stave off the end by prolonging the writing. His letter of 30 September, the last one we read, is a frantic and moving fight against conclusion:

> You are being carried off, you are going. [. . .] And with whom will you be now? Your little heart will be sad, sick and cold out there. [. . .] You will die out there, they will put you in the damp earth; there will be no one to weep for you there! [. . .] Why, how can such a thing be, Varinka? To whom am I going to write letters, *matotchka*?[13] [. . .] I shall die, Varinka, I shall certainly die; my heart will never survive such a calamity! [. . .] No, you must write to me again, you must write another letter about everything, and when you go away you must write to me from there, or else, my heavenly angel, this will be the last letter and you know that this cannot be, this cannot be the last letter! Oh no, I shall write and you will write. . . . Besides, I am acquiring a literary style. . . . Oh, my own, what does style matter now? I don't know, now, what I am writing, I don't know at all, I don't know and I don't read it over and I don't improve the style. I write only to write, only to go on writing to you . . . *matotchka*, my own, my Varinka. . . .

Dostoyevsky leaves us hanging on this plaintive suspended note, the blank space that follows representing the widening distance between him and the Varinka who is being carried away.

In closing *Poor People* Dostoyevsky is actually playing off the unfinished against the finished. On the one hand incomplete letters—letters that are interrupted or trail off in ellipsis—suggest that there is more to say, that these two souls could go on writing. Such unfinished letters are the tangible manifestation of a love that is never fully confessed and never comes to fruition; they leave us with a feeling of the incomplete; just as the last letters, though suggesting death, leave uncertain the fate of Varvara and Dyevushkin. On the other hand, the very cessation of the correspondence suggests an ending—and of more than just a relationship. For it is not merely the separation that drives Dyevushkin to distraction, but the impossibility of getting letters to Varvara ("So I keep on about our letters; who will carry them for us, my precious?" [29 September]). Letters are all these impoverished people have; to take away this simple treasure is to strip them totally. The end of the correspondence constitutes the ultimate destitution.

When we compare the end of *Poor People* to the conclusion of other love novels in letters, we better grasp this sense of the incomplete that characterizes Dostoyevsky's first work. Whereas in the *Lettres portugaises*, in Crébillon's *Marquise* and *Duchesse*, or in Mme Riccoboni's *Fanni Butlerd* the heroine's final letter constitutes a renunciation of both love and letter, *Poor People* leaves us with a promise to write and an expectation of more letters; it breaks off with a half-articulated statement of love from one writer and an effusion of sentiments from the other, who refuses to put down his pen. In the former group of novels the final blank space confirms resolutions; in *Poor People* it merely betrays hopes. In short, whereas the cessation of letters in narrative like the *Lettres portugaises* reinforces an already strong movement of closure, in Dostoyevsky the termination clashes with the will to continue, augmenting tension rather than producing resolution.

No character, not even Makar Dyevushkin, is more reluctant to put down his pen than Senancour's Oberman. Senancour makes three different attempts to end his autobiographical hero's volume of letters to a friend-confidant. The 1833 edition contains a continuation of the correspondence into the tenth year (the 1804 edition having ended in the ninth year), and the 1840 edition contains yet another supplement. Of Senancour's three attempts to end the collection of letters, none sounds the note of finality.

Such endlessness, however, is entirely consonant with the thematic emphases of the work. Oberman, a Romantic hero stricken with *le mal du siècle*, lives in a perpetual "état d'attente" (L. 10); another epistolary victim of ennui from the same period— D'Alembert in *Mademoiselle de Maupin*—describes this Romantic state with an epistolary metaphor: "Moi, je demande au messager la réponse à une lettre que je n'ai pas écrite" (p. 46).[14] Oberman complains repeatedly about "cette perpétuelle lenteur de toutes choses," a slowness that is reflected in the very languor of his own letters. Typically, from each new place he writes, "Rien ne se termine: les misérables affaires qui me retiennent ici se prolongent chaque jour" (L. 10). It is no surprise that a writer who declares "que m'importe ce qui peut finir?" (L. 18) should not bring his own correspondence to a close.

Oberman is constantly in search of both ending and end, of conclusion and purpose, of termination and goal; long before Beckett's protagonists, this writer expresses a preoccupation with "terme," "but," "fin," "finir," "résultat," in almost every letter:

> lorsque je pressens cet espace désenchanté où vont se traîner les restes de ma jeunesse et de ma vie . . . que trouvez-vous que je puisse attendre à son terme, et qui pourrait me cacher l'abîme où tout cela va finir? . . .
> Il faut que toute chose ait une fin selon sa nature. [L. 41]

Oberman entertains frequent thoughts of death and suicide, takes a morbid pleasure in autumn: "la saison où tout paraît finir" (L. 24). Yet his preoccupation with ends is abortive; the narrative leads us neither to a Wertherian suicide nor to a discovery of purpose in living. Each new postmark reflects the prolongation of this wanderer's search. Rather than lead us to an end in either sense, the letters merely continue, as endless and aimless as the life of the writer himself.

*Oberman* testifies perhaps more than any other work to the potential ongoingness of the epistolary form, just as its corollary piece, *Werther*, actualizes letter narrative's potential for finality. All of the works that we have examined, however, elaborate themselves in a context in which both continuation and discontinuation of the writing itself have a special meaning. Because the letter writer feels so frequently the need to justify both picking up the pen and putting it down, epistolary narrative adds to the usual dynamics of literary closure its own dynamic. By rendering explicit the forces and counterforces acting on the process of enunciation, letter narrative demands to be understood in terms of the very forces that bring it into being, propel it, and bring it—or fail to bring it—to a state of arrest.

It is tempting, in view of the recent polemics for openness in art forms and criticism, to ask whether letter narrative is an end-determined or an antiteleological form. Insofar as the letter poses as a real-life document (and it certainly did in the eighteenth century), it hardly lends itself to the kind of well-made plot that builds toward a climax and contains no gratuitous elements. The memoir novel, written in the light of the end, is much more amenable to such selective patterning of plot elements, whereas the letter writer, who presumably cannot know the outcome of events he narrates, must include unimportant details as well as those that are central to the main action. Are we to conclude then that letter narrative, insofar as it adheres to its documentary pretensions, is a shapeless mimesis of pure contingency? How can a letter novel that respects verisimilitude be end-determined?

To pose the question in the above way is, however, to raise a separate and new issue. What is particular about epistolary closure, as we have been stressing throughout this chapter, is that it depends as much on the act of narrating as on what is narrated. For us to sense a letter as final we must not only be satisfied that all important threads of the plot have been tied but that there is no longer any reason for the writing to continue. This chapter's survey has suggested the variety of ways in which this constraint becomes a structuring possibility and closural strategy. Indeed, one of the implications of this survey may be that in comparison to other early novelistic modes, epistolary literature developed relatively more codified, more formal, and more narratively integrated closural strategies. Motivated renunciation of writing (with comic, tragic, and thematic implications) assures the strongest closure in this kind of narrative, whereas the unanswered letter or the refusal to put down the pen leaves the novel open-ended. Beneath the structure of the plot, epistolary narrative spins out a network of communication with its own raison d'être; as the letter itself acquires a symbolic value for the correspondents (sign of life, love, neurosis, virtue), motivation for writing becomes as important as story. Resolution—if it occurs— must take place not only at the level of the narrative as fable but at the level of the narrative as communication.

Moreover, in epistolary closure the ultimate narrative events— those that actually terminate the "fable"—are typically not narrated; they are merely signified by a rupture in the process of narration that leaves marks in the text. Ricarda Huch's 1910 novel *Der letzte Sommer* comes to a halt on the printed letter "j——," which signifies that the Russian governor who has been typing this final letter has been assassinated by a bomb wired to detonate when his typewriter strikes the *j* key.[15] The epistolary form sets up possibilities for contrapuntal and referential interplay between narrating act, physical text, and narrative content, which letter novelists regularly exploit.

Finally, although epistolary literature exhibits both diverse and strong closural strategies, there is a very real sense in which the epistolary text is never closed. The letter collection is regularly presented by its fictitious editors as incomplete: it is a "selection" from a larger group of letters or one side of an exchange. Such presentation spawns publication of texts that are not so much sequels (the appropriate continuation for the episodic work) as efforts to fill in the gaps or present the other side of the previous text—*Charlotte's Letters to Werther* or Fielding's publication of the "real" letters of Mrs. Shamela Andrews. Furthermore, the epistolary text is regularly framed and reframed as part of an ongoing process of textual creation, transmission, and interpretation that is endless. Editorial prefaces to epistolary works rarely make the gesture of presenting the work as completed product to a public or patron.[16] An instructive contrast is offered by two Crébillon novels. Crébillon frames his memoir novel *Les Egarements du coeur et de l'esprit* with two prefaces, a short conventional dedicatory one, offering this "unworthy homage" to his father, and a second, justifying its narrative content; in both prefaces the work is presented as a completed product, whose content may be questioned but not added to. His *Lettres de la marquise*, however, is introduced by an "extract" (i.e., incomplete text) from a "letter" by Mme de ***, an acquaintance of the count to whom the marquise wrote. Mme de *** is in turn passing these letters on to a M. de *** for his reading and (intimated) publication pleasure; she has selected seventy out of more than five hundred letters but will show M. de *** the others if he would like to see them. In other words, this work consists of fragments framed by yet another "extract."[17]

The editor of the epistolary work is, after all, not primarily a writer: he is a selective reader. He may devote most of his preface to explaining his work as textual critic or translator. The editor of Crébillon's *Marquise* explains her criteria for selecting the seventy letters, whereas Laclos's editor protests that he wanted to make more changes but "had no authority." Typically the editor also worries about the consequences of printing and reading. Smollett frames *Humphry Clinker* with an exchange between Jonathan Dustwich and Henry Davis, publisher in London, in which they discuss the libel suits that publication of private letters may bring upon them.

Thus the chain of actions and consequences is perceived as unending, the circuit of communication is never closed. Epistolary texts engender prefaces, prefaces, and postfaces, which dialogue with each other and with the text proper, and which are a continuation of the text's dialogical model. In short, the very publication of the epistolary work is explicitly seen as having consequences; within the epistolary framework, frames are constantly broken, and even closural gestures have inaugural implications.

1. Barbara H. Smith, *Poetic Closure*, p. 36.

2. John Frank Kermode, *The Sense of an Ending*, p. 8.

3. Robert Martin Adams, *Strains of Discord: Studies in Literary Openness* (Ithaca, N.Y.: Cornell University Press, 1958); Alan Friedman, *The Turn of the Novel* (New York: Oxford University Press, 1966); Beverly Gross, "Narrative Time and the Open-Ended Novel," *Criticism* 8 (Fall 1966): 362–76.

4. Kermode, p. 7.

5. Indeed, when Upton Sinclair imitates Richardson in *Another Pamela; or, Virtue Still Rewarded* (1950), he uses the same kind of closings: "May God guard and spare such sufferings to / Your sister / Pamela."

6. Jacques Derrida's *Envois*, however, poses questions that are not unrelated to the issues at stake in Heloise and Abelard's correspondence. The problematic moment of framing and signing the letter occurs at several points in *Envois*: (1)

when the letter writer conceives the idea of publishing his correspondence: "cela me donne l'envie . . . de publier sous mon nom des choses pour *moi* inconcevables, invivables surtout, que je n'ai pas écrites moi-même, en abusant ainsi du crédit 'éditorial' que j'accumule depuis des années. . . . Ils vont encore me dire que je ne signerais pas n'importe quoi: *prove it*" (p. 251); and (2) whenever the act of addressing words of love to his correspondent provokes an awareness of the multiplicity of self and other: "*je t'aime* ne se poste pas . . . je peux toujours dire 'ce n'est pas moi' " (pp. 254–55); "d'autres croiront que nous sommes quatre. . . . Mais quel que soit le nombre arrêté, c'est toi que j'aime uniquement" (p. 260). The strong move toward definition of unique selves (signer and addressee of letters) is contradicted by a move that denies the uniqueness and definability of an endlessly differentiated self. Like Heloise with Abelard, Derrida's writer and addressee split in the very gesture of self-identification imposed by the signature.

7. E.g., *Lettres de la marquise, Werther*, Nodier's *Adèle, Clarissa, Ultime lettere di Jacopo Ortis*, Giovanni Verga's *Storia di una capinera*, Restif's *Les Posthumes.*

8. To demonstrate just how codified this type of closure is in classical epistolary novels, we might well contrast the typical comic reunion of correspondents with the opposite movement in a tragic novella such as Nodier's *Adèle. Adèle* consists mainly of the letters of Gaston de Germance to his friend Edouard de Millanges, telling about the vicissitudes in his courtship with the enigmatic Adèle. Gaston's last letter, in which all the mysteries of Adèle's past are cleared up, could easily close a comic narrative, with its invitation to Edouard: "Viens auprès de moi, Edouard . . . je suis heureux à jamais; ta présence manque seule à ma félicité." The letter that actually closes the novel, however, is the subsequent one from Gaston's valet announcing Adèle's death: "Oui monsieur, venez. . . . Il vous écrivait son bonheur—Il ne savait pas. . . . " Even while the valet is writing, more tragic events are transpiring, for his final line is "Mais quel bruit! . . . Hélas, monsieur Edouard, ne venez pas!" The change in movement here—to "ne venez pas"—is precisely the opposite of the comic denouement's invitation to a reunion. In fact, it is tempting to call this tragicomic alternation between two possible outcomes an epistolary tragicomedy, or—in this case—melodrama.

9. Saint-Preux's muteness corresponds to that of Wolmar and Claire. Claire writes, "Wolmar m'entend et ne me répond pas. . . . Moi seule je ne puis ni pleurer, ni parler, ni me faire entendre" (6:13).

10. These letters, being part of the harem sequence, which Montesquieu grouped together at the end, are not actually the last in chronological order but rather the last in order of presentation.

11. Roger Laufer, in his chapter on *Lettres persanes* in *Style rococo, style des "Lumières,"* pp. 51–72. The chapter originally appeared as an article, "La Réussite romanesque et la signification des *Lettres persanes* de Montesquieu," *Revue d'histoire littéraire de la France* 61 (1961): 188–203.

12. Laufer, p. 71.

13. Though all quotations are from the Constance Garnett translation of *Poor People*, I have substituted for "my darling" in the Garnett translation the original "matotchka." *Matotchka* is Dyevushkin's special term of endearment for Varvara, which he repeats with desperate frequency in his last letter.

14. Thirteen out of seventeen chapters of Gautier's novel are in letter form.

15. Huch does not, of course, explain how this letter survived the accident. But then, as a twentieth-century novelist, she is less bound to account for her sources.

16. A noteworthy exception is Richardson, who presents *Clarissa* as a "History," with its dramatis personae and its moral. Richardson's impulse to present his text as completed, moreover, governs his entire narrative technique: his text presents all documents relevant to Clarissa's story (including wills and contracts) and his correspondents try to "give all the particulars"; the text is designed as an authoritative version and the editorial comments attempt to impose an interpretative authority. The editor presents himself not as *a* reader but as *the* reader of this work, invested with ultimate authority.

17. Jacques Derrida seizes this self-fragmenting aspect of the letter as an apt emblem for his concept of dissemination. He develops this notion in *Envois*: "une lettre, à l'instant même où elle a lieu . . . se divise, se met en morceaux tombe en carte postale" (p. 90); but he had already articulated it in his 1975 essay on Lacan: "La structure restante de la lettre, c'est que, contrairement à ce que dit le séminaire [Jacques Lacan's well-known seminar on Poe's "The Purloined Letter"] en son dernier mot ('ce que veut dire "la lettre volée," c'est qu'une lettre arrive toujours à destination'), une lettre peut toujours ne pas arriver à destination. Sa 'matérialité,' sa 'topologie' tiennent à sa divisibilité, à sa partition toujours possible. Elle peut se morceler sans retour. . . . la dissémination menace la loi du signifiant et de la castration comme contrat de vérité" ("Le Facteur de la vérité," rpt. in *La Carte postale*, p. 472).

# CHAPTER SIX

# THE EPISTOLARY MOSAIC

If in chapter 5 we approached the epistolary work as process, we shall now examine it as product. This final chapter offers an approach to the work's composition through analysis of the arrangement or patterning of its constituent parts—distribution of letters among the various correspondents, ordering and juxtaposition of letters, narrative continuity and discontinuity from letter to letter—all of which are a function of the letter's dual status as unity and as narrative unit.[1] As we turn from what is particular to epistolary communication to what is particular to configurations of letters, we move from the plane of internal writer-addressee to that of external author-reader. Awareness of the arrangement of letters within a narrative work involves consciousness of the hand that arranges—that of the fictional "editor," or of the epistolary novelist.

## THE LETTER AS UNIT AND THE LETTER AS UNITY

Within the epistolary work the letter has both a dependent and an independent status. Like tesserae, each individual letter enters into the composition of the whole without losing its identity as a separate entity with recognizable borders. Each letter is defined by the blank space that surrounds it; each has its characteristic shape and coloration. The letter retains its own unity while remaining a unit within a larger configuration.

Montesquieu's *Lettres persanes* richly illustrates the letter's viability as a self-contained entity. Each of the philosophical letters is highly structured according to a particular rhetorical form, deals with a single subject, and delivers a message of its own. Thus letter 38 is constructed as a debate; Rica argues both sides of the question of woman's liberty. Other letters are written as demonstrations of a thesis set forth in the first sentence. Many follow an anecdotal formula that begins with the first person singular pronoun, establishing the situation ("J'allai l'autre jour voir une grande bibliothèque" [L. 133]), continues by presenting one aspect of French life through a satiric dialogue, and closes with a punch line (e.g., Ll. 32, 45, 49, 52, 54, 59, 61, 74, 133). As we might expect, the anecdotal formula is used most often by Rica, whereas Usbek prefers the dissertation letter. The philosophical letters are much more than the "digressions" that Montesquieu praised the epistolary form for permitting;[2] each is a minitreatise possessing a rigorous stylistic organization and unity. In Montesquieu's hands an ancient and time-honored rhetorical form—the epistle—becomes an instrument for creating highly organized internal structures absent from most other philosophical and satiric novels of the same period.

The esthetic of Montesquieu's work is less one of "digression" than that of Laclos's "variété des styles." As we move from letter to letter, the tone, style, and subject change abruptly; contrast by juxtaposition of discrete units is as central to Montesquieu's art as to that of Laclos.[3] We shall examine the effects of such juxtaposition later in this chapter, but the important consideration now is the independent status of the letter that permits it. The unity of the individual letter makes it a suitable instrument not only for highly structured presentation of ideas but also for structuring works of a more narrative nature. Because each letter of Crébillon's marquise or of Mme Riccoboni's Fanni Butlerd is in a different key, having its own characteristic emotional register, the narrative traces the heroine's sentimental journey as clearly as a graph. In narrative whose action is psychological, each letter, as Werther puts it, marks the hero's progress "Schritt vor Schritt" (8 August 1771).

So versatile an instrument is the letter that it seems tailored for works that range from the philosophical and rhetorical to the plot-oriented. A writer like Laclos capitalizes on the letter as discrete unit for suspense purposes, making the letter into a serial installment that breaks off at the most exciting moment. Valmont interrupts his account of the charity scene to go dine (L. 21), delighting moreover in his power to make his reader Merteuil await the continuation: "J'en suis fâché, car le reste est le meilleur." Rousseau pushes this technique even further, when he has Saint-Preux close a letter to Edouard promising to reveal Julie's "fatal secret" at his next writing and arranges for this installment to get lost in the mail for the next eighty pages. Richardson and Marivaux likewise use the blank space between letters for a suspenseful halt, designed to make the reader anticipate the next letter impatiently. When we are analyzing reader response in this fashion, however, it is important to differentiate between Laclos's or Rousseau's creation of a very real suspense for the *external* reader (by actually postponing the continuation for several letters) with Richardson's mere imitation of the suspense that Pamela's internal readers would feel (having to await her letters), a suspense that her external reader would feel less (being able to turn the page). Likewise, the blank space that separates the letters of Marivaux's heroine Marianne for the modern reader merely imitates or represents symbolically the suspenseful waiting period that Marivaux's original feuilleton readers would have shared with Marianne's fictional addressee.

Epistolary narrative is by definition fragmented narrative. Discontinuity is built into the very blank space that makes of each letter a footprint rather than a path. Yet as any observer of perceptual behavior knows, the illusion of a continuous line can be produced from a series of points. In constructing the mosaic of their narrative, epistolary novelists choose constantly between the discontinuity inherent in the letter form and the creation of a compensatory continuity.

NARRATIVE CONTINUITY AND DISCONTINUITY

To maximize continuity between letters, the epistolary novelist has only to adhere to the following rules:

1. A single plot
2. Linear time followed in strict chronological order
3. One writer, one addressee
4. Intervals between letters either not emphasized or filled in by what the letters report (technique of keeping the addressee up to date)

Numerous in particular are the English novels whose correspondents, following Pamela's example, write letters in journalistic sequence to keep their confidant abreast of events; the very titling of these letters in the text ("Evelina in continuation") reflects the cult of narrative continuity. This particular technique is largely limited to novels dominated by a single correspondent; yet a similar effect is often produced in multicorrespondent works. In fact, at times when a single plot line begins to dominate an epistolary work, we may observe—even in a multicorrespondent novel like *Clarissa* or *Delphine*—that narrative continuity frequently overrides epistolary discontinuity. Thus in *Delphine* there are long sections where Delphine, Mme de Lebensei, and Louise assume narrative responsibility in turn, and where the plot is more important than who is doing the narrating. In *Clarissa* (or *Grandison*) we note the same kind of distribution of narrative responsibility. As Clarissa, then Lovelace, and finally Belford successively assume the role of narrator we often find that we are simply following a continuous story through the eyes of the most omniscient observer at the time.

On the other hand, discontinuity is maximized when none of the above rules is obeyed, that is, in narrative with the following characteristics:

1. Multiple plots
2. Disruption of the temporal line by nonchronological ordering of letters
3. Multiple correspondents, with each writer and addressee giving his characteristic coloration to the letter
4. Lacunae: the letters punctuate the story rather than constituting the entire action. Intervals between the letters loom large and contribute to the shape of the narrative.

The fourth characteristic requires elaboration. A simple illustrative work is Crébillon's *Lettres de la marquise*, where the letters allude to an action that is going on in the intervals and that we as readers must guess. Thus the seduction scene is never narrated, as it is in Dorat's *Les Malheurs de l'inconstance* or in *Les Liaisons*, where one character keeps his correspondent up to date on his activities. The moment of seduction must instead be inferred from a change in tone from one letter to the next. In such instances the blank space between letters is as responsible for shaping the narrative as the letter itself. Often two or more factors of discontinuity reinforce each other, as at the end of *Lettres d'une Péruvienne*, when in the interval between two letters a meeting between the long-separated lovers Aza and Zilia has occurred. For the first time in Mme de Graffigny's novel, Zilia writes to a person other than Aza, penning her first lines to her French friend and admirer Déterville. The sudden switch in addressee reinforces the blank space of nonnarrated action between letters, producing a shock comparable to the shock Zilia has had in the interval—the discovery that Aza no longer loves her. The dislocation that the film medium might produce by a blackout is accomplished in *Lettres d'une Péruvienne* by a switch in addressee that emphasizes a narrative lacuna.[4]

More often than not, the discontinuity inherent in the form is played off against an illusion of continuity. Thus the division of *Pamela* into dated letters draws more attention to skipped days than would a simple first-person narration. The events themselves are no more discontinuous than they would be in a memoir novel, but the interruption of the narration creates a different effect—be it apprehension or simply the heightened awareness that we are tuning in on the heroine only every few days.

Even when the time interval between letters is abnormally long, the very proximity of the letters on the printed page can nonetheless create a contrapuntal illusion of temporal continuity. For example, in part 3 of *La Nouvelle Héloïse*, letters 5 through 17 probably span one year but occupy only twenty-five pages in the Pléiade edition. This grouping produces a distorted effect, since it seems as if one blow (Julie's marriage) too quickly follows another (Mme d'Etange's death and Saint-Preux's sacrifice of Julie). Such a telescoping of time accentuates the shock of the blows inflicted on Saint-Preux by presenting them in rapid staccato succession. Likewise, although the harem sequence at the end of *Lettres persanes* spans many years, the illusion of a rapid continuous succession of peripeteia is created by grouping all of the letters together.

Zilia, in *Lettres d'une Péruvienne*, explains the illusion of continuity that a letter sequence creates. After a long period of silence she writes, "Combien de temps effacé de ma vie, mon cher Aza! Le Soleil a fait la moitié de son cours depuis la dernière fois que j'ai joui du bonheur artificiel que je me faisais en croyant m'entretenir avec toi" (L. 18). Waxing even more philosophical in another letter, she offers an interesting description of the letter writer's temporal experience: "le temps ainsi que l'espace n'est connu que par ses limites. Nos idées et notre vue se perdent également par la constante uniformité de l'une et de l'autre, si les objets marquent les bornes de l'espace, il me semble que nos espérances marquent celles du temps, et que si elles nous abandonnent ou qu'elles ne soient pas sensiblement marquées, nous n'apercevons pas plus la durée du temps que l'air qui remplit l'espace" (L. 9). The letter is thus the marker of duration; when there are no letters, there is no experienced time. For the outside reader, and even for Zilia, the only durational sequence is the letter sequence; the illusion of a continuous narrative is created by what are actually discrete events.

The unfolding of the epistolary work thus depends on both the disjuncture inherent in a work composed of discrete units and the compensatory sense of continuity created by the author and perceived by the reader. A typical technique for connecting letters, for instance, is that of following an enigmatic statement in one letter with an explanation in the next. Thus Julie's mysterious dream, described by her in part 3, letter 13 of *La Nouvelle Héloïse*, is explained by Claire in letter 14. Lydia's curious dream (*Humphry Clinker*, 10 June) is never explained to her, but the letter from Jery that follows Lydia's clears up the enigma for the external reader. In fact, the more fragmented and disconnected the narrative appears, the more actively the outside reader seeks to discover the connections. The first five letters of *Humphry Clinker* are a kaleidoscope of changing names, places, and events that are incomprehensible to the external reader because each of the five correspondents is writing to a friend who does not share the eavesdropper's need for exposition. Not only can the external reader not comprehend the contents of any letter by itself, but it is not immediately clear to him why the letters of these particular correspondents are grouped together in the same collection. Certain constants appear, however; certain names and incidents are repeated from letter to letter, and before long the reader finds himself collating the various letters to discover the relationships between characters and how they all relate to the incidents described. One constant that runs through all the first letters is the Lydia-Wilson incident; in fact, this well-emphasized affair will be the only narrative thread continued throughout the work.

As readers of epistolary narrative we are often called upon to act as detective-collators, to perceive continuity from one letter to the next because the image of the first persists in our mind. At the beginning of *Les Liaisons*, Laclos winks briefly at his reader when he follows Merteuil's letter to Valmont describing the "gauche" Cécile with a letter from Cécile describing an unknown woman whom she has overheard at a soirée: "Ce qui m'inquiétait le plus était de ne pas savoir ce qu'on pensait sur mon compte. Je crois avoir entendu pourtant deux ou trois fois le mot de *jolie*; mais j'ai entendu bien distinctement celui de *gauche*, et il faut que cela soit bien vrai, car la femme qui le disait est parente et amie de ma mère" (L. 3). The marquise is immediately identifiable to the reader, though not to Cécile, by her language, which he has just heard in the previous letter. Already Laclos has lured the reader to the level of complicitous superiority that will be his vantage point for the rest of the novel.

Smollett counts on the reader's persistence of vision (retention of image from one letter to the next) to create a narrative continuity that is actually lacking in verisimilitude. Because his five travelers are making the same voyage, witnessing the same incidents, yet writing to different friends, Smollett must choose constantly between redundancy and lack of verisimilitude. Theoretically, each important event should be narrated five times. Occasionally Smollett does present correspondents' conflicting versions of the same incident, but if overused, this technique would become tiresome. Caught between Scylla and Charybdis, Smollett opts more frequently to avoid redundancy. The result, however, is that his correspondents often allude to events as if they had already described them, when in actuality it is another letter writer who had reported them to his friend. Jery, for example, refers in passing to "the ball" in his letter of 10 May, when he has never mentioned it before. The most extreme case in point is Win's allegorical letter of 14 June describing Clinker's imprisonment, which the outside reader—who has just heard

Bramble's straightforward version—finds hilarious but which Win's friend Mary Jones must find incomprehensible, since she has heard very little of Clinker from Win. Smollett creates narrative continuity for his outside reader by sacrificing continuity for the internal readers. Smollett has thus moved a long way from the technique of the opening letters, which were unintelligible to the external reader precisely because they made sense to the internal addressees. By the time we reach Win's letter it is clear that the complicity of author-reader is overriding that of the internal writer-addressee, in the interest of a more linear, less redundant narrative.

As any reader of Smollett knows, however, the narrative thread (adventures of the five travelers, romances of the three women) is subordinate to the multiple visions of reality that Smollett creates by refracting each event through the eyes of different observers. *Humphry Clinker* never produces the sense of unbroken narrative that occurs in certain sections of *Delphine* (e.g., 3:48–4:13), where we forget the narrator to follow the events narrated by whoever is the most privileged witness, and the narrative technique approximates that of omniscient third-person narration. In Smollett's work, even where the narrative thread is the most continuous, that is, when the various correspondents seem to continue one another's reporting of events in chronological sequence, each writer's reporting is so lacking in omniscience, so colored by his character, that we cannot fail to be conscious of his letter as a separate fragment. Smollett exploits both continuity and discontinuity, asking his reader to perceive both coherence and fragmentation simultaneously.

DISTRIBUTION OF LETTERS AMONG CORRESPONDENTS

The discussion of *Humphry Clinker* has led us necessarily to consider one of the most salient aspects of epistolary structure: the choice of correspondents and the distribution of letters among them. Montesquieu, Smollett, and Laclos choose particularly diverse characters and construct their novels as patterns of the perspectives particular to each correspondent. These novelists explore to the fullest the possibilities of epistolary language as a means of depicting personality. Smollett, as a matter of fact, discovers a possibility unique to the letter—that of characterization by orthography. Win's letters are full of spelling errors, which convey not only her dialect (as would the same language in a play) but also her illiteracy; these errors make her advice to Mary Jones all the more amusing: "mind your vriting and your spilling; for, craving your pardon, Molly, it made me suet to disseyfer your last scrabble" (3 June).

Correspondents are characterized not only by their styles in these novels but also by the topics on which they write. Thus during the *Clinker* group's travels through Great Britain, the elderly head of the household, Squire Bramble, chooses to discourse upon the economy, architecture, government, and layout of the cities they visit, whereas his young nephew Jery, a recent university graduate, is more interested in food, entertainment, and girls. Moreover, whereas Bramble is introspective, indulging in self-analysis, homesickness, and health worries, Jery is more oriented toward the exterior world. It is he who is responsible for almost all the portraits of secondary characters and who observes others in order to report anecdotes. We see Bramble in Jery's letters but rarely see Jery in Bramble's. Because Jery is more interested in what surrounds him than in his interior being, his perspective is kaleidoscopic: "for my part, I am continually shifting the scene, and surrounded with new objects" (17 May). If Bramble's letters are marked by the repetition of the themes of noise, filth, and health—concerns and repetitions that are natural to an elderly man—Jery's are marked by the absence of this sort of obsession, in keeping with his open-minded youth.

Interestingly, the two principal correspondents of *Humphry Clinker* resemble their counterparts in *Lettres persanes*. Bramble and Usbek, the older men responsible for governing a social unit, write about serious topics, wax homesick, and worry about their health, whereas Jery and Rica write in an anecdotal style about less weighty matters (e.g., social life) and adapt more easily to new environments. Smollett and Montesquieu develop within their novels a thematics of characterization that would make each letter's author recognizable even without the signature. Distribution of letters among correspondents in their work is thus distribution of styles and topics of concern.

Smollett transforms this thematics of characterization into a major principle of novelistic construction. Whereas Montes-

quieu's Persians usually write about different aspects of occiden-
tal life, Smollett's characters often describe the same milieu. Their
letters focus on the same phenomena, although they interpret
them differently. Thus a frequent sequence in *Humphry Clinker* is
the description of a city by Bramble, followed by Lydia's or Jery's
version, in which the same elements are mentioned, radically
transformed by the change in point of view. Bramble's letter on
Bath—"this place . . . is become the very center of racket and
dissipation. . . . here we have nothing but noise, tumult, and
hurry" (23 April)—is followed by Lydia's: "Bath is to me a new
world—All is gayety, good-humour, and diversion. The eye is
continually entertained with the splendour of dress and equipage;
and the ear with the sound of coaches, chaises, chairs, and other
carriages. . . . We have music in the Pumproom every morning" (26 April). The same sounds are described by Bramble and
Lydia, but it is in the coloration of the description that all the
interest lies. What is "noise" for one is "music" to the other. The
division of narrative among various correspondents in Smollett
produces a fragmentation and deformation of reality that emphasize the role of the deforming agent. Each letter in *Humphry
Clinker*—like the component units of those cubist paintings that
present the same face from various angles—is a fragment juxta-
posed with another to produce a total picture.

Multiple versions of the same reality are a common occurrence
in epistolary narrative with multiple correspondents. Clarissa and
Lovelace offer contrasting accounts of the dinner and rape
episodes; Saint-Preux and Julie describe their first meeting after
seven years in quite different terms. Henry James constructs both
of his epistolary short stories, "A Bundle of Letters" and "The
Point of View," entirely around incompatible descriptions of the
same phenomena. In both stories the travelogue technique used
by Montesquieu and Smollett serves a Jamesian theme—the
confrontation of American and European cultures. A Parisian
boardinghouse that harbors American, British, German, and
French travelers is the setting from which "A Bundle of Letters"
are mailed; as we might expect in James, the boarders offer
divergent views of each other as well as of Paris. In "The Point of
View" James crosses the ocean, as American exiles return home
with French and British tourists to comment upon their own and

each other's cultures. The same national stereotypes are seen in a different light by each observer.

When Laclos's characters offer contrasting accounts of the same phenomena, the result is different, however. If we examine, for instance, the three views of Cécile's seduction-rape (Valmont, Cécile, Mme de Volanges), or Valmont's and the présidente's conflicting accounts of the "charity" scene, or Merteuil's two versions of the Prévan episode (one told to Valmont, the other to Volanges), we recognize that in Laclos one version is always more enlightened, or enlightening, than the other. Whereas in Smollett or James different points of view serve a relativistic theme, emphasizing the varieties of existence and the extent to which reality depends on the observer, in *Les Liaisons dangereuses* they are part of Laclos's mythology of intelligence. The doubling of accounts is one example of the interplay between naive puppet and omniscient puppeteer that characterizes the novel in general.

Thus far we have been speaking of the variety of ways in which shifts from letter to letter in style, formal organization, subject matter, and perspective produce gestalts of both the writer and the reality he records. In letter narratives characters are created less by what they do than by what, and how, they write. The gestalts we form, however, are also a function of distribution of activity among correspondents. Even when novelists do not use multiple or particularly diverse correspondents, their choice of who writes, and with what frequency, is a determinant structure. The fact that a character is merely written about but is not a correspondent himself affects reader response. In Balzac's *Lettres de deux jeunes mariées*, for example, Louise's first and second husbands are presented by two different techniques. The man who will be her first spouse, Felipe, is introduced before Louise has met him, through letters that the exiled Felipe exchanges with his brother in Spain and that appear early in the novel. Such independent presentation of Felipe establishes him as a correspondent in his own right. Because he in his own letter, as well as Louise in her subsequent ones, describes his background and current situation, we sympathize more with him than with the widowed Louise's second husband, Gaston, whom we see only through Louise's letters, after we have learned to doubt her romanticized portraits. Of Felipe's character we are certain, having met him through his own letter before Louise even knows him. With Gaston, however, when Louise begins to suspect his fidelity, the reader has no more privileged view of him than she and must await the denouement to discover that he has not betrayed her.

The fact that d'Ossery is not a correspondent in Mme Riccoboni's *Lettres de Milady Juliette Catesby* is likewise significant. Juliette writes *about* him to her friend Henriette, but not *to* him, and the difficulty that she has in establishing a correspondence with d'Ossery ("qu'il m'est difficile de lui écrire" [L. 31]) is a reflection of the difficulty that the two have in renewing their former relationship. Rejecting d'Ossery's overtures, Juliette writes to Henriette rather than replying to him. Her latent love and her unconscious desire for a reconciliation, however, are revealed by the fact that in the middle of a letter to Henriette she addresses d'Ossery (L. 29). The resumption of epistolary communication with him in letter 37 heralds the reestablishment of their former relationship; the Juliette-d'Ossery marriage that concludes the novel follows almost immediately. Furthermore, as we have noted in the preceding chapter, Juliette's reunion with d'Ossery is textually marked and celebrated in epistolary fashion by a rapid extension of the circle of correspondents at the novel's close.

In *Clarissa* a sudden proliferation of correspondents conveys a different message. If we examine the distribution of letters in Richardson's novel, we observe that at several points Clarissa interrupts her regular correspondence with Anna Howe to send out a series of letters to all her friends and relatives. These rounds of letters are written at points of tension in the narrative—when Clarissa is locked up at her father's, after her abduction, after the rape, after her final escape—at times when the heroine is particularly helpless and isolated. Each round of letters is a new set of cries for help; the responses, however, are always negative. From the prison of her room (at her father's, in the house where Lovelace confines her, or in the rooming house where she lives out her waning existence), Clarissa sends out feelers in all directions, only to discover how strong are the walls of her confinement.

Careful analysis of the pattern formed by the distribution of letters among the various correspondents of an epistolary work is a basic step in interpretation. Answers to such simple questions as who writes and who is silent, who receives messages and who does not, underlie Jean Rousset's sensitive reading of *La Nouvelle Héloïse:* "La première Partie, qui est le temps du délire, de l'abandon à la passion, est presque uniquement composée de lettres des deux amants; c'est un long duo, exclusif de tout ce qui n'est pas lui. . . . vers la fin seulement s'intercalent quelques lettres de tiers ou à des tiers, qui interviennent précisément pour rompre ce dangereux tête-à-tête."[5] Distribution of epistolary activity is only one of the essential ways in which meaning is generated in epistolary narrative. In the next section we shall review the influence of the environmental context of each letter.

ORDER AND JUXTAPOSITION OF LETTERS

Constructed as a composite of discrete units, epistolary narrative lends itself to interplay between contiguous letters. Juxtaposition of letters of similar or contrasting tones is a frequent ornamental or emphatic device. Even in a sequence of two letters from the same writer to the same addressee, there may be a radical change in key. Thus Valmont ebulliently writes Merteuil on 2 October (L. 99) that he is on the eve of conquering Tourvel; so certain of victory is the vicomte that he is already anticipating his reward from Merteuil. If Valmont's letter closes emphasizing his "joie," the one immediately following opens with, "Mon amie, je suis joué, trahi, perdu; je suis au désespoir: Mme de Tourvel est partie" (L. 100). The distance between inflation and deflation is only that of a blank space.

The letters of Crébillon's marquise to her lover regularly offer abrupt contrasts. In letter 25 the marquise coldly dismisses the count, closing on a flippant note wishing him "prospérité et bon voyage." In the following letter, however, her amorous effusion takes over from the very first sentence: "Quelle est donc la puissance de l'amour!" The epistolary form is an apt instrument for transcribing the sudden switches and ironic inconsistencies that characterize a love affair.

In Rousseau's hands juxtaposition of letters from different writers serves to reveal how kindred are the souls of Julie and Saint-Preux. In letter 26 of part 1 (Saint-Preux to Julie), just as Saint-Preux finishes describing his state of passion, he receives

Julie's letter 25, where she describes herself in similar terms; he finds in this coincidence "un frappant exemple de ce que vous me disiez de l'accord de nos âmes dans les lieux éloignés!" In Smollett, on the other hand, juxtaposition highlights contrast in characters. Bramble's first letter, which reveals his generosity toward the poor, is followed immediately by a letter from Tabitha in which she expresses her distrust and stinginess toward servants (L1. 1, 2).

Such antiphony becomes a major principle of construction in *Les Liaisons*. Laclos builds an entire section (L1. 146–50) around alternation between the frivolous flirtations of Danceny and Merteuil (146, 148, 150) and the grave communications of Mme de Volanges and Rosemonde concerning the dying présidente (147, 149).[6] If the contrast between the two correspondences were not already ironic enough, Laclos sets up a subtle contrast in Volanges's letter 149 and Danceny's 150 that emblemizes and deepens the irony. In letter 149 Volanges reports an event that is actually the most immediate cause of the présidente's death: the mere sight of a letter from Valmont triggers Tourvel's final convulsions. In letter 150 Danceny also has a reaction to unread letters, which he expresses at length to his new mistress, Merteuil: "Enfin, quel que soit le temps, on finit par se séparer, et, puis, on est si seul! C'est alors qu'une Lettre est si précieuse; si on ne la lit pas, du moins on la regarde. . . . Ah! sans doute, on peut regarder une Lettre sans la lire, comme il me semble que la nuit j'aurais encore quelque plaisir à toucher ton portrait." Danceny's entire letter, which is a naive defense of his epistolary pleasures, appears all the more ironic, following so hard upon Volanges's exposure of the letter as the most lethal of weapons.

Laclos is, of course, the master of ironic juxtaposition. Valmont's serialized account of his staged act of "charity" is interrupted by the présidente's gullible view of it (L1. 21–23). Tourvel's anticipation of what will happen when the "converted" Valmont comes to return her letters to her (L. 124) clashes head-on with Valmont's announcement "La voilà donc vaincue, cette femme superbe . . . " (L. 125). Valmont's letter in turn transforms the following one, wherein Rosemonde congratulates Tourvel on her courageous resistance, into an exercise in pure irony.

Laclos's geometric patterning of letters is celebrated. Yet even in lesser-known works we find curious and revelatory arrangements. A sequence of letters near the end of *Lettres de la marquise*, for instance, constitutes a reproduction in miniature of the letters comprising the body of the narrative. The marquise is actually seduced twice in Crébillon's novel. The first seduction is long, psychologically complex, full of delicate changes of sentiment. After her betrayal by the count, the marquise is reseduced in letters 59 to 63; this much shorter sequence of letters is marked by repetition of many of the same techniques on the part of the count and the same reactions on the part of the marquise as during the first seduction. Prayers and protests are frequently verbatim the same as earlier ones (cf. Ll. 60 and 25); the same justification for writing is offered (cf. Ll. 62 and 40). The count in turn uses the same devices to maintain contact: a husband's intercession and a feigned illness. The parallels between this sequence and the earlier long one make the accelerated reseduction an ironic mirror of the first, as the marquise succumbs a second time to the same ploys.

In *Lettres persanes* Montesquieu judiciously positions the harem letters in order to shed a certain light on the philosophical letters and vice versa. The Troglodyte story is framed by two letters from the chief eunuch lamenting his condition (Ll. 9 and 15). Such a placement emphasizes the injustice of the eunuch's condition and the harem society by opposing them implicitly to the just rule of the Troglodyte society. The final grouping of harem letters is the most often discussed product of Montesquieu's arranging hand. In this artificially accelerated section devoted exclusively to the harem plot, Montesquieu offers a parallel to the immediately preceding letters on French life. Both the French letters and the harem sequence describe the growing disorder in a community whose absolutist leader is absent: Usbek's absence from the seraglio wreaks the same havoc as Louis XIV's death in France. The juxtaposition of such parallel sequences is further evidence of the "chaîne secrète" that has inspired so many articles on *Lettres persanes* in recent years.

It is not within the scope of this chapter to exhaust the possibilities of analysis but rather to expose the ramifications of a simple principle underlying any analysis of epistolary form.

That principle is the basic consideration with which we began our chapter—the particular status of the letter as both unity and narrative unit; in epistolary narrative the letter serves simultaneously as a text within itself and as a context informing the letters contiguous to it. Working with these particular qualities, the epistolary novelist creates patterns of implication, through juxtaposition, order, and distribution of letters among correspondents. The blank space between letters shapes his narrative as well as the letters themselves, making the question of ellipsis in epistolary writing a much more complex one than in other narrative forms.

The question of ellipsis in narration (unnarrated time) has usually been dealt with by both novelists and theoreticians as "dead time."[7] The particular ellipsis that is built into letter novels (leaps between letters), however, is anything but negligible and has to be dealt with differently from the more common type of ellipsis (which we would find *within* letters, for example) for at least two reasons. First of all, temporal ellipsis in a novel where a primary narrator has charge of narration is quite different from ellipsis in a novel where there is no reified voice assuming responsibility for the narrative as a whole. In the former case, the assumed reliability of the overall narrator (at least insofar as selection of important events is concerned) typically precludes any investigation into the nonnarrated time. That is, the first- or third-person narrators who write "two years later" elide more smoothly than the epistolary novelist; even at the zero degree of epistolary elision in which Pamela or Fanny Burney's Evelina writes letters "in continuation" the epistolary novelist must leave a hiatus between letters that is interruptive if not disruptive. Second, the interval between any two letters always represents simultaneously at least four kinds of ellipsis, each with its own implications: (1) a certain interval during which the correspondent does not write, (2) intervening events that have been omitted from the narrative, (3) the interval during which the internal reader awaits the letter, which differs temporally and psychologically from (4) the interval during which the external reader anticipates the following letter (cf. the difference in suspense experiences discussed earlier apropos of *La Vie de Marianne* or the illusion of accelerated peripeteia produced in *La Nouvelle*

*Héloïse*). The letter's status as both a discrete entity produced by an internal writer for an internal reader and a unit within the larger epistolary novel thus makes ellipsis in epistolary writing correspondingly more complex.

The very discreteness of the letter as a building block makes it theoretically impossible for the letter to enter seamlessly into a continuous narrative. Yet we have noted a strong impulse toward continuity, particularly in novels like *Pamela, Clarissa, Delphine,* and Fanny Burney's *Evelina,* where correspondents fulfill their journalistic vocation as reporters, and a switch in witnesses only serves to keep us closer to the hot line of events. On the one hand, narrative continuity in epistolary works is as illusionistically possible as pictorial continuity in pointillist paintings; on the other hand, the narrative discontinuity inherent in the epistolary form affords interesting possibilities for elliptical, allusive writing, the creation of suspense, and juxtaposition of contrasting views or episodes. In fact, just as we distinguished in chapter 2 between two basic writing styles in epistolary literature (confidentiality, coquetry), we can speak of two fundamental editorial styles, seamless and disjunctive, according to whether the novelist chooses to minimize or accentuate gaps. But whatever the editorial style, what always distinguishes epistolary fictions from nonfictional letters is the space of structured interplay they leave between letters. This space is the trace of the "editor," of that very editor who typically claims elsewhere to have played a minimal role. The epistolary novelist who effaces himself from the title page thus reappears in the text; but his most compelling voice is not the one that speaks to us in editorial prefaces and footnotes. The creator of the epistolary novel who disclaims authorship reclaims it elsewhere—in the very joint work that structures the epistolary mosaic as art.

1. As a narrative unit, the letter bears some resemblance to the chapter, whose role in structuring prose narrative has been discussed by Philip Stevick in *The Chapter in Fiction.* Because the epistolary form multiplies these units considerably, and because each letter may differ radically from the next in tone, narrator, and addressee, the letter must, however, be treated differently from the chapter.

2. In his often-quoted preface, "Quelques réflexions sur les *Lettres persanes*," which appeared in the supplement to the 1754 edition.

3. Solim's and Narsit's contradictory views of the harem's outing (L1.151 and 152), for instance, offer as striking a contrast as Mme de Volanges's and Cécile's interpretations of the night of Cécile's rape, or the présidente's and Valmont's accounts of the vicomte's "charity."

4. Compare Clarissa's similar, although much more prolonged, epistolary blackout after her rape, when the traumatized heroine is unable to write of her experience. What is *not* narrated here is more important than what *is* narrated; the ellipsis looms larger than the narrative line.

5. See *Forme et significtion*, pp. 89–93, for the continuation of Rousset's illuminating analysis, one of the few to deal with Rousseau's novel in terms of narrative, rather than philosophical, strategies.

6. The framing of this section by the Merteuil-Valmont exchange concerning the marquise's arrival in Paris (L1. 144, 151) is yet another example of that sense of geometric arrangement that is so typical of Laclos.

7. See Gérard Genette, *Figures III* (Paris: Seuil, 1972), pp. 139–41, for a clear summary of this position.

# CONCLUSION: THE
# PARAMETERS AND
# PARADOXES OF EPISTOLARITY

WHAT IS EPISTOLARITY?

> *"Quand vous écrivez à quelqu'un c'est pour lui et non
> pas pour vous: Vous devez donc moins chercher à lui
> dire ce que vous pensez que ce qui lui plaît davantage."
> (Merteuil to Cécile, L. 105)*

> *"Mon ami, quand vous m'écrivez, que ce soit pour me
> dire votre façon de penser et de sentir, et non pour
> m'envoyer des phases que je trouverai . . . dans le
> premier roman du jour." (Merteuil to Danceny, L. 121)*

When the marquise de Merteuil articulates her two theories of the
epistolary art in letters 105 and 121, it is clear that her advice is
governed by utility rather than consistency. If Merteuil's self-
contradiction in these two letters tells us nothing new about her
duplicity, her two statements are nevertheless quite revelatory
insofar as epistolary theory is concerned. The letter is no less
mutable in character than the marquise; depending on the writer's
aim, the letter can be either portrait or mask. This protean aspect
of the letter raises a serious question about our study of epistolarity. How can we speak of what is particular to the epistolary form
when the letter can in one context demonstrate properties that are
exactly the opposite of those revealed in other contexts?

Merteuil's contradictory definitions cannot, however, lead us
to conclude that the letter is a totally amorphous instrument in
the hands of its creator. The letter is unique precisely because it

does tend to define itself in terms of polarities such as por-trait/mask, presence/absence, bridge/barrier. These polarities guarantee the letter's flexibility and define its parameters, thus giving it recognizable dimensions of thematic emphasis and narrative potential. At those moments when letter writers speak self-consciously of their chosen form, they make these polarities clear; thus Merteuil in each of her above statements defines one epistolary pole by opposition to the other.

A brief description of some of the polar dimensions of the letter will remind us of those properties underlying the six approaches presented in this study:

1. Bridge/barrier (distance breaker/distance maker). The letter's mediatory property makes it an instrument that both connects and interferes. In *Clarissa* the letter is an imperfect intercessor, calling attention to estrangement, whereas in *Mitsou* it is a mediator without which two persons, even in the presence of each other, cannot communicate. As an intermediary step between indifference and intimacy, the letter lends itself to narrative actions that move the corre-spondents in either direction.

2. *Confiance/non-confiance.* If the winning and losing of *confiance* constitute part of the narrative content, the related oppositions *confiance / coquetterie* (or candor / dis-simulation) and *amitié / amour* represent the two primary types of epistolary style and relationship. These distinctions, as well as the blurring of these distinctions, are a function of the letter's dual potential for transparency (portrait of soul, confession, vehicle of narrative) and opacity (mask, weapon, event within narrative).

3. Writer / reader. The epistolary situation evokes simultane-ously the acts of writing and reading, as correspondents al-ternate, often within the same letter, between the roles of narrator and narratee, of encoder and decoder. Reader con-sciousness explicitly informs the act of writing itself. The movement from the private to the public in much of episto-lary fiction lays bare another paradox: as a reflection of self, or the self's relationships, the letter connotes privacy and intimacy; yet as a document addressed to another, the letter

reflects the need for an audience, an audience that may suddenly expand when that document is confiscated, shared, or published.

4. I/you, here/there, now/then. Letter narrative depends on reciprocality of writer-addressee and is charged with present-consciousness in both the temporal and the spatial sense. The letter writer is engaged in the impossible task of making present both events and addressee; to do so he attempts to close the gap between his locus and the addressee's (here/there) and creates the illusion of the present (*now*) by oscillation between the *then* of past and future.

5. Closure/overture; discontinuation/continuation of writing. The dynamics of letter narrative involves a movement between two poles: the potential finality of the letter's sign-off and the open-endedness of the letter seen as a segment within a chain of dialogue. Finality is actualized in epistolary terms by motivated renunciation of writing, the death of the writer, the arrival of the addressee, whereas enigmatic silence realizes the letter form's potential for open-endedness.

6. Unit/unity; continuity/discontinuity; coherence/fragmentation. The letter's duality as a self-contained artistic unity and as a unit within a larger configuration make it an apt instrument for fragmentary, elliptical writing and juxtaposition of contrasting discrete units, yet at the same time the very fragmentation inherent in the letter form encourages the creation of a compensating coherence and continuity on new levels.

The definition of epistolarity is thus charged with paradox and contradiction. The opposite of almost any important trait can be equally a characteristic of the letter form. When Walter Scott contrasts epistolary to third-person narrative in *Redgauntlet,* he describes the letter as a slow-motion form. Scott justifies his switch to third-person narrative after a long epistolary section by comparing himself first to the explorers of Mont Blanc who go painfully through the snow "and anon abridge their journey by springing over the intervening chasms . . . with the assistance of their pilgrim staves" and second to the "dragoons, who were trained to serve either on foot or horseback, as the emergencies of the service required" (p. 159). Yet the acceleration that Scott felt he could produce only by switching to third-person narrative can be produced by the epistolary form, as we have seen in chapter 6 when we examined certain sequences of *Lettres persanes* (final harem letters), *La Nouvelle Héloïse* (3:5–7), or *Lettres de la marquise* (L1. 57–63) that accumulate and link together a series of major events. If the dialogue ritardando seems more characteristic of the epistolary form, letter sequences can become accelerando precisely because they break with the accustomed tempo (as in the ironic accelerated reseduction of Crébillon's marquise). In fact, whatever the parameter, we will always find that epistolary narrative thrives in an atmosphere of contrary possibilities.

Throughout the history of the epistolary form, implicit or explicit concepts of the letter's nature have governed the writer's defense or description of his instrument. Such definitions of epistolarity—whether inferable from authorial comments like Scott's,[1] correspondents' reflections, or critics' reactions—always reveal as much about the writer's esthetic values as they do about the form itself. But is this not the danger of any ontology? When theoreticians of film began to reflect upon what is specifically cinematic, their definitions were bound up with esthetic choices. Whereas Eisenstein conceived the film image as a frame, within which an editor formally arranges lines, shapes, and movement, André Bazin believed it to be a window on the world. Eisenstein's esthetic is formalist and privileges the cinematic work's reference to itself as a work of art, whereas Bazin's is realist, grounded in the shot's constant reference to a real world that is being photographed. The telling distinction between these two major theoreticians' answers to "What is cinema?" is obviously a difference in perception of screen space: whereas for Eisenstein the screen's outer edge encloses the only reality, for Bazin it centrifugally impels the viewer's awareness toward off-screen reality, which is conceived as continuous with the space of the screen.

The frame/window opposition is instructive: though such metaphors clearly elevate esthetic preferences into ontologies, they derive their appeal from seemingly objective formal properties—the physical nature of screen space and the photographic image—just as Merteuil's alternate definitions of the letter as portrait/mask are grounded in epistolary language's status as expression of oneself/to another. Moreover, such ontologies have clearly been formative as well as descriptive of two major film styles, from Lumière and Méliès on, just as the portrait/mask opposition underlies two distinct styles of epistolary writing.[2] What we learn from these conflicting ontologies is not surprising: to create the ontological metaphor—"the film shot is a frame," "the letter is a portrait of the soul"—involves selective perception whereby some formal phenomena are highlighted and conflicting ones suppressed. Such selective perception is an integral part of style; as ontology, however, it is obviously reductive.

My own objective in exploring epistolarity has not been to suggest a simple ontology of the letter form but rather to provide a series of formal perspectives for reading epistolary novels, by tracking the pressure exerted by form on meaning in a broadly representative group of works. The relation between form and content in epistolary narrative is complex, and the conceptual dualities that I have just summarized in the preceding pages cannot do justice to that complexity. They do, however, remind us insistently of the extent to which the practice of writing and reading epistolary novels is governed by a formal dialectic, in which certain properties of the letter are developed in tension with others. In the preceding chapters I have tried to describe the conventions and field of play that create meaning in epistolary narrative. As a form, the letter constrains and permits the production of meaning in specific ways, which are best conceptualized as a dynamic or field of force set up by conflictual possibilities.

Epistolary language is polarly generated. We have noted throughout that the letter is both a reflection of the gap and an instrument for gap closing. Epistolary language and letter sequences are marked by hiatuses of all types: spatial separation between writer and addressee; time lags between event and recording, between message transmission and message reception; blank spaces and lacunae in the manuscript. The letter is a both-and, either-or phenomenon, signifying either bridge or barrier, both presence and absence. The external reader's perception of continuity in letter sequences is generated by their seeming discontinuity, and the continuation of a correspondence by the internal writers and readers acquires meaning only in relation to potential discontinuation. Oscillation between trust and mistrust, writing and reading, forms the thematic material of epistolary narrative. If such narrative speaks so self-consciously of its dualities, it is logical that we as readers should attempt to understand it through the poles that generate it. The paradox of epistolarity is that the very consistency of epistolary meaning is the interplay within a specific set of polar inconsistencies.

EPISTOLARITY: Approaches to a Genre

Thus far, my work has had a dual objective: to identify fundamental parameters of epistolarity and to demonstrate their influence on the creation of meaning in a variety of individual works. In so doing, however, I hope also to be laying a foundation for more serious consideration of epistolary literature as a genre. If the preceding section concluded my case for epistolarity as an interpretative concept, in this section I would like to open up the case for a number of generic approaches.

Is there an epistolary "genre"? To ask this is to raise once again the question of what constitutes a genre. As Paul Hernadi's encyclopedic survey of modern genre theory (*Beyond Genre*) reveals, there are at least as many theories as there are genres. Yet Hernadi is able to distinguish four principal concepts of genre—which he categorizes as expressive, pragmatic, structural, and mimetic—according to whether the theorist's criterion for genre divisions is based on (1) the mental attitudes of the author, (2) the effects on the reader, (3) the verbal medium, or (4) the subject matter and "message" of the evoked world. If we look at the praxis, rather than the theory of genre criticism, however, we find that Hernadi's last two concepts (structural and mimetic) underlie most studies of individual genres, which usually begin by identifying a genre either *structurally* as a fixed form (e.g., memoir novel, sonnet) or *mimetically* as a specifically evoked world (e.g., the western, the gothic novel). Whereas Claudio Guillén (*Literature as System*) and others have implied that for the practical critic the valid identification of a genre need not do more than discern *some* similarities between works, Tzvetan Todorov and Fredric Jameson have developed specific criteria similar to Hernadi's structural and mimetic (thematic) bases for genre description. In their respective work on fantastic literature and romance they have suggested specific guidelines for the identification and study of individual genres that it is useful to review and compare here.

Both Todorov, in his *Introduction à la littérature fantastique* (1970), and Jameson, in his account of "Romance as Genre" (1975), begin by distinguishing between what they call *syntactic* and *semantic* approaches to an individual genre.[3] For Todorov syntactic analysis accounts for the relations—logical, temporal, and spatial—between the parts of a work, whereas the semantic approach identifies its themes. Jameson similarly defines the semantic approach as one that aims to give an account of the meaning of a genre, that tends to deal with the "essence" of a genre in terms of a "mode." In contrast, the structural or syntactic approach is more scientific, more analytic, and deals with genre in terms of "fixed form." A semantic approach to comedy would deal with the comic "vision," opposing it to tragedy, whereas a syntactic approach would discover the precise laws of the comic, opposing it to the noncomic. Todorov's and Jameson's choice of the same terms may be coincidental; certainly their respective uses of them differ somewhat. Yet the fundamental distinction between the purely formal elements and the thematic thrust of a genre is maintained by both, as well as by Hernadi, and will be retained for our conclusions concerning the generic nature of epistolary literature.

Rather than prescribe one approach above the other, Jameson makes these two "seemingly incompatible tendencies" the basis for a fresh hypothesis about the nature of genre:

> The latter would then be defined as that literary phenomenon which may be articulated *either* in terms of a fixed form *or* in terms of a mode, and which *must* be susceptible of expression in *either* of these critical codes optionally. The advantage of a definition like this consists not only in its exposure of false problems (thus, it would no longer make any sense to wonder whether the novel *as such* can be considered a genre, inasmuch as one cannot imagine any determinate literary mode which would correspond to such a "form"); but also in its capacity to generate new lines of research, for example, to raise the question of the nature of the *mode* to which such a fixed form as the historical novel may be said to correspond, or that of the *fixed form* of which a familiar mode like that of the romance may be said to be the expression.[4]

In other words, though either a "semantic" or a "structural" description of a group of works may suffice to define it as a genre, the study of a genre does not become interesting until it includes both.

Following the implications of Hernadi's, Jameson's, and Todorov's methodologies, and tailoring their notions to our own needs, we can outline six distinct generic approaches to epistolary literature:

1. The *expressive* approach would focus on the mental attitudes that underlie the author's choice of the letter form.
2. The *pragmatic* would focus on the letter work's effect on the reader.
3. The *semantic* would study thematic constants in letter fiction.
4. The *structural* or *syntactic* would describe the parts of a work and their relations. (I use the terms *semantic* and *syntactic* loosely and metaphorically here, as do Todorov and Jameson in their genre studies.)
5. The *historical* approach would consider national, historical, or sociological variables affecting the origin, development, and decline of the genre.
6. The *subgeneric* would study subdivisions of the genre, using the same approaches that are applicable to study of the genre as a whole.

At the heart of genre study qua genre, however, are those two central approaches—the structural and the semantic—that form implicitly or explicitly the basis for most definitions of a genre and thereby constitute the basis for most of the other approaches.

If we return now to our original question—Is there an epistolary "genre"?—we should be in a position to answer it more meaningfully. Few would deny to epistolary literature the status of genre by Jameson's minimal definition. The epistolary novel is readily perceived as a fixed form (narrative implemented by letter sequences), as one type of verbal medium distinct from the diary novel, memoir novel, and theatrical dialogue, with which it has the closest formal affinities. The particular characteristics that distinguish this verbal medium from other types of discourse were examined in chapter 4, and other formal traits that invest epistolary literature with a particular dynamic and shape were discussed in chapters 5 and 6. Thus the real question is no longer "*Is* there an epistolary genre?" but rather, "Is the epistolary genre susceptible to coherent semantic or other descriptions as well?" In the remaining pages I shall offer partial answers to this question, speculating on the directions that further inquiry into the letter genre might take and using as my basis the six approaches outlined above.

I shall begin by dealing somewhat summarily with possible *expressive* and *pragmatic* approaches. Recognition of the "intentional fallacy" and the "affective fallacy" has led critics to shy away from literary criticism based on the author's attitudes toward a work or its effect on a reader. Yet certain observations we regularly make about letter authors and readers could lead us to revive some modified version of these approaches. Critics dealing individually with Richardson and Rousseau, for example, have often pointed out that these men were timid and frequently preferred written to oral communication with friends; we might be tempted to investigate the relation between other letter novelists' personalities and their choice of the letter form. The real question, however, whether one subscribes to the notion of the intentional fallacy or not, is whether epistolary novelists share common mental attitudes that are identifiable and significant enough in their implications for the genre to make what Hernadi calls the expressive concept of genre a meaningful approach. The letter novel's traits likewise raise a number of questions about the reader's experience of an epistolary text: With whom does the reader identify—writer, addressee, or editor—and what are the determinants of reader identification in the letter-reading experience? Do epistolary narratives have particular ways of playing to (or against) the reader's desire for mastery, his creative pleasure in coordinating fragments, his voyeurism? Why are so many internal readers in epistolary novels authority figures— parents, judges, censors, confessors, mentors—whose relationship to the letter writer seems to resemble that of the superego to the ego? In short, the *mise-en-abyme* within the novel of the writer-reader relationship invites speculation about the relationship of the real writer and reader to each other and to the text.

These speculations will remain vague and unsubstantiated, how-ever, unless supported by concrete analyses, with a solid base in rhetorical theory, biography, reception history, psychoanalytic theory, phenomenology, or affective stylistics.

A *semantic* approach to the epistolary genre is more promising. The recurring themes and polarities that we have identified seem sufficiently limited and related to the form itself to suggest that the epistolary genre can be described as a genre with a particular arsenal of thematic and narrative content. It is to be hoped that other critics might build upon these preliminary findings to produce a more thorough and systematic account of the semantic nature of the genre and that critics with a more philosophical orientation will investigate the implications of these recurring themes and polarities.

The *structural* approach, which was the basis for our initial definition of the genre, will be dealt with more expansively in the next section.

In my own study I have dealt with *historical* matters only when they became pertinent to formal questions. A glance at history in its own right, however, raises some new questions about letter forms. Why, for example, does there seem to be an evolution in the eighteenth century from monologue to polyphony, returning finally at the end, with *Werther's* influence, to the epistolary monologue? In any historical study of generic evolution we would need to investigate national variables also; the development of the epistolary novel in Germany is bound up with the diary form, in France with conversational and rhetorical arts, and in England with an esthetic that valued realistic, immediate description of phenomena. In general the German letter writer is a diarist, the English correspondent a witness,[5] and the French *épistolier* a verbal duellist. Whereas the German and English traditions tend to opt for the static method of narration (confidential letters), using language to present a seemingly unmediated transcription of internal and external reality, the French tradition of letter writing prefers the kinetic method (dramatic letters), in which the letter is used as a weapon and a mask. The difference between faith in the letter/language as candid portrait and skepticism regarding the letter/language as mask could also be roughly characterized as the difference between bourgeois and aristocratic ideologies. Only with Rousseau and imitators of Richardson (e.g., Mme Riccoboni, Diderot) does the bourgeois strain, with its espousal of candor, transparency, and Puritan values, enter French epistolary literature; even so, it enters in a dialectical tension with "aristocratic," gallant values. Thus a history of the epistolary genre is not complete without consideration of the specific cultural, sociological, and ideological values that constrain its forms.

The life of forms in art is of course a complex phenomenon to explain. The historical work that has been done on the letter form has concentrated on its origins (Kany, Black, Day); very few critics have pushed beyond the eighteenth century.[6] Indeed, most histories of the novel typically deal with the eighteenth and nineteenth centuries as if they were sealed off from each other. There is a need for careful assessment of the changes in society and esthetic ideals that underlie the decline of a form such as the letter novel; there is a need for a study, in other words, that would bridge the gap between eighteenth- and nineteenth-century novel studies by investigating more thoroughly the evolutionary or dialectical relations obtaining between the two.

Until such a study would nuance our sense of the form's history, we can only observe prima facie that the epistolary novel stands in an essentially diametrical relationship to the dominant traits of nineteenth-century narrative (with its third-person omniscient narrator, objective presentation, attention to the role of physical setting and environment, concern with historical and social surroundings). The epistolary novel's most visible affiliations are with the modern novel. Long before Proust, Woolf, Joyce, and other modern writers, epistolary novelists were experimenting with elliptical narration, subjectivity and multiplicity of points of view, polyphony of voices, interior monologue, superimposition of time levels, presentation of simultaneous actions. If the use of the letter form in the nineteenth century sticks out as an anachronistic throwback, twentieth-century novelists such as Montherlant, Colette, Grass, Bellow, Natalia Ginzburg, and Thornton Wilder have been able to reappropriate the letter innovatively—as one of a panoply of narrative vehicles available to them, while nonetheless displaying the motifs that we have come to associate with the form. Although there has been some research on the "included letter" in pre-eighteenth-century narrative,[7] almost no one has investigated the reappearance of the letter in mixed forms in twentieth-century narrative. In short, there is ample material for a history (or histories) of the epistolary novel since 1800; such a history would be particularly valuable if it compared modern uses of the form to earlier uses and situated the epistolary novel carefully within the context of mainstream novelistic production of various periods.

Within the larger corpus of epistolary literature there appear to be *subgenres*, which exhibit certain structural or semantic similarities. In my own survey, for example, I have been struck by the frequency with which the content of letter novels divides into two basic categories—erotic and educational. At the center of erotic correspondence stands the lover-seducer; crucial to the educational sequence is the mentor or guide. Abelard was, of course, both tutor and seducer. So omnipresent is the myth of Abelard and Heloise in epistolary fiction that it is tempting to consider it the prototype of these two important lineages (Heloise and Abelard's correspondence being, significantly enough, divided by traditional scholarship into two groups: the love letters and the letters of direction or instruction). The erotic impulse generates the epistolary seduction novel, whose specific forms we examined in detail in chapter 1. The educational impulse assumes primarily three forms. In the first the letter writer functions almost uniquely as teacher, and the entire letter collection is perceived as a primer. Most of Mme de Genlis's and Restif's novels—which are dominated by sequences of instructional letters on the sciences, the arts, philosophy, and ethics—would fall into this category. In the second the letter writer functions as guide, and the novel assumes the form of a travelogue or compilation of essays on contemporary society (e.g. *Humphry Clinker, Lettres persanes*, Goldsmith's *Citizen of the World*, Henry James). In the third, more narrative or dramatic strain, the mentor enters into competition with other teachers for influence over a pupil. The most common epistolary mentor is the corruptor-debaucher, who is called "my dear mentor" by his naive tutee and whose letters expounding upon his libertine philosophy are written down to be reread: "ma lettre . . . laissera par ce moyen des impressions plus profondes qu'un entretien trop tôt oublié," Gaudet asserts in *Le Paysan perverti*. The role of tutor-corruptor, which we associate with Laclos's vicomte and marquise, is basic to countless letter novels. The discovery of the corrupt mentor's letters by the representatives of virtue and their rebuttal letters of instruction to the protagonist are all part of the plot, which centers around the rivalry of two schools for a pupil. Restif's *Le Paysan perverti* is the best example of this organizational principle. Although works such as *Lettres portugaises* belong exclusively to the erotic strain, and Mme de Genlis's novels to the educational, works such as *La Nouvelle Héloïse* and Restif's *Lettres posthumes* combine the two types, thus returning to the initial Heloise-Abelard model.

Probably the most complex yet cohesive subgenre of epistolary literature is what we might call the "novel of dangerous connections." Laclos's novel is the best-known example of this form, but countless minor novels (e.g., *Delphine*, *Les Malheurs de l'inconstance*, *Les Lettres du marquis de Roselle*, Fanny Burney's *Evelina*) as well as *Clarissa* and *La Nouvelle Héloïse* can be seen to fit this type, as I shall briefly describe it. The type is definable by the character types or functions described in the table (p. 198) and by the following plot: Estranged from parents or husband, the heroine (or hero) chooses or is befriended by a surrogate parent. The hero and heroine write to respective confidants or correspond secretly and fall in love. Obstacles are posed by parents and the rival suitor. Conflict is expressed in the following ways: extended debate between the hero and heroine over the sexual nature of their relationship; rivalry between parents and confidants for the allegiance of the protagonists; opposition between an old and a new morality.

The interest of each particular work lies, of course, in the way in which the above functions are combined or split among characters, and in their psychological, ideological, and esthetic realization. Usually the outcome is tragic; Fanny Burney's *Evelina*, however, works essentially within this model in order to reverse its usual denouement, since the heroine's close ties (epistolary and psychological) with her adoptive father give her the strength she needs to resist the dangers of London society and persist in the virtuous path toward marriage with a noble suitor. This form is a quintessential eighteenth-century one, influenced by classical

## The Novel of Dangerous Connections

| | Liaisons | Nouvelle Héloïse | Delphine | Clarissa |
|---|---|---|---|---|
| Absent or weak parent or husband | Mme de Volanges M. de Tourvel | Julie's parents | Delphine's dead parents | Clarissa's "invisible" parents |
| Parent surrogate | Rosemonde Valmont Merteuil | Wolmar | Lebensei Louise Mme de Vernon | Mrs. Sinclair Lovelace |
| Heroine | Tourvel Cécile | Julie | Delphine | Clarissa |
| Heroine's confidant | Volanges and Rosemonde Sophie and Merteuil | Claire | Louise Mme d'Artenas Mme de Lebensei | Anna |
| Hero | Danceny | Saint-Preux | Léonce | Lovelace |
| Hero's confidant | Valmont | Edouard | Barton | Belford |
| Rival suitor | Gercourt | Wolmar | Mathilde Valorbe | Solmes |

theater and particularly adapted for the common eighteenth-century thematic opposition of libertinism to virtue. Yet many elements or variants of this subgenre can be found in Natalia Ginzburg's *No Way* (*Caro Michele* [1973]) and Bob Randall's *The Fan* (1977), two of the most recent revivals of the letter form. Essentially this type of novel portrays a network of destructive or ineffectual familial, erotic, and confidential connections through epistolary liaisons.

The epistolary genre is a highly conventional and imitative one, which delights in articulating its own imitativeness—hence titles like *La Nouvelle Héloïse, Le Nouvel Abélard, Shamela*. Recently, we have even witnessed the publication, three centuries after Guilleragues's landmark work, of the *New Portuguese Letters*. No historian of the genre can fail to note the importance of key texts like Guilleragues's *Lettres portugaises*, Montesquieu's *Lettres persanes*, or Goethe's *Werther*, which spawned countless imitations and variations. More often than not, imitators seized upon both the inner and the outer form, the narrative techniques as well as the content: countless love monologues were written in the wake of the Portuguese nun, and diarylike letters were produced by post-Wertherian suicidals. The six basic types identified by Jost in his typology of epistolary novels can be seen to have at their center one influential work that showed what could be done with the letter form and generated numerous imitations. This is obvious for Jost's "type portugais," "type Abélard," and "type Werther"; many of the works in the "type Clinker" category can be shown to have Montesquieu's work as historical model.[8]

As we move further away from the period dominated by the letter form we find fewer instances of works that fit into a subgenre. The principle of imitativeness—rarer in the modern period when the letter form is not a "popular" genre—can nonetheless be found: e.g., Upton Sinclair's *Another Pamela; or, Virtue Still Rewarded*. Certain modern works, moreover, which present no surface similarities to earlier epistolary literature, reveal underlying structures that suggest that the form itself is exerting some thematic pressure: Herzog's epistolary trauma is strikingly similar to that of Saint-Preux, Tourvel, and Clarissa. The frequent recurrence of both structural and semantic similarities is obviously both historically and formally conditioned, just as human behavior is to some extent both socially and genetically determined.

Literary genres and subgenres develop the greatest cohesion and complexity when they evolve within a limited sociohistorical context. Courtly lyrics, French classical comedy, American westerns—all developed their particular conventions within a fairly short time period and a specific cultural milieu. The epistolary novel, which flourished in the second half of the eighteenth century, developed recognizable conventions and a thematic cohesiveness that its predecessor, the memoir novel, did not have. Further historical, narratological, and semiotic work is necessary before we could offer more than partial explanations for this cohesiveness. But the simple conclusion should stand: in contrast to the autobiographical or memoir novel, which is definable essentially in terms of a narrative technique,[9] letter fiction is describable as a genre and invites exploration as such.

TOWARD A THEORY OF EPISTOLARY NARRATIVE

It should be evident from the preceding section that all studies of the epistolary genre, whatever their approach, depend most fundamentally on some concept—intuitive or systematic— of the genre's structural constituents. We cannot begin to study the life of the letter form in art (its origins, its decline) without some understanding of what the letter's "forms" are. Thematic emphases in letter fiction, we have observed, tend to grow out of, rather than to dictate, the choice of the form. The most convincing pragmatic and expressive approaches are those that find some basis for authorial attitude or reader response in concrete textual phenomena, such as the *mise-en-abyme* of the writer-reader relationship within the form itself. In short, it is the structural or syntactic approach that is logically prior to all other approaches. In this final section we shall sketch the directions that a structural description of the letter novel might take and the problems we are likely to encounter in undertaking such a description.

The general model below should help clarify the parameters that have to be taken into account. The horizontal line represents (albeit *not* chronologically) the creation and reception of an epistolary narrative; the concentric circles represent degrees of

removal from the action of the novel. We thereby have distinguished three broad diegetic levels.[10] (1) Clearly within the frame
of the world created by the narrative (the diegesis) are the
correspondents (writer and addressee). (2) Clearly outside the
frame of the diegesis, on the other hand, are the epistolary
novelist and his reader. (3) Between this clearly diegetic and
extradiegetic territory lies the domain of the intermediary figures:
the editor (who by selection and annotation participates in the
creation of the text) and the publisher (intermediary in the
transmission of the text).

Already this model encourages some historical distinctions and
speculations. As we observed in chapter 3, epistolary novels
posing as real-life products in the eighteenth century set up the
intermediary editorial frames only to blur the distinction between
the fictional world of the correspondents and the real historical
worlds of the novelist-reader, by making the expansion of
readership part of the diegesis, just as the creation of the Super
Reader figure makes exegesis part of the diegesis. The critical
climate of the time, which tended to define verisimilitude as

authenticity, fostered this incorporation of the outer circles of our model into the inner circle. In fact, our model might encourage us to relate this "authentication" of the action of a novel to the phenomenon of "presentification," which we studied in chapter 4, whereby the writer tries to create the illusion that both he and his addressee are immediately present to each other and to the action. In both cases we might speak of a vortex action that absorbs writers and readers into the narrative center; in both cases the action of the novel is authenticated by (pseudo)eradication of spatiotemporal distance between the narrated action and the writer, between the writer and the addressee, and ultimately between these two and the reader of the novel, who is encouraged to believe that only the time required for publication separates his world from that of the novel. Such tendencies suggest an eighteenth-century reading public whose dominant esthetic is contemporaneity; one might speculate on the dialectical relation-ship between the epistolary novel so popular in the latter half of the eighteenth century and the historical novel focusing on more distant events that ushered in a new kind of narrative in the nineteenth century.

Such tendencies typify also a public so interested in the private life of the ordinary contemporary individual that the movement from the fictional to the real world can be disguised as the movement from private to public reading, as the readdressing of private correspondences. The editor-publisher figure, by having one foot planted in the world of the correspondents and one in the world of the reader, seemingly guarantees the authenticity as well as the original privacy of the transmitted text. We might ask whether there is a comparable figure or diegetic domain in letter works published prior to or after the eighteenth century. The twentieth century has favored mixed forms that combine dia-logue, letter, and straight narrative sequences (e.g., *Mitsou, Herzog,* Natalia Ginzburg's recently published best-seller *Caro Michele*). It would be worth investigating narratorial presenta-tion of letters in these works as well as the narrator's relation to the outside reader to compare the esthetic ideals of the century that was dominated by the letter form with earlier and later periods.

Having scanned the basic diegetic levels of an epistolary

narrative, let us return to the inner circle that circumscribes the
world of the correspondents. In the more elaborate diagram
below I have added vertical dimensions that will help us visualize
the basic narrative options available to the epistolary novelist. In
the lower semicircle we would place all letter novels that develop a
single action (e.g., a segment of the life of a single protagonist, a
seduction, a voyage). In the upper semicircle we would locate all
works developing multiple plots. Under and above each category
of correspondent, moreover, we have indicated three numerical
options. We thereby describe three fundamental choices that the
epistolary novelist makes; in constructing his narrative he

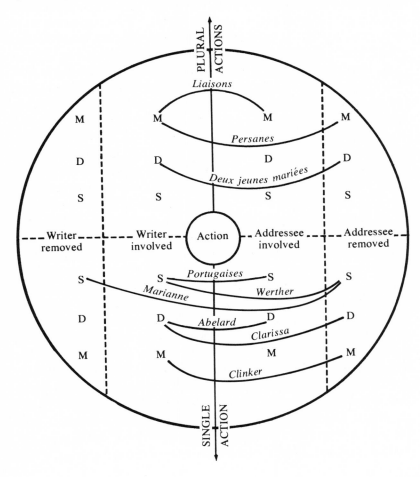

chooses either to limit himself to one basic plot or to interweave more than one; and he chooses to have that story told by single (S), dual (D), or multiple (M) writers to one (S), two (D), or more (M) addressees.

What we have now (besides a cluttered diagram) is a typology of epistolary narrative. This typology owes a great deal to François Jost's classification of epistolary narratives in his article "Le Roman épistolaire et la technique narrative au XVIIIe siècle" (summarized in the Introduction). Jost distinguishes only six types by essentially two criteria: number of correspondents and method of narration ("kinetic" or "static," according to whether the action proceeds through letters to protagonists or whether letters merely report events to confidants).[11] In my own diagram I have retained Jost's distinctions and examples but have systematized them, so that we can visualize not only those possibilities that have been actualized by well-known works but all theoretical possibilities. Some of these may never have been actualized, and for interesting reasons. We note, for example, that the "type Marianne" exists but there seem to be no novels composed by two or more correspondents removed from the action. This is largely because *La Vie de Marianne* and *La Religieuse*, like John Cleland's *Memoirs of Fanny Hill* (1745), grafted epistolary traits upon the memoir model, in which a single narrator recounts his life. Yet nothing precludes our imagining a novel that would interweave autobiographical letters or combine several correspondents' memoirs of the same past incident.[12]

In addition, I have added another parameter to those that Jost's classification suggests or implies—that of the number of actions narrated (vertical axis). This enables us to distinguish, for example, between two novels that Jost places in the same category: *Lettres persanes* and *Humphry Clinker*. Although these two novels are similar in their travelogue composition (some of these similarities are discussed elsewhere in this study), the interweaving of letters that develop the harem plot and those devoted to a critique of French society is crucial to Montesquieu's novel. Smollett presents nothing comparable. On the other hand Smollett, who offers us not two but five travelers, develops fully the possibilities for multiple perspective, which Montesquieu had hardly explored. Usbek is involved in two different worlds, which fragment his mind; Smollett's characters are involved in one and the same world, of which they give us fragmented views.

If I insist on the importance of the number of actions it is not merely to distinguish between novels. Jost implies that the privilege of narrating simultaneous actions is reserved for the "type Laclos," the kinetic polylogue.[13] Yet we have just seen a static polylogue (i.e., *Lettres persanes*) that develops two actions. In fact, the epistolary novel has time and again experimented with the narration of multiple and simultaneous actions, and not only in multicorrespondent or kinetic novels. Balzac's *Lettres de deux jeunes mariées* consists of the letters of two women who lead separate lives and whose reciprocal confidences constantly juxtapose two contrastive life-styles in diptych fashion. Let us contrast this novel with *Clarissa*, where two writers (Lovelace and Clarissa) likewise carry most of the narrative: *Clarissa* narrates a single action but offers us a female and a male perspective on it. In general, epistolary narratives of multiple actions (e.g., those above our horizontal axis) specialize in interweaving related actions, whereas those that narrate a single action emphasize the subject's perspective on events.

At the center of our model, and undiscussed thus far, is the small circle marked "action." How do we describe an epistolary "action," i.e., the narrative content of an epistolary work? If we take our lead from structuralist narratology, we will be concerned to give an accurate account of that "story" (*histoire*) that is separable from its linguistic medium. Accepting the principle that there are a limited number of elements that generate stories and that can be expressed or translated into any medium, we would proceed to a structural analysis of the plots of a representative sampling of letter novels. This analysis would produce a morphology or a grammar describing the constituent elements of an epistolary narrative and the rules for their combination. Such an undertaking is obviously beyond the scope of this chapter. We can, however, speculate here on the possible conclusions of such a morphological study. Assuming that it will have followed the same methods of analysis as other narratologists have used, either we will find that our grammar of epistolary narrative looks just like other morphologies of nonepistolary corpuses or we will find that letter narrative favors certain plots and functional combinations above others. My own work suggests that the conclusion would depend on what we take as our corpus—all works in letter form (including those that are closer to diary or memoirs) or those that concentrate traits of epistolarity—i.e., exhibit the properties of the letter as we have elaborated them. The novelist who uses the letter as a diary or memoir to report external events as they happen or happened independently of the letter writing can choose any type of "story." The novelist who chooses to make the letter an integral part of the action, on the other hand, will have a more limited repertory; seduction, conspiracy, the formation and dissolution of relationships will be his central narrative material.

Before any analysis of narrative content could be undertaken, however, we would have to specify what constitutes a narrative event. What do we do with letter novels that do not tell "stories" in the way that Boccaccian novellas or Russian folktales do? Whereas some letter writers concentrate on telling what happened, others may spend most of their time emoting, justifying, describing the world around them, confessing, persuading—and, above all, writing. One could easily argue that structural analysis of any novel poses the same problem, since all novels are complex forms, having lyrical, descriptive, philosophical, and dialogue passages that do not preclude our analyzing them as narrative. Yet the letter novel presents a special case. As a fragmented, dialogical form, in the hands of novelists who would rather explore the letter's formal potential than use it to tell a story, epistolary literature begins to look like modern experimental works where nothing "happens" except that characters spend a great deal of time talking or writing and authors invest a great deal of energy playing with a medium's formal elements. If we limit our analysis of narrative content to the kind of anecdotal action that is described in most morphologies, we will account for very little of the text.[14] Shall we conclude that most epistolary literature, and indeed much modern literature, is not "narrative"? Or do we rethink our definition of a narrative event?

If epistolary narrative problematizes the definition of the narrative events constituting its "action," it is for a simple reason: the storytelling impulse behind letter narrative is constantly constrained and modified by the letter's discursive nature. The letter cannot be *histoire* without passing through *discours*.[15] Its narrativity (defined as stories we can abstract from a narrative medium) is profoundly affected, if not limited, by its medium. The implications of discourse for narrative are numerous in letter fiction. Let us summarize the most important ones here:

1. Letter narrative proceeds through a *doubly oblique narration*. Narrated events are always reported *by* someone *to* someone. As Merteuil's different accounts of the Prévan episode illustrate, events are colored by addressee as well as by writer; in the context of epistolary discourse they are refracted through not one prism but two.

2. Letter narrative is *elliptical narration*. Paradoxically, many of its narrative events may be nonnarrated events of which we see only the repercussions. In the letters of Crébillon's marquise to her seducer, we never get an account of the actual scene of her submission, which is a climactic event; we must surmise it from a change in tone in her letters to her lover. In the epistolary situation where an addressee may already know of events, or a writer may be reluctant to report them, dialogue may simply reflect rather than report external events.

3. Thus far we have dealt with the implications of discourse for narrative insofar as the reporting of external events is concerned. Clearly, however, not all of letter fiction's narrat*ive* events are narrat*ed* events. In the epistolary work, acts of communication (confession, silence, persuasion, and so on) constitute important events; they are enacted rather than reported in discourse. Analytic models drawn from drama theory, speech act, or other types of communication theory may come closer than narrative models to describing what is "happening" in an epistolary work.[16]

We should now be in a better position to describe how a letter narrative is put together. Any model we construct must take into account the epistolary novel's discursive as well as its narrative dimensions. In the following basic model we shall distinguish between three levels or registers of action in epistolary narrative: (1) the register of reported events ($e_1, e_2, e_3, \ldots$); (2) the register of the writer reporting them, since writing itself is a primary activity in epistolary novels ($w_1$ = writer one, $w_2$ = writer two, and so forth); and (3) the register of the reader to whom they are reported, since reading is likewise an action ($r_1$ = first reader, and so on).[17]

Let us begin by taking examples of letter narrative where there is minimal interference from discourse:

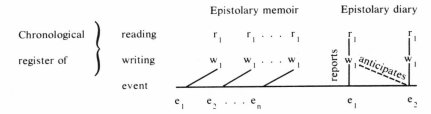

In an epistolary memoir like *La Vie de Marianne*, all events reported ($e_1, e_2, \ldots e_n$) precede the first moment of writing and occupy the bulk of the writing; dialogue between the single writer and addressee is minimal, detracting rarely from the continuum of reported events.[18] In an epistolary diary like *Pamela* and *Werther* we begin to get more interference from the register of writing. Tomorrow's events are unknown today; the writer's expectations regarding events begin to alternate with his reporting of events, thereby giving discursive elements added weight in the text.

As soon as we have more than one writer or more than one reader, discourse begins to take over from and deform "story." In the diagram below we have taken an imaginary epistolary novel that chains together letters relating a story composed of events 1–5 ($e_1$–$e_5$). Each segment of the diagram illustrates a common case of interference between discourse and story.

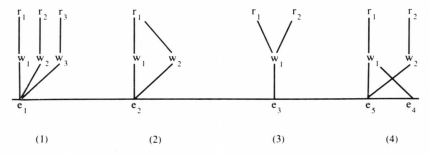

(1)                    (2)                    (3)                    (4)

1. In the first segment all of our writers are introduced in three consecutive letters. Each reports the same event to his respective confidant, offering different, perhaps contradictory perspectives. (*Humphry Clinker* makes extensive use of this technique.)

2. Now two writers report the same event to the same reader. When Merteuil receives two reports of Cécile's rape, one from Cécile and one from Valmont, she is in a privileged position as reader of both versions. Here, in contrast to the previously cited example from Smollett, it is the reader's rather than the writer's perspective that is highlighted; the narrative focus has been displaced from the register of events to the register of reading, and the reading event will generate consequent narrative events.

3. In this segment the same writer reports the same event differently to different readers (e.g., Merteuil writes two versions of the Prévan episode, one for Valmont and one for the general public).

4. A writer refrains from reporting an event ($e_4$) to a particular addressee or reports it out of sequence. (Clarissa undergoes an epistolary blackout after her rape and cannot report it until long afterward.)

The above diagram illustrates some of the implications of dialogue for narrative in cases where the story is constituted by reported events. In letters exchanged between lovers, or novels where the major vicissitudes are psychological and may result from acts of communication, our bottom line (the register of narra*ted* events) would have to be bracketed entirely, since all action would be transpiring at the level of writing and reading. *Lettres portugaises* comes closest to this kind of purely discursive narrative. Yet even in novels of intrigue the nature of the medium requires much of the action to be enacted in discourse rather than reported. Valmont, for example, does not report to Merteuil the machinations whereby he gains access to Tourvel's house in Paris; we as readers must surmise his plans through the letters we see from Valmont to Tourvel's priest.

The complexities of the interrelationship between *histoire* and *discours* are particularly visible in epistolary fiction, where *histoire* can be generated only through *discours*, and where the actions constituting *histoire* are not simply narrated but often enacted, and occasionally nonnarrated. To put it another way, the writer of epistolary fiction has a fundamental problem: the letter novelist (A) must make his letter writer (B) speak to an addressee (C) in order to communicate with a reader (D) who overhears; how does he reconcile the exigencies of story (communication between novelist and reader) with the exigencies of interpersonal discourse (communication between correspondents)?

The epistolary novel is a product of communicative impulses that are not entirely compatible. If a single impulse takes over

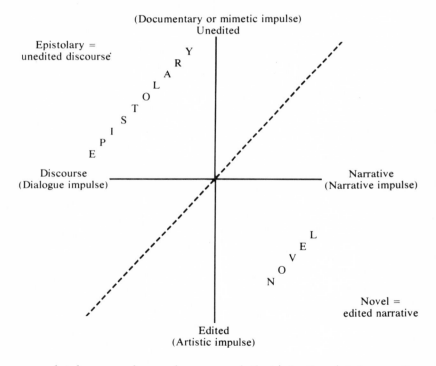

(Documentary or mimetic impulse)
Unedited

Epistolary =
unedited discourse

Y
R
A
L
O
T
S
I
P
E

Discourse
(Dialogue impulse)

Narrative
(Narrative impulse)

L
E
V
O
N

Novel =
edited narrative

Edited
(Artistic impulse)

completely, we no longer have a work that is both epistolary and a novel. The very qualities that guarantee the letter work's epistolarity in the mimetic sense (predominance of discursive elements and absence of an editor, which produce what Barthes would call the "effet de réel" and make the letters look like real letters) work against its narrativity, making the entire concept of an "epistolary fiction" as paradoxical as that of the nonfiction novel. Yet a writer like Laclos maximizes all four impulses in what is the most epistolary of all novels, simultaneously affirming and challenging the letter's authenticity and narrativity. The as-yet-unwritten history of epistolary literature will perhaps give a clearer account of the interplay between these four impulses in various eras and areas.

The epistolary novel was born in an age when novelists like Diderot and Sterne had moved beyond storytelling to playful reflection upon history, fiction, and the very means by which fictional or historical events are recounted. There is ample evidence that the epistolary form is experiencing a renaissance in the postmodernist era when so much fiction is questioning the representational status of writing, when discursive self-consciousness is overtly challenging the novel's traditional narrativity.[19] The discovery of the letter as a narrative medium, like the discovery of the movie camera in our era, had three principal appeals: documentary, narrative, and formal. The esthetic ideals behind letter works have much in common with those of *cinéma-vérité*, classical Hollywood narrative, and Eisensteinian formalism, according to the way the epistolary author composes and edits his "shots" (letters). (1) *Lettres-vérité*: the editor apologizes for the lack of style in the letters and emphasizes the aleatory construction of the work.[20] (2) Classical narrative: the editing is invisible, and the disjuncture inherent to the form is disguised by narrative continuity whenever we pass from letter to letter following a plot line without noticing a switch in perspective. (3) Formalist esthetic: the artistic hand of the editor is visible in the style and structure of individual letters, in the architectural composition (montage) of the novel. The letter novel is one of the first genres constituted by discovery of a medium and exploration of its potential. In that, it resembles many of the experimental forms of the twentieth century that question the subordination of medium to message. It is yet another paradox of epistolarity that we should be able to characterize letter fiction as a relatively codified genre that is nonetheless experimental.

The visible, often contradictory impulses behind epistolary fiction can be generalized, with appropriate modification, to other narrative forms, if not to virtually all literature. Although epistolary literature seemingly constitutes a highly particular, historically limited literary subgenre (whose particularities, indeed, have been the emphasis of my study), there is a very real sense in which it metaphorically "represents" literature as a whole. By its very *mise-en-abyme* of the writer-reader relationship, the epistolary form models the complex dynamics involved in writing and reading; in its preoccupation with the myriad mediatory aspects involved in communication, in the way that it wrestles with the problem of making narrative out of discourse, in its attempts to resolve mimetic and artistic impulses, epistolary literature exposes the conflicting impulses that generate all literature.

In fact, what makes this form so intriguing to study (as the concentric diagram at the beginning of this section implies) is the way in which it explicitly articulates the problematics involved in the creation, transmission, and reception of literary texts. By the very structural conditions of the letter-writing situation (which involves absence from the addressee and the constitution of a "present" addressee, removal from events and yet also the constitution of events) epistolary literature intensifies awareness of the gaps and traps that are built into the narrative representation of intersubjective and temporal experience. My work is only a prolegomenon to a study that would investigate more deeply—historically and philosophically—Jacques Derrida's suggestion in *Envois* that "l'histoire de la philosophie, comme la littérature, tout en rejetant la lettre dans ses marges, tout en affectant de la considérer comme un genre secondaire, comptait avec elle, essentiellement" (p. 69). Epistolary fiction tends to flourish at those moments when novelists most openly reflect upon the relation between storytelling and intersubjective communication and begin to question the way in which writing reflects, betrays, or constitutes the relations between self, other, and experience. At those crisis moments the letter form foregrounds—in its very consciousness of itself as a form—questions that are basic to all literature. Perhaps the final paradox of epistolarity is that the very parameters that help us define the form as a specific instance of writing should afford us perspectives on the discipline of "letters" in its broadest sense.

> *la lettre, l'épître, qui n'est pas un genre mais tous les genres, la littérature même—Derrida, "Envois"*

1. Réal Ouellet, in "La Théorie du roman épistolaire en France au XVIIIe siècle," studies authorial conceptions of the form in the prefaces of some two hundred epistolary novels. His remarks are not conclusive. J. von Stackelberg, in a subsequent article, "Der Briefroman und seine Epoche," tries to distill from Ouellet's and his own research a relationship between sensibility and the epistolary form.

2. I have discussed these two styles in chapter 2 above and from a somewhat different perspective in my article "Addressed and Undressed Language in Laclos's *Liaisons dangereuses.*" In that essay I use Laclos's novel as an opportunity to look more closely at the conflictual relationship between the rhetorical impulse (what I call "addressed language") and the autobiographical impulse (what I call "undressed language") in epistolary writing. In this article I also take up the complementary and related issues of "redressing" (rewriting letters) and "readdressing" (circulation of letters) and the infinite layers of differential meaning that these possibilities imply.

3. Tzvetan Todorov, *Introduction à la littérature fantastique* (Paris: Seuil, 1970), p. 24, and Fredric Jameson, "Magical Narratives: Romance as Genre," *New Literary History* 7 (1975): 135–63. Some aspects of Todorov's book, one of the few structuralist studies of a specific genre, have subsequently been criticized. See, for example, David Richter's review article "Pandora's Box Revisited," *Critical Inquiry* 1 (1974): 473, and John Reichert's perceptive delineation of "The Limits of Genre Theory" in J. P. Strelka, ed., *Theories of Literary Genre*, pp. 66–74 of which are devoted to Todorov. Since most of these criticisms center on discrepancies between Todorov's theory and practice, they need not be taken up here, where I am concerned only with the implicit relationship between his and other genre theories. Todorov has more recently returned to a discussion of literary genres in *Les Genres du discours* (Paris: Seuil, 1978).

4. Jameson, pp. 137–38.

5. In fact, in English letter fiction we even find numerous novels whose principal correspondent writes as an observer primarily about the actions of a third party. *The Memoirs of Sir Charles Goodville and his Family* (1753), for instance, begins, "I have, at last, sat down, to fulfill the engagement I am under of giving you as distinct an account, as I am capable, of the remarkable transactions in the family of Sir Charles Goodville." F. G. Black, in his article "The Technique of Letter Fiction in English from 1740 to 1800," p. 304, makes the frequency of this type clear. It is rare in French fiction.

For a richly documented, subtle discussion of diary writing and its relation to fictional forms in eighteenth-century Germany, see James P. Pusack, "German Monologic Fiction in the Eighteenth Century" (Ph.D. diss., Indiana University, 1977).

6. Two exceptional studies have appeared recently, however. Bernard Bray describes "Transformation du roman épistolaire au XXe siècle en France" in a 1977 article that I shall cite in more detail later; and L. Versini's *Le Roman épistolaire* (1979) notably brings out the popularity of the form with exiles from the French Revolution and with nineteenth-century woman novelists. (The implications of this phenomenon are worth exploring.)

7. See, for example, R. B. Johnson, Jr., "Anatomy of a Literary Device: The Included Letter."

8. See F. C. Green, "Montesquieu the Novelist and Some Imitations of the *Lettres persanes*."

9. Indeed, Philip Stewart has admirably traced the French memoir novel's contributions to narrative technique in *Imitation and Illusion in the French Memoir-Novel, 1700–1750* (New Haven and London: Yale University Press, 1969).

10. I am using the terms *diegetic* and *diegesis*, as Gérard Genette and other narratologists (particularly those working with cinematic narrative) use them, to designate the fictional world of the primary narrative. This use differs from Plato's original conception of *diegesis*: in the third book of the *Republic*, when Socrates opposes *diegesis* to *mimesis*, he is essentially contrasting authorial presentation to dramatic representation.

11. Jost's distinction of the "type Marianne" from the "type Werther" (both of which have a single, "static" correspondent), is, however, based implicitly on what I have chosen to establish as an independent third parameter—the narrator's distance from the events narrated.

12. Indeed, since drafting this Conclusion I have come across *Les Noces d'or* (1974), by Arlette and Robert Bréchon, an epistolary duologue in which husband and wife exchange recollections of their conjugal life. The novel itself is an interesting "marriage" of the autobiographical impulse toward construction of the personal self through an account of the past viewed as a totality, and the epistolary impulse toward exchange, in which the *other* constantly interferes. The male correspondent articulates the complexity of this particular merger of the memoir and letter forms, where it is not just a question of one *I* or even two *I*'s confronting relationships with the past *I* and present *you*, but of a *we* confronting its past and present composition. With an awareness of the implications of personal pronouns that is so typical of recent literature, the husband writes: "le *nous* de ce livre n'est pas la somme d'un *je* et d'un *tu*, mais un perpétuel compromis, le résultat d'une plus ou moins constante négociation" (p. 307). Of obvious interest, moreover, in this novel and other collaborative works (e.g., *New Portuguese Letters*, recently coauthored by the "three Marias") is the question of joint authorship and the relationship between those who sign the book and those who sign (or do not sign) the letters.

13. Jost, p. 416.

14. I am referring to work on large corpuses like Propp's on the folk tale, Souriau's on theater, and Todorov's on the *Decameron*. I do not mean to imply that structural analysts of narrative like Bremond and Todorov are unaware of the problems posed by complex forms. In fact, Todorov attempts two different (and not uninteresting) segmentations of *Les Liaisons* in *Littérature et signification* and concludes that these are unsatisfactory. Bremond's elaborate model for analysis in *Logique du récit* appears more appropriate for complex narrative, yet in fact most of Bremond's examples are drawn from anecdotal and episodic works.

15. I draw the opposition of *histoire* to *discours* from Benveniste's well-known essays on "L'Homme dans la langue" (section 5 of *Problèmes de linguistique générale*, 1:225–66). Benveniste's influential work has inspired many analyses and a great deal of discussion; moreover, since Benveniste's articles appeared G. Genette has used the two terms somewhat differently in his "Discours du récit" (*Figures III*).

16. Ronald Rosbottom is to my knowledge the only reader to have systematically applied a complex communication theory to analysis of an epistolary novel. See his "Dangerous Connections: A Communicational Approach to *Les Liaisons dangereuses*." Rosbottom uses as a critical model recent work in interactional psychotherapy (the writings of the Palo Alto group of communicational therapists) to analyze most sensitively various communicational circuits in Laclos's novel.

17. Elsewhere I have explored the implications of these three registers for time structures in epistolary narrative: "The 'Triple Register': Introduction to Temporal Complexity in the Letter-Novel."

18. That there is nonetheless more digressive dialogue with the addressee in a work like Marivaux's *Marianne* than in his *Paysan parvenu* is at least in part a function of the epistolary form of the former. Talbot Spivak ("Marivaux's *Le Paysan parvenu:* A Study of Thematic Structure and Narrative Voice" [Ph.D. dissertation, University of Iowa, 1976]) points out that Rousset's concept of the "double register" (in which the older narrator's voice remains distinct from the voice of the character whose life he is narrating) holds less validity for *Le Paysan* than for *Marianne*.

19. Bernard Bray, in "Transformation du roman épistolaire au XXe siècle en France," describes a number of recent epistolary novels, including the form's modern avatar, the "roman téléphonique," and moves toward this conclusion. Jacques Derrida suggests in *Envois* a slightly different hypothesis, more closely tied to his own meditations throughout *La Carte postale* on communication circuits, dissemination, and the letter's (language's) potential to "ne pas arriver à destination": "Dans l'histoire, c'est mon hypothèse, les fictions épistolaires se multiplient quand arrive une nouvelle crise de la destination" (p. 249). This speculation merits further exploration in careful historical terms.

20. Godard's film esthetic of "on doit tout mettre dans un film" is not unlike Montesquieu's epistolary esthetic: "Dans les romans ordinaires les digressions ne peuvent être permises que lorsqu'elles forment elles-mêmes un nouveau roman. . . . Mais dans la forme de lettres, où les acteurs ne sont pas choisis, et où les sujets qu'on traite ne sont dépendants d'aucun dessein ou d'aucun plan déjà formé, l'auteur s'est donné l'avantage de pouvoir joindre de la philosophie, de la politique et de la morale à un roman" ("Quelques réflexions sur *Les Lettres persanes*"). Montesquieu has already discovered Godard's formula "discours = cours discontinu": "Au cours d'un film—dans son discours, c'est-à-dire son discours discontinu—j'ai envie de tout faire, à propos du sport, de la politique, et même de l'épicerie. . . . On peut tout mettre dans un film. On doit tout mettre dans un film" (*Jean-Luc Godard par Jean-Luc Godard* [Paris: Belfond, 1968], pp. 392–93).

# SELECTED BIBLIOGRAPHY

## EPISTOLARY WORKS

I have listed only those works cited in my study. Whenever the date of original publication differs from the date of the edition used (not infrequently the case, since I have tried to use relatively available, reliable editions for quoting purposes), the date of the original publication is indicated in brackets.

Abelard, Pierre, and Heloise. "The Personal Letters between Abelard and Heloise: Introduction, Authenticity, and Text." Edited by J. T. Muckle. *Mediaeval Studies* 15 (1953): 47–94.

———. *The Letters of Abelard and Heloise.* Translated by Betty Radice. Middlesex, Eng.: Penguin, 1974.

Balzac, Honoré de. *Mémoires de deux jeunes mariées.* In *La Comédie humaine,* edited by Pierre Citron, 1:103–77. Paris: Seuil ("L'Intégrale"), 1965. [1841–42]

Barreno, Maria-Isabel; Horta, Maria-Teresa; and Velho da Costa, Maria-Fátima. *New Portuguese Letters.* Translated by Helen R. Lane. Garden City, N.Y.: Doubleday, 1975. [1972]

Behn, Aphra. *Love-Letters between a Noble-Man and His Sister.* In *The Novel in Letters,* edited by Natascha Würzbach. Coral Gables: University of Miami Press, 1969. [1694]

Bellow, Saul. *Herzog.* Greenwich, Conn.: Fawcett Crest, 1965. [1964]

Boursault, Edme. *Lettres à Babet.* Paris: Maison Quantin, 1886. [1669]

———. *Treize lettres amoureuses d'une dame à un cavalier.* In *Lettres nouvelles.* Paris: Veuve Brunet, 1699.

Bréchon, Arlette, and Bréchon, Robert. *Les Noces d'or.* Paris: Albin Michel, 1974.

Burney (later d'Arblay), Frances. *Evelina; or, The History of a Young Lady's Entrance into the World.* Edited by Edward A. Bloom. London: Oxford University Press, 1968. [1778]

Butor, Michel. *Illustrations III.* Paris: Gallimard, 1973.

Colette, Sidonie Gabrielle. *Mitsou, ou comment l'esprit vient aux filles*. Paris: Fayard (Flammarion), 1970. [1919]

Crébillon, fils, Claude-Prosper Jolyot de. *Lettres de la duchesse de \*\*\* au duc de \*\*\**. In *Collection complète des oeuvres de M. de Crébillon le fils*, vol. 7. London, 1772. [1768]

————. *Lettres de la marquise de M\*\*\* au comte de R \*\*\**. Edited by Ernest Sturm and Lucie Picard. Paris: Nizet, 1970. [1732]

Derrida, Jacques. *Envois*. In *La Carte postale de Socrate à Freud et au-delà*, pp. 5–273. Paris: Flammarion, 1980.

Diderot, Denis. *La Religieuse*. In *Oeuvres*, edited by André Billy, pp. 235–393. Paris: Gallimard ("Pléiade"), 1951. [Written 1760, publ. 1796]

Dorat, Claude-Joseph. *Les Malheurs de l'inconstance, ou lettres de la marquise de Syrcé et du comte de Mirbelle*. 2 vols. Amsterdam and Paris: Delalain, 1772.

Dostoyevsky, Fyodor. *Poor People*. In *Three Short Novels By Fyodor Dostoyevsky*, translated by Constance Garnett, pp. 141–273. New York: Laurel, 1960. [1846]

Elie de Beaumont, Anne-Louise Dumesnil-Molin. *Lettres du marquis de Roselle*. 2 vols. London and Paris: Louis Cellot, 1764.

Epinay, Louise de La Live d'. *Les Pseudo-mémoires de Mme d'Epinay: histoire de Mme de Montbrillant*. Edited by Georges Roth. 3 vols. Paris: Gallimard, 1951. [Probably 1756–70]

Fielding, Henry. *An Apology for the Life of Mrs. Shamela Andrews*. Berkeley and Los Angeles: University of California Press, 1953. [1741]

Fontenelle, Bernard le Bouyer de. *Lettres galantes de monsieur le chevalier d'Her \*\*\**. Leipzig: Jean Gothofroi Müller, 1764. [1683, 1687]

Foscolo, Ugo. *Ultime lettere di Jacopo Ortis*. Torino: Einaudi, 1963. [1802]

Gautier, Théophile. *Mademoiselle de Maupin*. Edited by Adolphe Boschot. Paris: Garnier, 1966. [1835]

Genlis, Stéphanie-Félicité de. *Adèle et Théodore, ou lettres sur l'éducation*. 3 vols. Paris: M. Lambert et F. J. Baudouin, 1782.

————. *Les Petits Emigrés, ou correspondance de quelques enfants: ouvrage fait pour servir à l'éducation de la jeunesse*. 2 vols. Paris: Onfroy, 1798.

Goethe, Johann Wolfgang von. *Die Leiden des jungen Werthers*. Munich: Deutscher Taschenbuch Verlag, 1962. [1774; final version, 1787]

Gourmont, Rémy de. *Le Songe d'une femme: roman familier*. Paris: Mercure de France, 1899.

Graffigny, Mme Françoise d'Issembourg d'Happancourt de. *Lettres d'une Péruvienne*. Paris: Duchesne, 1752. [1747]

Guilleragues, Gabriel-Joseph de Lavergne de. *Lettres portugaises*. Edited by Frédéric Deloffre and J. Rougeot. Paris: Garnier, 1962. [1669]

Huch, Ricarda. *Der letzte Sommer*. Edited by Dieter Cunz. New York: Norton, 1963. [1910]

James, Henry. "A Bundle of Letters" [1879]; "The Point of View" [1882]. In *The Complete Tales of Henry James*, edited by Leon Edel, 4:427–519. London: Rupert Hart-Davis, 1962.

Kafka, Franz. *Briefe an Milena.* In *Gesammelte Werke: Briefe*, vol. 7, edited by Willy Haas. Frankfurt: S. Fischer, 1952. [written 1920–23]

Laclos, Pierre-Ambroise-François Choderlos de. *Les Liaisons dangereuses.* Edited by Yves Le Hir. Paris: Garnier, 1961. [1782]

Marivaux, Pierre Carlet de Chamblain de. *La Vie de Marianne ou les aventures de Madame la Comtesse de \*\*\*.* Edited by Frédéric Deloffre. Paris: Garnier, 1963. [1728–41]

Montesquieu, Charles de Secondat, baron de la Brède et de. *Lettres persanes.* In *Oeuvres complètes*, edited by Roger Caillois, pp. 127–386. Paris: Gallimard ("Pléiade"), 1949. [1721]

Montherlant, Henri de. *Les Jeunes Filles.* 4 vols. Paris: Gallimard, 1936–39. Vol. 1, *Les Jeunes Filles* (1936). Vol. 2, *Pitié pour les femmes* (1936). Vol. 3, *Le Démon du bien* (1937). Vol. 4, *Les Lépreuses* (1939).

Nodier, Charles. "Adèle." In *Romans de Charles Nodier*, pp. 243–317. Paris: Charpentier, 1840. [1820]

Ovid (Publius Ovidius Naso). *Heroides and Amores.* With an English translation by Grant Showerman. London and New York: Macmillan (Loeb Classical Library), 1914. [First century B.C. or A.D.]

Randall, Bob. *The Fan.* New York: Random House, 1977.

Restif de la Bretonne, Nicolas-Edme. *La Malédiction paternelle; lettres sincères et véritables de N\*\*\* à ses parents, ses amis, et ses maîtresses; avec les réponses; recueillies et publiées par Timothée Joly, son exécuteur testamentaire.* 3 vols. Paris: Veuve Duchesne, 1780.

———. *Le Nouvel Abélard; ou lettres de deux amants qui ne se sont jamais vus.* 4 vols. Neuchâtel and Paris: Veuve Duchesne, 1778.

———.*Le Paysan et la paysanne pervertis.* In *L'Oeuvre de Restif de la Bretonne*, edited by Henri Bachelin, vol. 6. Paris: Editions du Trianon, 1931. [1787]

———. *La Paysanne pervertie, ou les dangers de la ville: histoire d'Ursule R\*\*\*, soeur d'Edmond, le paysan, mise au jour d'après les véritables lettres des personnages.* Edited by Béatrice Didier. Paris: Garnier-Flammarion, 1972. [1784]

———. *Le Paysan perverti, ou les dangers de la ville: histoire récente, mise au jour d'après les véritables lettres des personnages.* Edited by François Jost. 2 vols. Lausanne: L'Age d'Homme, 1977. [1776]

———. *Les Posthumes: lettres reçues après la mort du mari, par sa femme, qui le croit à Florence.* 4 vols. Paris: Duchêne, 1802. [Comp. 1786–96, publ. 1802]

Riccoboni, Marie-Jeanne Laboras de Mézières. *Lettres d'Adélaïde de Dammartin, comtesse de Sancerre, à M. le comte de Nancé, son ami.* Paris: Belin, 1786. [1766]

———. *Lettres d'Elisabeth-Sophie de Vallière à Louise-Hortence de Canteleu, son amie.* Paris: Humblot, 1775. [1771]

———. *Lettres de Milady Juliette Catesby à Milady Henriette Campley, son amie.* Paris: Belin, 1785. [1759]

———. *Lettres de Mistress Fanni Butlerd à Milord Charles Alfred, comte d'Erford.* Amsterdam and Paris: Belin, 1792. [1757]

Richardson, Samuel. *Clarissa; or, The History of a Young Lady.* 8 vols. Oxford: B. Blackwell (Shakespeare Head edition), 1930. [1747–48]

——. *Pamela; or, Virtue Rewarded.* New York: Norton Library, 1958. [1740–42]

Rousseau, Jean-Jacques. *La Nouvelle Héloïse.* In *Oeuvres complètes de J.-J. Rousseau,* edited by Henri Coulet and Bernard Guyon, vol. 2. Paris: Gallimard ("Pléiade"), 1961. [1761]

Sand, George. *Mademoiselle La Quintinie.* Paris: Michel Lévy frères, 1863.

Scott, Sir Walter. *Redgauntlet, a Tale of the Eighteenth Century.* Paris: Baudry's Foreign Library, 1832. [1824]

Sénac de Meilhan, Gabriel. *L'Emigré.* In *Romanciers du XVIIIe siècle,* edited by René Etiemble, 2:1541–1912. Paris: Gallimard ("Pléiade"), 1965. [1797]

Senancour, Etienne Pivert de. *Oberman.* Paris: Bibliothèque 10/18, 1965. [1804, 1833, 1840]

Sévigné, Marie de Rabutin-Chantal, marquise de. *Lettres.* 3 vols. Edited by Gérard-Gailly. Paris: Gallimard ("Pléiade"), 1953–57.

Shklovsky, Viktor B. *Zoo; or, Letters Not about Love.* Translated and edited by Richard Sheldon. Ithaca: Cornell University Press, 1971. [1923]

Sinclair, Upton. *Another Pamela; or, Virtue Still Rewarded.* New York: Viking Press, 1950.

Smollett, Tobias. *The Expedition of Humphry Clinker.* London: Oxford University Press, 1966. [1771]

Staël, Germaine de. *Delphine.* Paris: Garnier, 1875. [1802]

Verga, Giovanni. *Storia di una capinera.* Milano: Fratelli Treves, 1905. [1869]

Voltaire (François-Marie Arouet). "Les Lettres d'Amabed, traduites par l'abbé Tamponet." In *Romans et Contes,* edited by Henri Benac, pp. 424–68. Paris: Garnier, 1960. [1769]

Wilder, Thornton. *The Ides of March.* New York and London: Harper, 1948.

CRITICAL STUDIES

The following list, although selective, should constitute a working bibliography for the study of epistolary literature. Although there is too much overlap to permit a listing in separate categories, essentially this bibliography includes (1) studies devoted specifically to the letter novel or the letter form, (2) helpful studies of related forms, (3) books and articles that offer closely related readings of those individual works that I have focused on in my study, and (4) general works that offer particularly useful methodological or historical perspectives for reading epistolary literature.

Abbott, H. Porter. "Letters to the Self: The Cloistered Writer in Nonretrospective Fiction." *PMLA* 95 (1980): 23–41.

Altman, Janet Gurkin. "Addressed and Undressed Language in Laclos's *Liaisons dangereuses.*" In *Laclos: Critical Approaches to "Les Liaisons dangereuses,"* edited by Lloyd Free, pp. 223–57. Madrid: José Porrúa Turanzas (Series Studia Humanitatis), 1978.

——. "The 'Triple Register': Introduction to Temporal Complexity in the Letter-Novel." *L'Esprit créateur* 17 (1977): 302–10.

Arban, Dominique. *Les Années d'apprentissage de Fiodor Dostoievski*. Paris: Payot, 1968.

Bakhtine, Mikhail. *La Poétique de Dostoievski*. Translated by Isabelle Kolitcheff. Paris: Seuil, 1970.

Baude, Michel. "Une Structure insolite: les anniversaires dans le journal intime." In *Le Journal intime et ses formes littéraires*, edited by V. Del Litto, pp. 163–71. Geneva: Droz, 1978.

Benton, John F. "Fraud, Fiction, and Borrowing in the Correspondence of Abelard and Heloise." In *Pierre Abélard, Pierre le Vénérable: les courants philosophiques, littéraires et artistiques en Occident au milieu du XIIe siècle*, edited by René Louis, Jean Jolivet, and Jean Châtillon, pp. 469–511. Paris: CNRS, 1975.

Benveniste, Emile. *Problèmes de linguistique générale*. Paris: Gallimard, 1966.

Beugnot, Bernard. "Débats autour du genre épistolaire: réalité et écriture." *Revue d'histoire littéraire de la France* 74 (1974): 195–203.

Black, F. G. *The Epistolary Novel in the Late Eighteenth Century*. Eugene: University of Oregon Press, 1940.

———. "The Technique of Letter Fiction in English from 1740 to 1800." *Harvard Studies and Notes in Philology and Literature* 15 (1933): 291–312.

Blum, Carol O'Brien. "The Epistolary Novel of the Ancien Regime: Document and Dissemblance." Ph.D. dissertation, Columbia University, 1966.

Boyer, Henri. "Structuration d'un roman épistolaire: énonciation et fiction." *Revue des langues romanes* 80 (1972): 297–327.

Brady, Patrick. "Structural Affiliations of *La Nouvelle Héloïse*." *L'Esprit créateur* 9 (1969): 207–18.

Braudy, Leo. "Penetration and Impenetrability in *Clarissa*." In *New Approaches to Eighteenth-Century Literature: Selected Papers from the English Institute*, edited by Phillip Harth, pp. 177–206. New York: Columbia University Press, 1974.

Bray, Bernard. *L'Art de la lettre amoureuse: des manuels aux romans (1550–1770)*. The Hague and Paris: Mouton, 1967.

———. "Communication épistolaire et intersubjectivité dans *Les Illustres Françaises*." *Revue d'histoire littéraire de la France* 79 (1979): 994–1002.

———. "L'Epistolier et son public en France au XVIIe siècle." *Travaux de linguistique et de littérature* 11, no. 2 (1973): 7–17.

———. "Transformation du roman épistolaire au XXe siècle en France." *Cahiers d'histoire des littératures romanes* 1 (1977): 23–39.

Brooks, Peter. *The Novel of Worldliness*. Princeton: Princeton University Press, 1969.

Brown, Homer. "The Errant Letter and the Whispering Gallery." *Genre* 10 (1977): 573–99.

Bullen, John Samuel. *Time and Space in the Novels of Samuel Richardson*. Monograph Series 12, no. 2. Logan: Utah State University Press, 1965.

Butor, Michel. "L'Usage des pronoms personnels dans le roman." *Les Temps modernes* 16 (1961): 936–48.

*Cahiers de l'Association internationale des études françaises* 29 (1977): 131–241, 348–59. Papers and discussion from colloquium on "Le Roman par lettres."

Articles by B. Bray, B. Beugnot, J. Rougeot, F. Jost, L. Versini, R. Fortassier, and M. Delcroix.

Carr, J. L. "The Secret Chain of the *Lettres persanes.*" *Studies on Voltaire and the Eighteenth Century* 55 (1967): 333–44.

Carroll, John J., comp. *Samuel Richardson: A Collection of Critical Essays.* Englewood Cliffs, N.J.: Prentice-Hall, 1969.

Carroll, M. G. "Morality and Letters in *La Nouvelle Héloïse.*" *Forum for Modern Language Studies* 13 (1977): 359–67.

Cherpack, Clifton C. *An Essay on Crébillon fils.* Durham: Duke University Press, 1962.

―――. "A New Look at *Les Liaisons dangereuses.*" *Modern Language Notes* 74 (1959): 513–21.

―――. "Space, Time, and Memory in *La Nouvelle Héloïse.*" *L'Esprit créateur* 3 (1963): 167–73.

Conroy, Peter V. *Crébillon fils: Techniques of the Novel. Studies on Voltaire and the Eighteenth Century* 99 (1972).

Coulet, Henri. *Le Roman jusqu'à la Révolution.* New York: McGraw-Hill and Armand Colin, 1967.

Cowler, Rosemary, comp. *Twentieth-Century Interpretations of "Pamela": A Collection of Critical Essays.* Englewood Cliffs, N.J.: Prentice-Hall, 1969.

Crosby, Emily A. *Une Romancière oubliée: Mme Riccoboni, sa vie, ses ouvrages, sa place dans la littérature anglaise et française du XVIIIe siècle.* Paris: F. Rieder, 1924.

Daniel, Georges. *Fatalité du secret et fatalité du bavardage au XVIIIe siècle: la marquise de Merteuil, Jean-François Rameau.* Paris: Nizet, 1966.

Darnton, Robert. "Reading, Writing, and Publishing in Eighteenth-Century France: A Case Study in the Sociology of Literature." *Daedalus* 100 (Winter 1971): 214–56.

Day, R. A. *Told in Letters: Epistolary Fiction before Richardson.* Ann Arbor: University of Michigan Press, 1966.

Deloffre, Frédéric. "Le Problème de l'illusion romanesque et le renouvellement des techniques narratives de 1700 à 1715." In *La Littérature narrative d'imagination*, pp. 115–29. Colloque de Strasbourg, 1959. Paris: Presses Universitaires de France, 1961.

Derrida, Jacques. *De la grammatologie.* Paris: Minuit, 1967.

Dottin, Paul. "Samuel Richardson et le roman épistolaire." *Revue anglo-américaine* 13 (1935–36): 481–99.

Duchêne, Roger. *Réalité vécue et art épistolaire.* Vol. 1, *Madame de Sévigné et la lettre d'amour.* Paris: Bordas, 1970.

―――. "Réalité vécue et art épistolaire: le statut particulier de la lettre." *Revue d'histoire littéraire de la France* 71 (1971): 177–94.

Dussinger, John A. *The Discourse of the Mind in Eighteenth-Century Fiction.* The Hague: Mouton, 1974.

Eigeldinger, Marc. *J. J. Rousseau et la réalité de l'imaginaire.* Neuchâtel: A la Baconnière, 1962.

Ellrich, Robert J. "The Rhetoric of *La Religieuse* and Eighteenth-Century Forensic Rhetoric." *Diderot Studies* 3 (1961): 129–54.

————. *Rousseau and His Reader: The Rhetorical Situation of the Major Works.* Chapel Hill: University of North Carolina Press, 1969.

*L'Esprit créateur* 27 (1977), no. 4. Issue devoted to "Epistolary Literature of the Eighteenth Century." Articles by Ronald Rosbottom, Janet Altman, Marsha Reisler, Edward Knox, Timothy Scanlan, Manfred Kusch, and Louise Smith.

Fellows, Otis. "Naissance et mort du roman épistolaire français." *Dix-Huitième Siècle* 4:17–38. Paris: Garnier, 1972.

Gassman, Byron. "The Economy of Humphry Clinker." In *Tobias Smollett: Bicentennial Essays Presented to Lewis M. Knapp,* edited by G. S. Rousseau and P. G. Boucé, pp. 155–73. New York: Oxford University Press, 1971.

Gauglhofer, Wolfgang. "Geschichte und Strukturprobleme des europäischen Briefromans im besonderen Hinblick auf die romanischen Literaturen." Dissertation, University of Innsbruck, 1968.

Genette, Gérard. *Discours du récit: essai de méthode.* In *Figures III,* pp. 65–282. Paris: Seuil, 1972.

Ghent, Dorothy van. *The English Novel: Form and Function.* New York: Harper, 1961.

Gilson, Etienne. "La Méthode de Monsieur de Wolmar." In *Les Idées et les lettres,* pp. 275–98. Paris: J. Vrin, 1932.

Girard, René. *Mensonge romantique et vérité romanesque.* Paris: Grasset, 1961.

Giraud, Yves. *Bibliographie du roman épistolaire en France des origines à 1842.* Fribourg, Switz.: Editions universitaires, 1977.

Green, Frederick Charles. "Montesquieu the Novelist and Some Imitations of the *Lettres persanes.*" *Modern Language Review* 20 (1925): 32–42.

————. "Some Observations on Technique and Form in the French Seventeenth- and Eighteenth-Century Novel." In *Stil- und Formprobleme in der Literatur,* edited by P. Böckmann, pp. 208–15. Heidelberg: Carl Winter, 1959.

Grosclaude, Pierre. "Rôle et caractère de l'analyse intérieure chez Rousseau." In *J.-J. Rousseau et son oeuvre,* pp. 317–26. Commémoration et Colloque de Paris. Paris: Klincksieck, 1964.

Guillén, Claudio. *Literature as System.* Princeton: Princeton University Press, 1971.

Hernadi, Paul. *Beyond Genre.* Ithaca, N.Y.: Cornell University Press, 1972.

Hopp, Lajos. "Le Genre épistolaire hongrois." *Zagadnienia Rodzajów Literackich* 14 (1972): 51–72.

Hughes, Helen Sard. "English Epistolary Fiction before *Pamela.*" In *The Manly Anniversary Studies in Language and Literature.* Chicago: University of Chicago Press, 1923.

Ince, Walter. "L'Unité du double registre chez Marivaux." In *Les Chemins actuels de la critique,* edited by G. Poulet, pp. 71–85. Paris: 10/18, 1968.

Iser, Wolfgang. *The Implied Reader: Patterns of Communication in Prose Fiction from Bunyan to Beckett.* Baltimore: Johns Hopkins University Press, 1974. Originally published as *Der implizite Leser: Kommunikationsformen des Romans von Bunyan bis Beckett.* Munich: Wilhelm Fink, 1972.

————. "Wirklichkeit und Form in Smolletts *Humphry Clinker.*" In *Europäische Aufklärung,* edited by H. Friedrich and F. Schalk, pp. 87–115. Munich: Wilhelm Fink, 1967.

Jacobson, Howard. *Ovid's "Heroides."* Princeton: Princeton University Press, 1974.

Johnson, Roger Barton, Jr. "Anatomy of a Literary Device: The Included Letter." Ph.D. dissertation, University of Illinois, 1968.

Jost, François. "Le Roman épistolaire et la technique narrative au XVIIIe siècle." *Comparative Literature Studies* 3 (1966): 397–427. Amplified and reprinted in his *Essais de littérature comparée* as "L'Evolution d'un genre: le roman épistolaire dans les lettres occidentales," 2:89–179, 380–402. Fribourg, Switz.: Editions universitaires, 1968.

Kany, Charles E. *The Beginnings of the Epistolary Novel in France, Italy, and Spain*, pp. 1–158. University of California Publications in Modern Philology, vol. 21, no. 1. Berkeley: University of California Press, 1937.

Kearney, Anthony. "*Clarissa* and the Epistolary Form." *Essays in Criticism* 16 (1966): 44–56.

Kermode, John Frank. *The Sense of an Ending: Studies in the Theory of Fiction.* New York: Oxford University Press, 1967.

Kimpel, Dieter. "Entstehung und Formen des Briefromans in Deutschland: Interpretationen zur Geschichte einer epischen Gattung des 18. Jhs. und zur Entstehung des modernen deutschen Romans." Dissertation, University of Vienna, 1961.

Kristéva, Julia; Milner, Jean-Claude; and Ruwet, Nicolas, eds. *Langue, discours, société: pour Emile Benveniste.* Paris: Seuil, 1975.

Laufer, Roger. *Style rococo, style des "Lumières."* Paris: Corti, 1963.

Lecercle, Jean-Louis. *Rousseau et l'art du roman.* Paris: Armand Colin, 1969.

Lee, Vera G. "Decoding Letter 50 in *Les Liaisons dangereuses.*" *Romance Notes* 10 (1968): 305–10.

Lejeune, Philippe. *L'Autobiographie en France.* Paris: Armand Colin, 1971.

———. *Je est un autre: l'autobiographie, de la littérature aux médias.* Paris: Seuil, 1980.

———. *Le Pacte autobiographique.* Paris: Seuil, 1975.

Leopold, Keith. "Ricarda Huch's *Der letzte Sommer:* An Example of Epistolary Fiction in the Twentieth Century." University of Queensland Papers, Faculty of Arts, vol. 1, no. 5 (1962), pp. 19–30.

Lizé, Emile. "*La Religieuse*, un roman épistolaire?" *Studies on Voltaire and the Eighteenth Century* 98 (1972): 143–63.

Lotringer, Sylvère. "Vice de forme." *Critique* 286 (1971): 195–209.

Macchia, Giovanni. "Il sistema di Laclos." In *Il paradiso della ragione*, pp. 216–29. Bari: Laterza, 1960.

Marks, Elaine. *Colette.* New Brunswick, N.J.: Rutgers University Press, 1960.

Martin, Angus; Mylne, Vivienne G.; and Frautschi, Richard. *Bibliographie du genre romanesque français 1751–1800.* London: Mansell, 1977.

May, Georges. *Diderot et "La Religieuse."* New Haven: Yale University Press; Paris: Presses Universitaires de France, 1954.

———. *Le Dilemme du roman au XVIIIe siècle: étude sur les rapports du roman et de la critique (1715–1761).* New Haven: Yale University Press; Paris: Presses Universitaires de France, 1963.

_____. "La Littérature épistolaire date-t-elle du dix-huitième siècle?" *Studies on Voltaire and the Eighteenth Century* 56 (1967): 823–44.

McKillop, A. D. "Epistolary Technique in Richardson's Novels." *Rice Institute Pamphlet* 38 (1951): 36–54.

Mercier, Roger. "Le Roman dans les *Lettres persanes*: structure et signification." *Revue des sciences humaines*, n.s. 108 (1962): 345–56.

Monfrin, Jacques. "Le Problème de l'authenticité de la correspondance d'Abélard et d'Héloïse." In *Pierre Abélard, Pierre le Vénérable: les courants philosophiques, littéraires et artistiques en Occident au milieu du XIIe siècle*, edited by René Louis, Jean Jolivet, and Jean Châtillon, pp. 409–24. Paris: CNRS, 1975.

Mylne, Vivienne. *The Eighteenth-Century French Novel: Techniques of Illusion*. New York: Barnes & Noble, 1965.

O'Reilly, Robert F. "The Structure and Meaning of the *Lettres persanes*." *Studies on Voltaire and the Eighteenth Century* 57 (1969): 91–131.

_____. "Time and Consciousness in the *Lettres portugaises*." *Romance Notes* 11 (1970): 586–90.

Ouellet, Réal. "Deux Théories romanesques au 18e siècle: le roman bourgeois et le roman épistolaire." *Etudes littéraires* 1 (1968): 233–50.

_____. "La Théorie du roman épistolaire en France au XVIIIe siècle." *Studies on Voltaire and the Eighteenth Century* 89 (1972): 1209–27.

Pelous, J. M. "A Propos des *Lettres portugaises*: comment interpréter l'apostrophe initiale 'Considère, mon amour. . . '?" *Revue d'histoire littéraire de la France* 72 (1972): 202–8.

Picard, Hans Rudolf. "Die Illusion der Wirklichkeit im Briefroman des 18. Jahrhunderts." Dissertation, University of Heidelberg, 1971.

Pizzorusso, Arnaldo. "Boursault et le roman par lettres." *Revue d'histoire littéraire de la France* 69 (1969): 525–39.

_____. "La concezione dell'arte narrativa nella seconda metà del seicento francese." *Studi mediolatini e volgari* 3 (1955): 125–34.

Porter, Charles. *Restif's Novels*. New Haven: Yale University Press, 1967.

Poulet, Georges. "Chamfort et Laclos." In *Etudes sur le temps humain*. Vol. 2, *La Distance intérieure*, pp. 56–80. Paris: Plon, 1952.

Preston, John. "*Les Liaisons dangereuses*: An Epistolary Narrative and Moral Discovery." *French Studies* 24 (1970): 23–36.

Prince, Gerald. "The Diary Novel: Notes for the Definition of a Sub-genre." *Neophilologus* 59 (1975): 477–81.

_____. "Introduction à l'étude du narrataire." *Poétique* 14 (1973): 178–96.

Raymond, Agnès G. "Encore quelques réflexions sur la 'chaîne secrète' des *Lettres persanes*." *Studies on Voltaire and the Eighteenth Century* 89 (1972): 1337–47.

*Revue d'histoire littéraire de la France* 78 (1978), no. 6. Issue devoted to "La Lettre au XVIIe siècle." Articles by Beugnot, Gérard, Duchêne, and Nies are of interest.

Richter, David H. *Fable's End: Completeness and Closure in Rhetorical Fiction*. Chicago: University of Chicago Press, 1974.

Roelens, Maurice. "Le Texte et ses conditions d'existence: l'exemple des *Liaisons dangereuses.*" *Littérature* 1 (1971): 73–81.

Romberg, Bertil. *Studies in the Narrative Technique of the First-Person Novel.* Translated by M. Taylor and H. Borland. Stockholm: Lund, 1962.

Rosbottom, Ronald. *Choderlos de Laclos.* Boston: Twayne, 1978.

————. "Dangerous Connections: A Communicational Approach to *Les Liaisons dangereuses.*" In *Laclos: Critical Approaches to "Les Liaisons dangereuses,"* edited by Lloyd R. Free, pp. 183–221. Madrid: José Porrúa Turanzas (Series Studia Humanitatis), 1978.

————. *Marivaux's Novels: Theme and Function in Early Eighteenth-Century Narrative.* Rutherford, N.J.: Fairleigh Dickinson University Press, 1975.

————. "Motifs in Epistolary Fiction: Analysis of a Narrative Sub-genre." *L'Esprit créateur* 17 (1977): 279–301.

Roussel, Roy. "Reflections on the Letter: The Reconciliation of Distance and Presence in *Pamela.*" *ELH* 41 (1974): 375–99.

Rousset, Jean. "La Monodie épistolaire: Crébillon fils." *Etudes littéraires* 1 (1968): 167–74.

————. *Narcisse romancier: essai sur la première personne dans le roman.* Paris: Corti, 1973.

————. "Une Forme littéraire: le roman par lettres." In *Forme et signification: essais sur les structures littéraires de Corneille à Claudel*, pp. 65–108. Paris: Corti, 1962.

Rustin, Jacques. "*La Religieuse* de Diderot: mémoires ou journal intime?" In *Le Journal intime et ses formes littéraires*, edited by V. Del Litto, pp. 27–46. Geneva: Droz, 1978.

Schérer, Jacques. *La Dramaturgie classique en France.* Paris: Nizet, 1959.

Seylaz, Jean-Luc. "*Les Liaisons dangereuses" et la création romanesque chez Laclos.* Geneva: Droz, 1958.

Showalter, English, Jr. *The Evolution of the French Novel, 1641–1782.* Princeton: Princeton University Press, 1972.

Singer, Godfrey Frank. *The Epistolary Novel: Its Origin, Development, Decline, and Residuary Influence.* Philadelphia: University of Pennsylvania Press, 1933.

Smith, Barbara H. *Poetic Closure: A Study of How Poems End.* Chicago: University of Chicago Press, 1968.

Spacks, Patricia Meyer. *Imagining a Self: Autobiography and Novel in Eighteenth-Century England.* Cambridge: Harvard University Press, 1976.

Spitzer, Leo. "*Les Lettres portugaises.*" *Romanische Forschungen* 65 (1954): 94–135.

————. "A Propos de *La Vie de Marianne.*" *Romanic Review* 44 (1953): 102–26.

Stackelberg, Jürgen von. "Der Briefroman und seine Epoche: Briefroman und Empfindsamkeit." *Cahiers d'histoire des littératures romanes* 1 (1977): 293–309.

Starobinski, Jean. *J.-J. Rousseau, la transparence et l'obstacle.* Paris: Plon, 1957.

Stevick, Philip. *The Chapter in Fiction: Theories of Narrative Division.* Syracuse: Syracuse University Press, 1970.

Stewart, Joan Hinde. "Colette: The Mirror Image." *French Forum* 3 (1978): 195–205.

―――. *The Novels of Mme Riccoboni.* North Carolina Studies in the Romance Languages and Literatures, no. 8. Chapel Hill: University of North Carolina Press, 1976.

Stewart, Philip R. *Imitation and Illusion in the French Memoir-Novel, 1700–1750: The Art of Make-Believe.* New Haven: Yale University Press, 1969.

―――. *Le Masque et la parole: le langage de l'amour au XVIIIe siècle.* Paris: Corti, 1973.

Strelka, Joseph P., ed. *Yearbook of Comparative Criticism.* Vol. 8, *Theories of Literary Genre.* University Park: Pennsylvania State University Press, 1978.

Terras, Victor. *The Young Dostoevsky (1846–1849): A Critical Study.* The Hague: Mouton, 1969.

Testud, Pierre. "Les *Lettres persanes*, roman épistolaire." *Revue d'histoire littéraire de la France* 66 (1966): 642–56.

―――. *Rétif de la Bretonne et la création littéraire.* Geneva: Droz, 1977.

Thelander, Dorothy R. *Laclos and the Epistolary Novel.* Geneva: Droz, 1963.

Todorov, Tzvetan. *Littérature et signification.* Paris: Larousse, 1967.

Versini, Laurent. *Laclos et la tradition: essai sur les sources et la technique des "Liaisons dangereuses."* Paris: Klincksieck, 1968.

―――. *Le Roman épistolaire.* Paris: Presses Universitaires de France, 1979.

Voss, E. Th. "Erzählprobleme des Briefromans." Dissertation, University of Bonn, 1960.

Watt, Ian. *The Rise of the Novel: Studies in Defoe, Richardson, and Fielding.* Berkeley and Los Angeles: University of California Press, 1964.

Weinrich, Harald. *Tempus: besprochene und erzählte Welt.* Stuttgart: W. Kohlhammer, 1964.

Wohlfarth, Irving. "The Irony of Criticism and the Criticism of Irony: A Study of Laclos Criticism." *Studies on Voltaire and the Eighteenth Century* 120 (1974): 269–317.

Wolpe, Hans. "Psychological Ambiguity in *La Nouvelle Héloïse.*" *University of Toronto Quarterly* 28 (1958–59): 279–90.

Würzbach, Natascha. "Die Struktur des Briefromans und seine Entstehung in England." Dissertation, University of Munich, 1964.

# INDEX

I have divided the index into two sections. The first, Subjects, includes a number of topics that I have only touched upon in my work; I hope that this separate listing will not only facilitate access to my discussion on a topic but also encourage further inquiry. The Authors and Titles section lists titles separately from authors. The reader who is interested in my discussion of a particular author should therefore look also under individual titles, referring to the Selected Bibliography for a complete listing by author of epistolary texts cited.